MW01036556

Dreaming of Dixie

The University of North Carolina Press   Chapel Hill

Dreaming of Dixie

How the South Was Created in American Popular Culture

KAREN L. COX

© 2011 The University of North Carolina Press
All rights reserved
Manufactured in the United States of America

Designed by Courtney Leigh Baker and set in Merlo and Society
Page by Rebecca Evans.

Library of Congress Cataloging-in-Publication Data
Cox, Karen L., 1962–
Dreaming of Dixie : how the South was created in American
popular culture / Karen L. Cox.
p. cm.
Includes bibliographical references and index.
ISBN 978-0-8078-3471-8 (cloth : alk. paper)
ISBN 978-1-4696-0986-7 (pbk.   )
1. Southern States—In popular culture—History. 2. Nostalgia—
Southern States. 3. Romanticism—Southern States. 4. Popular
culture—United States—History. I. Title.
F209.C68 2011
975—dc22   2010041421

cloth   15 14 13 12 11   5 4 3 2 1
paper   17 16 15 14 13   5 4 3 2 1

THIS BOOK WAS DIGITALLY PRINTED.

CONTENTS

ILLUSTRATIONS

ACKNOWLEDGMENTS

This book is the result of my long and abiding interest in southern history and culture, which in this instance prompted me to investigate how Americans living outside of the region developed their understanding of the South in the period that marked the rise of mass consumption. I sought to do this through an examination of various forms of popular culture that were part of people's everyday lives and experiences—advertising, music, literature, movies, and radio shows. What I found was that regardless of the medium the image of the American South was consistent. Southern belles and gentlemen, mammies and uncles, white-columned mansions, fields of cotton and, literally, moonlight and magnolias were employed to suggest *Dixie*. One could certainly find such icons within the post–Civil War mythology of the Lost Cause, but southerners were not responsible for marketing and disseminating this imagery for national consumption. On the contrary, Madison Avenue's advertising agencies, Tin Pan Alley's music makers, Chicago's radio stars, and Hollywood's filmmakers were the ones who found profit in selling the romantic South to American consumers. Southerners, I discovered, also wanted in on this scheme, and they created a tourist trade to meet the demand of the thousands of northerners and midwesterners who came by trains, planes, and automobiles to see Dixie for themselves. This, too, became part of the story I wanted to tell.

I often say that the reason I love to study the South is that it sometimes reminds me of a sideshow at a county fair—you don't want to look, but you can't help yourself. I also love popular culture, contemporary and historical. This particular study combines my interest in history with that in popular culture and has been a real adventure. It has helped me to better comprehend national perceptions of the region and its people, which include me. I am a native of West Virginia, my family moved to North Carolina when I was twelve, and that's where I attended high school and college. I have also lived in the southern states of Mississippi and Kentucky, so it is fair to say that I know a thing or two about southern stereotypes.

This study has meant traveling to fascinating archives and repositories, some of which I had never before visited. The help of librarians and archivists is essential to any book of history, and I appreciate the assistance of the many professionals with whom I worked—at the Library of Congress, the New York Public Library, the Georgia Historical Society, the Virginia Historical Society, and the Mississippi Department of Archives and History. I am especially grateful to Lynn Eaton at the John W. Hartman Center for Sales, Advertising & Marketing History at Duke University; Michael Henry at the Library of American Broadcasting at the University of Maryland; and Ron Mandelbaum with New York–based Photofest, which is a wonderful repository of film stills. A special thank you goes to Marilyn Schuster in the J. Murray Atkins Library at the University of North Carolina at Charlotte (UNCC), who assisted me with scanning images in the late stages of the project.

The ability to travel to archives requires both funding and time. In 2006–7, I had the opportunity to serve as faculty-in-residence for the UNC in Washington program, during which it was my good fortune to live within two blocks of the Library of Congress, where I conducted some of my earliest research. A faculty research grant from my home institution, UNCC, allowed me to conduct research around the South and in New York. I also received a Mellon Research Fellowship from the Virginia Historical Society, a wonderful library and archive that has the added benefit of being in one of Richmond's most beautiful neighborhoods. The time needed to write most of this book was made possible by a sabbatical during 2008–9, provided by my department's Cotlow Fellowship, and a faculty research leave funded by UNCC's College of Liberal Arts and Sciences. The college also provided funds to assist with permission fees for the many images that accompany this book.

Writing this book has been an enjoyable enterprise, due in large part to wonderful friends, family, and colleagues who have indulged my questions, listened as I explained what this book was about, and even tried the Scarlett O'Hara cocktail recipe I discovered during my research. My first stab at this project came during a small symposium called the Dixie Emporium, which was hosted by the Watson-Brown Foundation in Georgia and organized by Anthony Stanonis. There, my research began to take new shape, and that meeting provided me with the opportunity to get to know better some of the most talented scholars of southern history and culture, including Fitz Brundage, Patrick Huber, Nicole King, Ted Ownby, and Eric Plaag. That gathering also led to a friendship with Anthony Stanonis, who later hosted me at Queen's University in Belfast, where I shared some of my research with his students.

As a member of UNCC's Department of History, I am fortunate to work with a talented, and genuinely congenial, group of colleagues who have provided useful feedback on portions of this work during our brown bag luncheons and, more generally, have been good friends. I especially want to thank my former colleague Heather Thompson for her interest in this project. Heather, in particular, is a dear friend and great supporter of my work. Amanda Pipkin and Ritika Prasad, two recent additions to our department, have both been good to remind me to relax and not take myself too seriously. My office neighbor and titan of colonial Latin American history, Lyman Johnson, has been very supportive, and I have enjoyed our discussions, both serious and humorous, in our two offices. I am also lucky to work with wonderfully talented colleagues in other areas of the university, including Katie McCormick and Ceily Hamilton, whom I consider friends. Current and former students have offered their encouragement as well. Jason Harpe, Brandon Lunsford, and Nicole Moore make me proud every day, and a special thanks goes to Bill Jeffers, who provided research assistance in the final days of manuscript preparation.

I wrote most of this book in coffeehouses in Charlotte (hat tip to the Caribou on East Boulevard), working alongside my friend La Shonda Mims. While she prepared to take her comprehensive exams at the University of Georgia, I wrote my chapters. We kept one another motivated, talked a lot about our chosen profession, laughed, drank lots of tea and coffee, and, when not working so hard, indulged in an adult beverage or two. I am happy to say that she passed her exams and I finished this book. So, big thanks to La Shonda, who is on course to make her own contribution to the field of southern history.

My pals in the Southern Association for Women Historians (sawh) have also been important to sustaining me through this process, whether they knew it or not. As many of us know, the sawh is an organization that not only shapes careers; it creates an atmosphere of support in which long-lasting friendships are made. Particular thanks go to Angela Boswell, Megan Shockley, Shannon Frystak, Alecia Long, Joan Johnson, Anne Rubin, Rebecca Montgomery, and Kathleen Clark. I found that Facebook was not just a social network but could also be used as motivation. Each time I posted my writing progress, I was cheered on by my extended network of friends, including Janet Allured, Victoria Bynum, Melissa Walker, Rebecca Sharpless, Shep McKinley, Tonya Thames Taylor, Bill Mulligan, Tom Ward, Susannah Ural, Andy Wiest, Kathy Barbier, Catherine Clinton, Thomas Chase Hagood, Tracey Yost, Sarah Fuelleman, and my BFF, Sheri Rawls. I also want to thank my mother, Flora Carter, and my aunt, Wilma

Smith, for their love, encouragement, and interest in this project. If it is possible to thank my dog, Phoebe—and I think it is—then I have appreciated her loyal companionship, too.

Finally, during the writing of this book, I had the good fortune to meet one Carann Beth Brown, affectionately known to me as "the Oracle of Hopkins." Carann has enriched my life in ways I could not imagine and has made me happier than I knew I could be. She has become my biggest cheerleader and provides me with the respite I need from my life in academia. She also knows how to keep me in check. For this and so much more, I am very grateful.

Dreaming of Dixie

INTRODUCTION

Cultural anthropologist Ruth Landes wrote an essay in 1945 entitled "A Northerner Views the South," which was at once a critique of the region and an honest assessment of how Dixie was perceived by nonsoutherners. "Of all the United States," she wrote, "the South is most trapped by poverty and disease, illiteracy, political corruption, and deep want of ambition." The Columbia-educated Landes, who was one of Gunnar Myrdal's research assistants for *An American Dilemma: The Negro Problem and Modern Democracy*, condemned white southerners for their false sense of loyalty to "their negroes" and yet was clearly frustrated with how (her criticisms aside) northerners seemed to have an "ineradicable feeling of appreciation for the South." Much of that feeling was not based on reality but on the way the region was presented in popular culture. Films, best-selling books, advertising, radio, and even popular music offered the American public what Landes described as "beguiling picturizations of the antebellum South as some country [where] men were chivalrous and ladies glamorous, and their former slaves were attached to them by silken bonds." The region, she noted, was "gilded in sentimentality" to such an extent that northerners did not really *know* the American South at all.[1]

Although Landes's focus was on northern perceptions of Dixie, the truth was that most Americans during the first half of the twentieth century saw the South and southerners through this same magnolia-shaped lens. White southerners, to be sure, believed in the regional myths they associated with the Lost Cause; this belief permeated their culture. Not so in the North, in the Midwest, or even on the West Coast. So how did nonsoutherners come to accept and subscribe to these same myths? The answers lay in historical developments of the late nineteenth century, which included a post–Civil War culture of reconciliation between the North and the South, rapid industrialization and urbanization, anxiety about modernity, the rise of mass consumerism, and the emergence of mass culture.

The Culture of Reconciliation
Sectional reconciliation following the Civil War was by no means limited to reunions of veterans, nor was it simply a matter of politics. The

process of reconciliation was also broadly evident in American culture. Novels that centered on the marriage of a northern man and a southern woman—the literary equivalent of reunification—were popular in the late nineteenth century. Songs of reconciliation, from T. Brigham Bishop's "A Knot of Blue and Gray" (1876) to George M. Cohan's "Wedding of the Blue and the Gray" (1906), were played in the parlors of American homes. White supremacy was central to the culture of reconciliation, too, because northern and southern whites shared similar views on African Americans. In truth, northern whites sympathized with the South regarding the "Negro," not only because of the migration of southern blacks to their cities but because they held similar attitudes toward immigrants from southern and eastern Europe, who also made their homes there. The enormous success of Thomas Dixon's racist novels of Reconstruction, for example, was made possible by this shared belief in white racial superiority. The fact was, all across America, white readers regarded Dixon's not-so-subtle commentary on southern blacks as historical truth.[2]

The culture of reconciliation could also be found in post–Civil War tourism. As one Union veteran asserted in 1877, tourism to the South was "the surest method of reconciliation" because it allowed for the "intermingling of the people" from both sections.[3] Chapters of the Grand Army of the Republic (GAR) organized trips to the South as early as 1881, well before there were veterans' reunions. Not only did these veterans visit southern battlefields; they also became participants in the postwar southern tourist trade by visiting historic sites and returning home with souvenirs. In 1899, for example, the Grand Army Club of Massachusetts organized a steamboat tour to Virginia. In addition to visiting battlefields on which they had fought, the group also toured the Confederate Museum (now the White House of the Confederacy), as well as St. John's Church and the Old Capitol in Richmond.[4]

Toward the end of the nineteenth century and into the twentieth, Civil War monuments served as both the art and tangible sites of reconciliation. The Confederate monument in Arlington National Cemetery, for example, was heralded by its sculptor, Moses Ezekiel, as a monument of reconciliation, and the speeches given at its unveiling in 1914 stressed those same themes. President Woodrow Wilson was on hand to receive the monument as a "gift to the nation" from the United Daughters of the Confederacy (UDC), and his speech focused on its meaning for a reunified country. The rituals of monument unveilings like the one at Arlington were calculated to reflect a spirit of reunification. Government officials from both sections, Union and Confederate veterans, and women from the UDC as well as the Daughters of the American Revolution were all in attendance.[5]

Reconciliation was also an important plot line in stories developed for the new medium of film, most notably D. W. Griffith's *The Birth of a Nation* (1915). In Griffith's take on Thomas Dixon's novel *The Clansman*, sectional reconciliation was depicted through the marriage of a northern woman to a southern man. While Elsie Stoneman and Ben Cameron's marriage was used to symbolize reconciliation, Griffith also employed the theme of Anglo-Saxon brotherhood, which brought together white people in the cause of destroying a common enemy—black southerners. Such themes of reconciliation continued to be portrayed on film throughout the twentieth century and played an important role in the culture of reconciliation through World War II.[6]

Reaction to Modernity

The response to modernization in the urban-industrial centers of the North also contributed to perceptions of the South from outside of the region. Rapid industrialization and urbanization in the late nineteenth and early twentieth centuries created social as well as economic conditions that led to Americans' anxiety about modernity, and in the mediums of popular culture the South was frequently represented as its antithesis. The reactions to a society that was in flux were often at odds with one another. On the one hand, Americans felt an antipathy toward modernity and longed for a return to America's pastoral and romantic past, with its emphasis on leisure and individualism. Such a dream seemed elusive in the urban factory settings of the North but still possible in the American South. On the other hand, there were the benefits of modernity, which made possible a world where the new technologies employed by industry produced and distributed cheaper consumer goods accessible to people from all walks of life. The conflict between "backward-looking pastoralism" and the impulse toward modernity seemed incompatible; however, popular culture helped to bring both ideas together in the marketplace, and frequently the antebellum South acted as the conduit. That is to say that pastoral images and themes of the Old South and of southerners were used to sell goods and entertainment to American consumers, all of which was made possible by the modern urban-industrial world in which they lived. This was not lost on the producers of popular culture. They were keenly aware of consumers' anxiety about modernization, and they cleverly linked their products—from pancake flour to movies—to the idyllic images conjured up by the Old South.[7]

Contemporary writers, too, wrote explicitly about the South as the repository of America's rural values. In 1896, the northern travel writer Julian Ralph published a book about his visit to the South entitled *Dixie; or Southern Scenes and Sketches*, which first appeared as a series of articles in *Harper's Weekly*. Ralph, who also reported for the *New York Sun*, traveled south via steamboat down the Mississippi River. He wrote fondly about his adventure as an escape from the frenetic North, pronouncing the South to be a place where he could "cast [his] lines off from the general world of today to float back into a past era, there to loaf away a week of utter rest, undisturbed by telegraph or telephone, a hotel elevator or a clanging cable-car, surrounded by comfort, fed from a good and generous kitchen, and at liberty to forget the rush and bustle of that raging monster the French call the *fin de siecle*."[8] His observations captured the mood of many Americans concerning the intrusion of modernity into their lives. And it was in the South, the least modernized region of the country, where he and others found comfort.

Historians, too, have written about the impact of modernity on American society. Robert Wiebe, in his now-classic work *The Search for Order*, described America at the turn of the twentieth century as a "distended society" in which people felt "dislocation" and "bewilderment."[9] The literature of the day often idealized the past and the loss of virtues associated with that past, whether it was "the valiant men of the Wild West, the touching warmth between master and slave, or the quiet peace of the New England village." In the midst of rapid industrialization and urbanization, especially in the North and the Midwest, Americans were obsessed with what Wiebe described as the "peculiar ethical value of an agricultural life," which Americans had "long taken for granted."[10]

T. J. Jackson Lears, likewise, sought to understand this end-of-the-century anxiety in his book *No Place of Grace*, about antimodernism and the transformation of American culture.[11] What Wiebe described as feelings of "dislocation" Lears called "feelings of unreality." The response to these feelings, Lears argued, was that people "yearn[ed] for an authentic experience," whether it was physical, spiritual, or emotional. Although the language Lears used differed from that of Wiebe, they both recognized that a key component to understanding the rapid social and economic changes occurring at the turn of the twentieth century was the inherent contradiction between wanting the benefits of modernity while at the same time longing for the pastoral ideal.[12]

The rise of mass consumerism, in particular, highlights the ambivalent relationship American society had with modernization, and popular culture provides insights into how the benefits of industrialization, such as mass-produced consumer goods, could be sold and still appeal to people's need to connect with a simpler, preindustrial past. As Americans became consumers on a mass scale, they also consumed ideas about the products they purchased. When those products were marketed using southern imagery very often it was the South of the American imagination. Advertising, movies, early radio, popular literature, and even music all worked in tandem to shape national perceptions of the South. It was represented as a region that upheld its links to the rural past and the one least spoiled by urbanization and industrialization. The irony was that this narrative of southern identity was being disseminated for consumption by industries from outside of the South, whether they were New York advertising agencies, radio shows broadcast from Chicago, or Hollywood films. This is not to say that white southerners did not see themselves as preservers of the "southern way of life" or contribute to this perception. Rather, the industries responsible for the spread of popular culture nationally were located outside of Dixie and had far more influence over what ideas Americans consumed about the South than did native southerners themselves.

The South in Popular Culture

The South in popular culture is a subject that historians have, for the most part, avoided, as not serious enough to warrant their attention. To be sure, Jack Temple Kirby addressed it in *Media-Made Dixie* more than thirty years ago by surveying images of the South, especially those developed by native southerners like D. W. Griffith and Thomas Nelson Page. The book, however, provided a somewhat cursory overview of the South in popular culture, and contemporary reviewers regarded it as more anecdotal than scholarly.[13] The subjects of popular culture, however, deserve to be taken seriously and certainly merit more in-depth attention by southern historians. This is not to say that there have not been important historical contributions to the study of popular culture, only that the South in popular culture represents one of the least-investigated areas of study, especially for historians of southern identity. By examining the various topics of popular culture—from advertising to films—historians can further their understanding of the South in a national, and even global, context.[14]

Southern historians who do write about the South and popular culture often turn to the work of sociologists, particularly John Shelton Reed, who has examined southern culture for more than thirty years. As early as 1972, Reed was grappling with the issues of regionalism and national identity. In *The Enduring South: Subcultural Persistence in Mass Society*, he wrote about the effects of American mass culture on the South, especially of the national media. The South, he argued, may have been engaged with the national media, but the national media was "subservient to community values" that existed within the region. Moreover, he argued, even though the South was not (at least in 1972) creating mass culture through the popular media, the region did use such media to perpetuate and maintain regional and local cultural values. Reed's overarching conclusion—that, on the whole, southerners did not create mass culture—is important and has a basis in fact. That is to say, the South did not—and, as a rule, does not—manufacture mass culture. Publishing houses, television and film studios, and advertising firms are headquartered in New York or Los Angeles and have long been responsible for the way in which nonsoutherners perceive the region.[15]

Scholars in other fields, from literature to film studies, have addressed the role of the South in popular culture through the lens of their various disciplines. The most recent of these include Leigh Anne Duck's *The Nation's Region: Southern Modernism, Segregation, and U.S. Nationalism*; Tara McPherson's *Reconstructing Dixie: Race, Gender, and Nostalgia in the Imagined South*; and Allison Graham's *Framing the South: Hollywood, Television, and Race during the Civil Rights Struggle*. Duck explores how the literary modernism of southern writers, from Thomas Dixon to Erskine Caldwell, helped shape national perceptions of the South. McPherson, a professor of cinema studies, employs feminist theory to explore what she terms the "nostalgia industry," which has constructed an "imagined South" in the period from the 1930s to the present. Graham's work on film and television is much more focused on the period of civil rights, but she also argues that national perceptions of the region can be linked to the media's interpretations of race, class, and gender in the South.[16]

This book represents an effort to take popular culture seriously as a topic of historical investigation and to understand its implications for the region in a national context. Through a study of the South in popular culture in the period from the late nineteenth century through World War II, the book analyzes how perceptions of southern identity have been shaped from outside of the region. In chapters on advertising, popular music, early radio, travel literature, and the movies, it examines how popular culture has influenced and colored how Americans viewed the region and its people. This study also examines the southern tourist trade to show how the South responded to national perceptions of the region. Southern state and local governments, as well as individual entrepreneurs, not only understood the region's identity in the national imagination but sought to capitalize on it by providing nonsouthern tourists, especially those from the North and the Midwest, with exactly what they had come to expect of the South, whether it was being able to see blacks working in cotton fields, taking tours of old plantations, or experiencing that ubiquitous feature of life in Dixie known as southern hospitality.

National perceptions of the South were, undeniably, often oversimplified. During the period of this study, the South was frequently portrayed in popular culture as a region that was either primitive or exotic and was seen through the haze of moonlight and magnolias. Southern identity in the national imagination encompassed many regional icons, including the old Confederate colonel, the mammy, the belle, the opulent plantation big house, bolls of cotton, and the hillbilly. Such representations of the region became part of the catalog of southern imagery that was employed in everything from advertising to movies. In popular culture, the South was used to represent the pastoral ideal and to recall a premodern America. These themes were not isolated in any one area of popular culture; they were evident in *all* of them. Thus, the southern mammy was more than an advertising icon. She appeared in popular music, on early radio shows, in Hollywood movies, and in popular literature. This was also true of the antebellum plantation, which served as the locale for novels, advertisements, and films about the South throughout the period of this study, which concludes in the years immediately following World War II.

Such perceptions not only perpetuated ideas of a romantic, premodern South. They also helped sustain beliefs about race that were particularly detrimental to African Americans nationally. White Americans, on the whole, subscribed to the mythology that blacks were happy in servitude and needed white supervision or were exotic creatures who provided entertainment. Overcoming these southern racial stereotypes found in popular culture proved to be a difficult task and hurt the cause of civil rights nationally. As Claude Barnett, a leading black journalist of the period, argued, such characterizations also damaged black morale and symbolized how the nation had capitulated to the South.[17]

Coda

Fugitive poet John Crowe Ransom observed in 1930: "It is out of fashion these days to look backward rather than forward. About the only American given to it is some unreconstructed Southerner." Ransom, of course, was concerned about the preservation of the "southern way of life" and was emphasizing the desirable qualities of the region's agrarian tradition. Clearly, he had not fully examined representations of the South in popular culture, for had he done so he would have recognized that the mediums of national culture not only looked backward but used the South to do so. Several years later, Ransom's fellow southerner David Cohn wrote a book about the region in which he lamented how difficult it was to "[make] others see the South plain." Cohn, a native of Greenville, Mississippi, observed that the antebellum traditions of the South and its image in the national imagination remained intact despite the work of historians and sociologists to demystify Dixie. In the "minds of outsiders," the South was imbued with qualities that applied to no other region of the country, causing Cohn to conclude, "Men love what they imagine and worship what they create." The South of the American imagination was, and still is, very often created by the industries of popular media. During the period marked by the rise of mass consumption, those industries produced an image of the South that contributed to perceptions of the region as the custodian of America's pastoral traditions. It was portrayed as a place where those traditions still had meaning, and where Americans, if they ventured South, might get to experience the Dixie of their dreams.[18]

CHAPTER 1

Dixie in Popular Song

Jack Yellen, a Jewish immigrant to the United States from Poland, was an unlikely person to write songs about the American South. His family immigrated to Buffalo, New York, in 1897 when Yellen was five years old. He went to college at the University of Michigan and returned to Buffalo to work as a journalist. He enjoyed writing songs on the side, and though he had never visited the South, he wrote lyrics to some of the most popular songs about the region to come out of New York's Tin Pan Alley—the center of music publishing in the early twentieth century. As Yellen recalled, "Dixie songs were then the craze, and like all other writers of our limited talents . . . we started out by imitating."[1]

Yellen achieved his greatest fame for the songs "Happy Days Are Here Again" (1929) and "Ain't She Sweet" (1927), but his early success as a lyricist was with the songs "All Aboard for Dixieland" (1913) and "Are You from Dixie?" (1915). During the early twentieth century, hundreds of songs about Dixie that became popular American music were not written by southerners or even Americans who had spent time in the South. Tin Pan Alley's composers were primarily first- and second-generation Jewish immigrants who lived in New York, had never traveled below the Mason-Dixon Line, and did not have the faintest idea what the region was like. Yet they wrote reams of songs about Dixie that became popular music during the years leading up to and beyond World War I and which later had a renaissance on early radio and in movies.

The music that emerged from Tin Pan Alley often focused on romantic themes and exotic places. When the focus was on the South, the region symbolized a place where people living in hectic urban environments like New York or Chicago could psychologically escape. More famously, Irving Berlin and George Gershwin joined Yellen and numerous other song men of Tin Pan Alley to write songs about the pastoral and preindustrial South—a region that was distinct from the rest of the country and yet distinctly American.[2] The South served as the place where many Americans believed that the rural ideal could still be achieved, and songs about Dixie perpetuated that ideal through plantation images of the region—a trend that was also taking place in books about the South and in the advertising of consumer goods.[3]

It did not matter that the sentimental South they wrote about was mythological—through their songs, Tin Pan Alley musicians, lyricists, and composers helped sustain a familiar image of the region most Americans identified as southern. Moreover, it was an image they readily consumed when they purchased sheet music, which sold by the millions. Songs about the South contrasted sharply with the urban environment where Yellen and others plied their trade. Certainly, Tin Pan Alley publishers had enormous success with sentimental ballads of all types, but the theme of Dixie proved particularly profitable. In 1930, Isaac Goldberg, an early documentarian of Tin Pan Alley, commented on this trend, offering his own explanation for why the South provided northern composers with lyrical inspiration. "Paradise is never where we are," he wrote. "The South has become our Never-never Land—the symbol of the Land where the lotus blooms and dreams come true." The fact that the region had been destroyed by war and that a life of leisure was one perpetuated by slavery seemed inconsequential. More important, songs about Dixie sold well.[4]

This nostalgia for the South was part of a long development in the history of American popular music that stretched back to the minstrel stage of the 1840s. Popular music of any era generally offers a reflection on American character and culture at specific points in time, and from the days of minstrelsy through the heyday of Tin Pan Alley, popular songs about the South consistently perpetuated an image of the region as primitive, exotic, and pastoral. Throughout most of the nineteenth century, nostalgic songs with southern themes were born out of the minstrel tradition on stage and in songs that emphasized an idyllic and monolithic South. This tradition remained strong into the twentieth century as minstrel songs continued to be performed on the vaudeville stage and, later, on early radio. Between 1890 and 1920, sales of sheet music about Dixie soared into the millions thanks to the expansion of the music publishing industry in New York. Throughout this period, songs about Dixie never strayed far from themes of a romanticized South. As Isaac Goldberg suggested, the South served as inspiration for songwriters who saw a paradise in mythological Dixie, regardless of whether it matched reality.[5]

Tin Pan Alley's song men built on the legacy of nineteenth-century American composers who wrote what were known as "Ethiopian" or minstrel songs—the most famous of which were the plantation melodies by Stephen Foster but also those of Daniel Decatur Emmett. Foster's

aid in the
Lost Cause

"Old Folks at Home" (1851), also known as "Swanee River," and Emmett's "Dixie's Land" (1859), better known as "Dixie," became instantly popular with American audiences and were the forebears of a song tradition centered on the theme of the plantation South. Significantly, the most successful popular songs about the region from the mid-nineteenth century through the early twentieth century—from Stephen Foster's compositions to those of Irving Berlin—were written and published by northerners and were extremely popular with northern audiences, which shared the composers' nostalgia for the South and sentimentalized its race relations. As an 1861 editorial, entitled "Songs for the South," explained, Emmett's "Dixie's Land" was, "like most articles of Southern consumption . . . imported from the North—Northern men perpetrating both words and music." However, the reality was that nonsoutherners were even larger consumers of southern songs then and for years to come.[6]

Stephen Foster and Daniel Decatur Emmett were among the progenitors of a tradition of northerners who wrote songs about an idyllic South. Foster was born in Lawrenceville, Pennsylvania, near Pittsburgh, and Emmett was from Mount Vernon, Ohio. Foster is considered America's first major composer and certainly had considerably more success than Emmett. But both composers attained their greatest success as writers of minstrel songs. Emmett was important to the development of American minstrelsy and founded the Virginia Minstrels in 1843. He wrote "Dixie's Land" for the Bryant Minstrels while living in New York. The tune was intended as a "walk around," the closing number performed in a minstrel show, and it swiftly became popular throughout the country. It appealed to America's nostalgia for the antebellum South and was an upbeat song that was easy to sing. Although not intended as a rallying song for southern armies, it nonetheless became associated with the Confederacy, even though numerous other writers of the period composed different lyrics for the song, including northern versions such as "Dixie for the Union" and "Dixie Unionized." More than fifty years later, a writer for *Outlook* magazine commented on how "Dixie" was still "the most popular patriotic song in this country," in part because "the Northern people like the Southern people," suggesting that although the song was fixed in the American imagination as a southern tune it was still admired by the rest of the nation. Its lyrics, however, make clear Emmett's effort to capitalize on the sentimental appeal of a preindustrial South—"I wish I was in the land ob cotton,/Old times dar am not forgotten"—incorporating the theme of a black man who longs to return "home" to the plantation where he was most happy, a popular theme in minstrel songs as the issue of slavery became increasingly divisive and the nation headed toward civil war.[7]

Foster's impact on American popular music was more far-reaching than Emmett's, and his compositions are credited with helping to shape American identity both within and outside of the United States. Only twenty of his two hundred songs were influenced by the minstrel tradition, but his blackface dialect songs have had the longest impact on American music and are the best remembered. The song "Old Folks at Home," better known as "Swanee River," is arguably his most famous. The tune, about the Suwanee River in Florida, a place Foster never visited, has been performed and recorded by countless artists and has influenced some of the most highly regarded composers of the twentieth century. Irving Berlin's first hit, "Alexander's Ragtime Band" (1911), paid homage to "Swanee River"; George Gershwin's first hit song was "Swanee" (1919); and Duke Ellington composed "Swanee River Rhapsody" (1930).

Foster's song was originally sold and performed as a "plantation melody," owing to its dialect. During the nineteenth century, the Christy Minstrels—the nation's best-known minstrel troupe—helped to popularize the song. New York music publisher Firth, Pond & Company, which published Foster's song, as well as "Dixie" and numerous other minstrel tunes, had difficulty keeping up with the demand for the sheet music for "Old Folks at Home." In twentieth-century parlance, the song was a "hit." The lyrics capitalized on northern sentimentality toward southern blacks, employed dialect, and were nostalgic for the antebellum South, as the line "Still longing for the old plantation," suggests. Foster initially did not want his name linked with the song because of its association with minstrelsy, yet the song's success inspired him to write to Edwin Christy in 1852 requesting that his name be reinstated to the piece. According to Foster, he decided to "pursue the Ethiopian business without fear or shame" after all and sought to "establish [his] name as the best Ethiopian song writer."[8]

Indeed, Foster went on to write more songs in the minstrel tradition, including the tune "Old Black Joe," published in 1860. It tells the story of a former slave who is being called by his departed friends "from the cotton fields" when his "heart was young and gay," employing the common trope of a minstrel song in which a black man, presumably now living in the North, longs for the time when he lived on a plantation and worked alongside his friends. For decades, several lyricists incorporated the line "the land of Old Black Joe" into their own minstrel songs as a way of linking their compositions to the American South, and the song has had enormous longevity as popular American music. During the 1930s, the Sinclair Minstrels, made up of four white men, performed the song as the opening number of their radio program in Chicago, some seventy-five years after its publication, and "Old Black Joe" has been recorded by Tommy Dorsey and more modern artists from Jerry Lee Lewis to Van Morrison.[9]

Foster's songs became popular because they were appreciated by a cross section of the American public; their appeal traversed regional, ethnic, and class lines. Moreover, printing technology by the mid-nineteenth century made it possible to reach a mass audience. Indeed, it was the improvement in this technology, combined with advertising, that eventually made sheet music a commodity available to Americans across the country, and the sale of sheet music became the litmus test by which songs became popular music. Music swiftly became a profitable commodity in the late nineteenth century, and in 1887, Ticknor & Company of Boston reissued Foster's songs "My Old Kentucky Home" and "Swanee River" in a "full gilt" publication. The book was illustrated with a "typical Southern mansion," "the possum and the coon," "the field where sugar canes grow . . . and other pathetic scenes and incidents of the old slave life in Dixie." Such fare sold very well among American consumers, who enjoyed Foster's music and whose image of the South was not far removed from such illustrations.[10]

By the mid-1890s, New York City had the greatest concentration of song publishers in the country, and it was during that decade that a new genre of popular song, also linked to the American South, took the country by storm—the "coon song."[11] Throughout the nineteenth century, most minstrel songs were written and performed by whites, who caricatured blacks to comedic effect for white audiences, most especially as "Zip Coon" and "Jim Crow." "Zip Coon" was the urban black dandy, very often living in a northern city, who tried to emulate white dress and manners. As played on the minstrel stage, the clothes were loud and flashy, and the character often mangled the English language. "Jim Crow" was portrayed as a plantation Negro who spoke slowly, shuffled his feet, and wore tattered clothing. Both figures were firmly entrenched in the American imagination by the time of the Civil War, and during the second half of the nineteenth century this ensemble of minstrel figures expanded to include the greedy, money-hungry, black woman. Beginning in the 1880s, all three figures appeared on the vaudeville stage in performances of this new genre known as coon songs, which were much more vicious in their portrayals of blacks.[12]

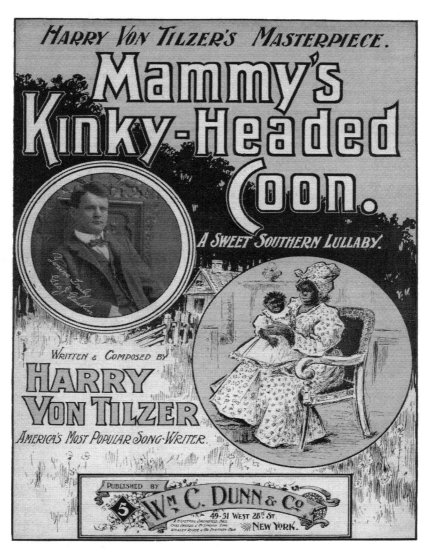

"Mammy's Kinky-Headed Coon," sheet music cover, 1899. (Courtesy Lilly Library, Indiana University, Bloomington, Indiana)

The term "coon" was not used to describe blacks until the 1880s and can be attributed to the popularity of coon songs, which became a trend in music publishing that lasted through the first decade of the twentieth century. Whites associated southern blacks with eating raccoons, and in coon songs they also became known as chicken-thieving, watermelon-eating, razor-wielding oafs. These tunes were enormously popular in the decade of the 1890s, not surprisingly during the period of heightened racial violence nationally. In that decade, over 600 coon songs were produced as sheet music and performed in music halls and vaudeville shows around the country. In effect, coon songs expressed American racism and were important to popularizing black stereotypes. Such music also supported the rise of the music publishing industry in New York, which profited handsomely from their sale. These songs, as expressions of the larger culture, played a unique role in perpetuating Jim Crow racism across the country. Their lyrics made fun of blacks and kept alive racist stereotypes often associated with the South; however, such stereotypes were held more broadly in American culture, which was what made them profitable to the music publishers of Tin Pan Alley.[13]

Ironically, many coon songs were written and performed by blacks. Sam Lucas, Ernest Hogan, and even Paul Laurence Dunbar—best known for his dialect poetry—wrote lyrics for coon songs. Hogan's "All Coons Look Alike to Me" (1896) was the first song of its type to become a big hit. Published in 1896 by M. Witmark & Sons, the song stereotypes a black woman as only having an interest in men with money and black men as "coons" who are indistinguishable from one another:

All coons look alike to me, I've got another beau, you see
And he's just as good to me as you, nig! Ever tried to be
He spends his money free, I know we can't agree
So I don't like you no how, All coons look alike to me.[14]

It is well documented that Hogan later regretted writing the song, as African Americans generally resented coon songs. However, at the time of his composition, he also understood that writing such songs provided him and other black composers an opportunity, albeit demeaning to their race, to earn money by performing in musical theater, at a time when most black men worked as laborers. Moreover, the acceptance of coon songs by white audiences provided black musicians an opportunity to legitimize ragtime—a syncopated style developed by African Americans—since coon songs were ragtime.[15]

Coon songs represented a more complex shift in perceptions of blacks in American popular culture at the turn of the twentieth century. Increasing racial violence in both the North and the South contributed to the stereotype of the dangerous, razor-wielding black man—a theme not only evident in coon songs but also in popular literature. Thomas Dixon's *The Leopard's Spots*, published in 1902, capitalized on the fear of the rapacious black man and helped to perpetuate southern racist stereotypes used to justify lynching. Yet his books, just like coon songs, also appealed to racist assumptions held by whites outside of the South. Indeed, the book sold several hundred thousand copies. Both novels and coon songs can be understood in the context of the post–Civil War process of reconciliation between northern and southern whites, who sought common ground and found it in their shared beliefs about Anglo-Saxon supremacy.[16]

Coon songs, and the Tin Pan Alley songs that followed in this ragtime tradition, were, in effect, the musical expression of these broader cultural trends, which lasted well into the 1930s. In his visit to the South in 1916, northern journalist John Martin Hammond commented on the fact that sentimental historians and fiction writers had defined the South as a place where people "[spoke] in lazy accents somewhat resembling a cross between a coon song and a man too tired to speak."[17] So, too, had vaudevillians and, later, radio personalities, who continued to perform minstrel and coon songs. During the 1930s there were several minstrel troupes that performed Stephen Foster tunes and Emmett's "Dixie." In 1930, the NBC network briefly carried a radio show on which a white woman named Marie Cahill performed "negro characterizations," played the banjo, and "introduce[d] many of the old-time coon songs" to a national audience and a new generation of Americans. Such performances not only perpetuated an archaic image of the American South and African Americans but also contributed to its longevity in the American imagination.[18]

The popularity of coon songs may have waned by 1910, but they were swiftly replaced by an entire genre of what were known as "back-to-Dixie" songs, which sold in the millions. Hundreds of songs with "Dixie" in the title or songs that played on the names of southern states were extremely popular in the decade between 1910 and 1920. Jewish immigrants who were pounding out a living in New York's Tin Pan Alley—and with few exceptions had never been to the places that were the subject of their songs—wrote nearly all of them. "I Want to Be in Dixie" (1912), "All Aboard for Dixieland" (1913), "I Guess I'll Soon Be Back in Dixieland" (1915), "I Love the Name of Dixie" (1915), "Everybody's Crazy over Dixie" (1919), "Anything Is Nice If It Comes from Dixieland" (1919), "Dixie Lullaby" (1919), and "Dixie Girls Are Good Enough for Me" (1923) offer a brief overview of Dixie titles. Southern states, too, provided fodder for Tin Pan Alley songsters. "I'm Going Back to Alabam'" (1914) complemented "I'm Going Back to Carolina" (1913), "On the Mississippi" (1912), "Down Kentucky Way" (1919), "Memories of Virginia" (1918), and "Everything Is Peaches Down in Georgia" (1918) celebrated other states of the former Confederacy. The character of "mammy" also found her way into the music of the period, in titles like "Carolina Mammy" (1922), "I Want My Mammy" (1921), "Mammy's Little Coal Black Rose" (1916), and "Mammy's Shufflin' Dance" (1911).[19]

Dixie was the muse for songwriters and song pluggers, who wrote and promoted music that appealed to the nation's fascination with the South and its regional mythology, which was long evident in American popular culture. Such tunes not only brought in huge profits for the New York–based music publishing industry but they also boosted the careers of vaudevillians and were used to popularize Broadway musicals. These songs became a livelihood for singers like Al Jolson and Eddie Cantor—both Jewish immigrants who had very successful careers as blackface performers.[20]

Dixie songs, like most Tin Pan Alley songs, were very formulaic, because the goal of the publisher was to create a song whose tune was catchy and sold well. Indeed, Tin Pan Alley was "one of the first industries geared to standardization and mass marketing."[21] Songs were a commodity manufactured for sale. The music was frequently written before the lyrics, and many of the lyricists could neither read sheet music nor play the piano. They were, very often, men like Jack Yellen who knew how to write lyrics that fit the tune. Popular music often reflects popular taste and sells to a mass audience because its listeners immediately recognize the tune. During the 1910s and 1920s, Dixie songs achieved this familiarity by conforming to popular taste for the sentimental South, and, given the millions of pieces of sheet music sold on the very topic, the nation was clearly in step with Dixie.[22]

The lyrics of back-to-Dixie songs generally repeated the well-worn southern themes of moonlight, cotton fields, and singing "darkies." Those images were frequently accompanied by the theme of longing to return to a southern home. The lyrics of "Carolina Sunshine" (1919), for example, created this imaginary scene:

Down in Carolina where the sunbeams play
Down where all the world seems bright
Pickaninies romping all the day,
In the cotton fields of white
How my heart is yearning to be there once more
Just to hear the darkies' song
Carolina sunshine calls me back to where I belong.[23]

The same events could take place in other southern states as in the song "In the Evening by the Moonlight in Dear Old Tennessee" (1914). Here, moonlight shines over Dixie, too, where the song's protagonist "dreams of snow fields of cotton" and can hear the "darkies sweetly singing." Dixie was the South of America's imagination.[24]

Tin Pan Alley tunes, from coon songs to those of the back-to-Dixie variety, were primarily distributed and consumed as sheet music. Beginning in the 1880s, the mass production of pianos contributed to the demand for sheet music, and by the 1890s music publishing houses were sprouting up all around Union Square in New York City. A decade later, the industry had moved to Twenty-eighth Street between Fifth and Sixth Avenues; by 1900, the firms of Joseph Stern, Leo Feist, Jerome Remick, and M. Witmark & Sons were well established. Music publishing houses were purposely situated near vaudeville theaters, which became the best place to employ song "pluggers" to help sell a song. If a famous vaudeville performer were persuaded—and in many cases paid—to sing a song, the song could find a mass market because of the increasing numbers of vaudeville houses on the national circuit, which had grown to 1,000 by the 1920s. Jack Yellen explained how this worked with the Dixie song he wrote with Milton Ager entitled "Lovin' Sam, the Sheik of Alabam'" (1922). Eddie Cantor was originally offered the song, but after trying it out he did not have much success. Another vaudevillian, Grace Hayes, asked for a copy, performed it in a Broadway show as a cabaret song, and turned it into a hit for Yellen. As he noted, "The reason we were able to achieve some kind of success with our songs was that we wrote songs that vaudevillians needed." Moreover, Yellen noted, "people went to those [vaudeville] theaters. They got their popular songs from the actors who came through and sang them, and then they bought them in the stores, at the music counters."[25]

By 1900, Tin Pan Alley had a monopoly on the manufacture and distribution of popular songs, and it was rare for a song to achieve national popularity if published outside of New York City. This monopoly was strengthened in 1914 with the founding of the American Society for Composers, Authors and Publishers (ASCAP). It was organized to protect the copyright of songs held by publishers and composers and to collect fees when those songs were performed, but it also ensured that music publishers—the majority of whom were located in New York City—controlled the use of popular songs on radio and in film. ASCAP, Tin Pan Alley, and, later, Hollywood studios maintained their control over American popular music until the beginning of World War II. Only then did other types of music and new publishing houses have a real opportunity to popularize songs from other genres, including jazz and country.[26]

If the lyrics of Dixie songs left any doubt as to the stereotypical images nonsoutherners had of the region, the artwork of the sheet music did not. It generally served as a visual representation of the lyrics, and it might also include a portrait of the singer who achieved renown for performing the song. Sheet music art was often colorful, and when the song employed southern places or black dialect, the illustrations commonly included images of the South and southern blacks. The artwork for coon songs exaggerated the features of African Americans by showing them with bulging eyes and large red lips. The artwork for Dixie songs moved beyond extreme black caricatures found on the sheet music for coon songs, but it was nonetheless stereotypical. Mammies frequently appeared on the covers of songs about the South, as did images of blacks dancing and playing banjo in front of log cabins or eating watermelon. "Little Puff of Smoke, Good Night—A Southern Croon" (1910), with lyrics describing mammy and her "pickaninny" child, who is the "puff of smoke," features a log cabin, the mammy in a kerchief and dress with an apron holding her "little colored child," and, in the foreground, a photograph of the young white man who wrote the music. The artwork for "Floatin' down the Mississippi (On Our Honeymoon)" (1918) features a "honeymoon houseboat" with a white couple in silhouette. A group of blacks play banjoes and sing as if to serenade the honeymoon couple. The grouping includes several stereotypical figures—the black dandy in top hat, the black field hand with patches on his overalls, a small black child often used to represent a "pickaninny," and the mammy in kerchief. All of them have large red lips and all appear to be happy as they sing.[27]

One of the most popular songs of the genre was Jack Yellen's "Are You from Dixie? ('Cause I'm from Dixie, Too!)," published in 1915. The sheet music for the tune features two white men shaking hands as they stand in the foreground of a cotton field of a southern plantation. Immediately

"Little Puff of Smoke, Good Night—A Southern Croon," sheet music cover, 1910. (Author's collection)

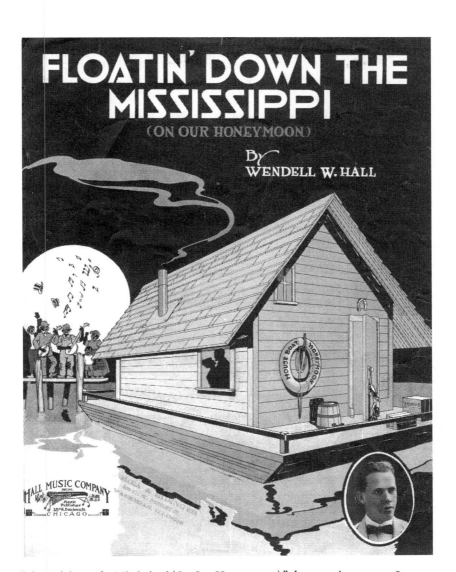

"Floatin' down the Mississippi (On Our Honeymoon)," sheet music cover, 1918.
(Author's collection)

behind them are blacks picking the cotton, and in the distance sits the plantation's "big house." The dress of the two men suggests that one is from the South and the other, from the North, as the lyrics reveal, is simply a southerner who wants to return to Dixie. He wears a modern suit and spats, while the southern gentleman wears a long waistcoat, large brimmed hat, and what is known as a plantation necktie.[28]

The image matches the lyrics of "Are You from Dixie?," which are quintessential in their sentiments of displaced southerners who want to return to the South. The song is a conversation between two men and the desire of one to come back to Dixie:

> Hello there stranger! How do you do!
> There's something I'd like to say to you.
> Don't be surprised, You're recognized!
> I'm no detective but I've just surmised
> You're from the place where I long to be
> Your smiling face seems to say to me,
> You're from my own land, My sunny homeland,
>   Tell me can it be?
> Are you from Dixie? I said from Dixie!
> Where the fields of cotton beckon to me
> I'm glad to see you, Tell me how be you,
>   And the friends I'm longing to see.
> If you're from Alabama, Tennessee or Caroline
> Any place below the Mason-Dixon line
> Then you're from Dixie, Hurray for Dixie! '
>   Cause I'm from Dixie too![29]

The song, published by M. Witmark & Sons, expressed the northern fascination with the South as a "sunny" place with cotton fields and good friends who recognize one another as such. As compared to the impersonal and urban North, the South was cast as a simpler and friendlier place. In his book about the Witmark publishing house, Isidore Witmark admitted as much. Dixie not only represented the "land of peace and plenty and love," he wrote. "The South, in Tin Pan Alley, has become the symbol of that land of milk and honey." Indeed, the themes of nature, home, family, and romance were all linked to the plantation ideal.[30]

Probably the most famous American composer to write Dixie songs was Irving Berlin. Born Israel Baline, he immigrated to New York from Russia in 1892 at the age of four, and by the time he was twenty-one, he was a

"Are You from Dixie? ('Cause I'm from Dixie, Too!)," sheet music cover, 1915.
(Author's collection)

staff lyricist for the Ted Snyder Company. A few years later, he became a partner in the music publishing firm of Waterson, Berlin & Snyder. Most of his early songs were written for vaudeville performances in which the majority of the audience was working class. He began his career plugging songs for the Snyder Company and often performed coon songs and other ragtime tunes. He also wrote several ethnic novelty songs about Italians, Jews, Germans, and Irish, but like many Tin Pan Alley lyricists he wrote songs that employed black dialect and sentimentalized the South.[31]

Berlin's coon songs, which included "Colored Romeo" (1910) and his back-to-Dixie songs, were written in a vein similar to his ethnic novelty songs in that they addressed immigrants—although in this case the "immigrants" were southern blacks who had migrated to northern cities.[32] Like other lyricists who wrote songs for blackface performance, Berlin's Dixie songs were written primarily in the second decade of the twentieth century although Tin Pan Alley lyricists continued to write such songs throughout the 1920s. In these Dixie tunes there is often a black male protagonist who longs to go home to the South where he "belongs." He might pick cotton and call for his mammy, and the lyrics are often in what was known as "blackface dialect," though not always. Even when written without dialect, early recordings of these songs reveal that they were performed in the dialect commonly used by white blackface performers.[33] For example, although the race of the protagonist in Berlin's "When It's Night Time Down in Dixieland" (1914) is unclear, the theme of the sentimental South is not. The chorus features "darkies strolling hand in hand," "Southern melodies, floating on the breeze," "listening to crickets," and even "Vet'rans of the civil war telling stories by the score." Yet Berlin expanded on that scene by suggesting that racial harmony existed in the South, with the lines "Dixie land embraces the happiest of races / All you see is smiling faces, when it's nighttime in Dixieland." As Berlin's lyrics suggest, he and other songwriters were content to perpetuate this blissful image of the region, even though lynching and other forms of racial violence was the reality on the ground.[34]

During these years, tunes written about the mythical South and the southern mammy were being churned out by the hundreds, performed in vaudeville and on the Broadway stage. They were also being recorded, and they eventually made their way onto radio and into film through the performances of Al Jolson and Eddie Cantor, who made a career out of performing blackface. Indeed, Al Jolson made his Broadway debut in 1910 performing a "coon" song and later helped popularize George Gershwin's best-selling song "Swanee" (1919) on Broadway. Cantor, too, performed blackface throughout his career, although he expanded his comedic repertoire once he became a radio personality. Jack Yellen appropriately credited songs about the South and their performance to the minstrel tradition. "These Dixie songs which I wrote and a lot of other writers wrote," he explained, "were the last of the minstrel show influence."[35]

Historical developments in this decade contributed to the increase in Dixie songs and their focus on the preindustrial South. The northern migration of southern blacks intensified the anxiety the native white population already held for immigrants from southern and eastern Europe. This decade also witnessed an increase in nativist and racist sentiment, the rise of the Ku Klux Klan, and, in 1915, the debut of D. W. Griffith's *The Birth of a Nation* to very appreciative white audiences around the country. There was also intensifying competition for unskilled jobs in northern cities between newly arrived immigrants and African Americans. Thus, back-to-Dixie songs had a very real meaning for northern writers, publishers, and immigrant audiences, who may have really wanted blacks to return to the South.[36]

Significantly, the theme of sectional reconciliation was also evident in Dixie songs, because the reconciliation between the regions and their white populations was cultural as well as political. The long reconciliation between North and South following the Civil War was ongoing in the early twentieth century, and a critical element of that reconciliation was to cement a sectional relationship based on the commonly held values of Anglo-Saxonism. Reunions of the Blue and the Gray, which had been taking place since the 1880s, were not only events but the topic of song. George M. Cohan, an Irish immigrant best known for his song "Yankee Doodle Dandy," also wrote a song called the "Wedding of the Blue and the Gray" (1906). It, too, was a patriotic song; however, the focus was on a southern soldier who had gone to fight for both "Dixie" and "Uncle Sam."[37]

In 1917, the writing team of Edgar Leslie and Harry Ruby wrote the song "The Dixie Volunteers," paying homage to southern soldiers in the American army who were headed to France. The lyrics allude to the soldiers' Confederate heritage and give a nod to Stephen Foster. The Dixie volunteers were "from the land of Old Black Joe," and "those great big Southern laddies / Just like their dear old daddies / They are proud to go." Moreover, "they're going to be / Fighting men like Stonewall Jackson and Robert E. Lee." The song became popular during World War I in part because patriotic songs were popular but also because it was performed in

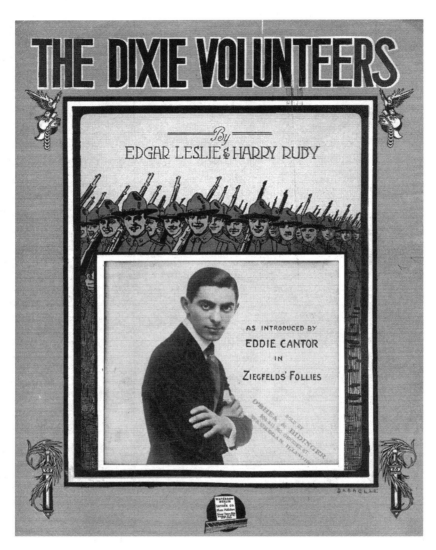

"The Dixie Volunteers," sheet music cover, 1917. (Author's collection)

the Ziegfeld Follies—the highly successful and long-running Broadway show—by one of its best-known stars, Eddie Cantor.[38]

Increasingly, popular songs about the South made their way onto Broadway and eventually to radio and film via the songwriters of Tin Pan Alley and the vaudeville performers who made the transition to these new forms of media. These changes to the music industry were accompanied by changes in popular music, as jazz emerged from the South to make its mark as an American art form. Much of this transformation in American popular music must be understood in the context of modernization during the interwar period and its impact on consumer culture. As Isidore Witmark noted, "Tin Pan Alley is the Newspaper Row of music. It is a species of song-and-dance journalism, intimately bound up with the current trend of events." In other words, the music industry continued to tell the story of American life and was consciously aware of its link to changes in culture, such that the industry adapted to changes in the way music was distributed and consumed.[39]

The 1920s witnessed important changes to American popular music. Broadway began to appeal to broader tastes in music and became what one scholar has referred to as "a glittering song supermarket." This decade also saw the recording of blues and jazz music for distribution to southern markets, and yet these "race records" began to influence the music of Tin Pan Alley—indeed, Tin Pan Alley transformed blues and jazz compositions by African American composers into popular songs, even though jazz remained controversial with music critics throughout the decade. Talking pictures also began to influence how Americans consumed popular songs, beginning with *The Jazz Singer* (1927). The film starred Al Jolson and was the first time that American audiences heard music on film. By the end of the decade, the technological revolution that occurred with the invention of radio meant that not only would the marketing and consumption of songs drastically change but new types of music could be heard. All of these trends signaled the beginning of the end of Tin Pan Alley's monopoly on American popular music. Regardless, the image of the South in song remained consistent.[40]

At the beginning of the decade, George Gershwin composed his biggest-selling song, "Swanee." Although Irving Caesar wrote the song's lyrics in 1919, it was made popular by Al Jolson's performance of the tune in the Broadway show *Sinbad* in 1920. The song's lyrics play off of Foster's influence and his song "Old Folks at Home." For example, the refrain to "Swanee" includes these lines:

My dear old Swanee I'd give the world to be
Among the folks in D-I-X-I-Even though my Mammy's
Waiting for me praying for me Down by the Swanee
The folks up north will see me no more
When I go to the Swanee shore.

Such lyrics made it a back-to-Dixie song, and yet few of that type achieved
the success of "Swanee," which sold 2 million recordings and more than a
million copies of sheet music. The song remained popular for two decades
because of its association with Jolson, who not only performed it on stage
but also recorded it and sang it in three different films.[41]

"Swanee" was a hit, and yet it was a hit that continued to perpetuate the
image of a southern black man who sought to return "home" to the South
and the care of his "mammy." It was an image from which popular songs
that mentioned the South were slow to change, and although not as many
songs of this type were written and popularized during the 1920s, when
a song set in the South or with a southern theme did emerge as a popular tune the same lyrical devices were employed. "Black" dialect was used,
a mammy was present, and the South remained a primitive culture with
primitive people. One song, for example, was simply titled "My Mammy,"
and it, too, was performed in the same Broadway show as "Swanee" and
became one of Jolson's signature songs.[42]

The 1920s also witnessed the influence of jazz on some of Tin Pan Alley's
best-known composers, including Irving Berlin, George Gershwin, and Jerome Kern. Gershwin and Kern, in particular, have been credited for popularizing jazz. Like its progenitor, ragtime, jazz was considered vulgar and
primitive, and white music critics argued vociferously about its legitimacy
as an art form. Gershwin, however, was a fierce defender of jazz, which he
considered "not Negro, but American." Yet even he would contradict himself by referring to jazz as having "developed out of ragtime" and as being
"the plantation song improved and transformed into finer, bigger harmo-
nies."[43] He had a keen respect for the music, which many of his generation
did not. As he argued in 1926, "No student of singing can afford any longer
to ignore jazz music or to sniff at it as a thing of low estate and of negative
cultural value."[44]

It was Gershwin's style of jazz, however, that became established in Tin
Pan Alley, on Broadway, and in films. While New Orleans is recognized as
the birthplace of jazz and Chicago is seen as the place where jazz matured,
it was the symphonic jazz performed by white artists like Gershwin, Kern,

"Swanee," sheet music cover, 1919. (Courtesy Lilly Library, Indiana University, Bloomington, Indiana)

and Paul Whiteman that achieved popularity. Certainly, white jazz leaders like Whiteman borrowed liberally from the work of black jazz musicians or adapted the "primitive" jazz of New Orleans and Chicago. Yet it was the symphonic jazz white artists performed that the listening and buying public wanted and that ultimately became popular American music. In fact, Paul Whiteman, whose orchestra played symphonic jazz, was publicly known as the "king of jazz" in the 1920s. He was a self-promoter, to be sure, and the "king of jazz" was a moniker he gave himself. Yet the symphonic jazz played by his orchestra achieved popularity even though he was adapting music by black artists. As Duke Ellington put it, "Mr. Whiteman deserves credit for discovering and recognizing ability or genius in [black] composers whose works would not normally be acceptable," adding, "[He] makes it possible to commercialize these works." Gershwin's "Rhapsody in Blue" (first performed by the Paul Whiteman Orchestra in 1924) even moved one music critic to remark, "He [Gershwin] is the beginning of the age of sophisticated jazz."[45]

Throughout this same period, Duke Ellington and his orchestra were performing jazz, and although Ellington personally referred to his music as "Negro music," an early jazz scholar argued that his music was really "just jazz," as though jazz was not an African American invention and art form.[46] Such comments reflect what was a serious issue with American popular music of the interwar period, which is that even though Gershwin, Kern, and many other successful white composers were influenced by jazz and blues—musical genres that emerged from the American South—black composers who drew on these same African American traditions in music were not taken as seriously for their contributions to American popular song.

The medium of radio without a doubt expanded the definition of what made a song "popular." Tin Pan Alley had long determined which songs became hits, but radio became the great equalizer. Certainly, the songs of Tin Pan Alley were the most played and listened-to songs on the air in the early days of radio. However, before national networks were established, in 1926, local radio stations were more likely to play music with regional appeal. Before country music achieved mass appeal, the music known as "hillbilly" music, for example, was popular with rural audiences across the country, especially in the South. Even Tin Pan Alley lyricist Jack Yellen recognized how radio had changed the music industry. Speaking of hillbilly songs and their popularity, Yellen remarked: "The radio made a song of that kind possible. [It] provided the audience which wanted that type of song." Certainly, hillbilly music of the 1920s and 1930s was being recorded and had considerable commercial success. It also reached a national audience via radio programs large and small, but especially through Chicago's *National Barn Dance* and Nashville's *Grand Ole Opry*. Yet scholars agree that country music's major breakthrough came during World War II, and more especially after the war, when its increasing popularity contributed to its integration into the national popular culture. The image of the southerner-as-hillbilly, moreover, did not emerge because of the content of hillbilly songs; rather, it was the creation of music promoters, the recording industry, radio, and Hollywood—addressed in other chapters of this book.[47]

Broadway, radio, and movies were all important vehicles for popularizing songs, and, during the 1920s and 1930s, the songs that focused on Dixie in each of these mediums continued to romanticize the South or showcase it as a primitive or exotic region. Jerome Kern and Oscar Hammerstein, for example, wrote the music and lyrics for one of the most successful Broadway shows—*Show Boat*—which debuted in 1927. The story was based on Edna Ferber's novel about a show boat that traveled the Mississippi River, and the songs Kern and Hammerstein composed for the show reiterated the themes found in "coon" songs from the early days of Tin Pan Alley and employed the dialect common to those tunes. "Ol' Man River," the signature song from the show, became one of America's best-known songs and employed the dialect commonly used to denote both the "South" and the "Negro." *Show Boat* had such success as a Broadway musical that Maxwell House sponsored a popular radio version of the show in the mid-1930s. Hollywood adapted it to the large screen in 1928, 1936, and again in 1951.[48]

As soon as the technology of sound could be melded with films to create the "talking picture," music became part of Hollywood filmmaking. Movies became a primary vehicle for selling songs and a venue for popular singers to revive songs from early Tin Pan Alley or introduce new songs to the American public. Al Jolson began the trend with *The Jazz Singer* (1927) and later *The Singing Fool* (1928), in which he performed "Swanee" and parlayed his blackface stage performances to the big screen. Many of the earliest Hollywood films began as Broadway musicals, like *Show Boat*, which brought with it familiar images of the South—steamboats on the Mississippi River, white women in hoop skirts, and blacks singing happily as they worked. To ensure that new films had musical accompaniment, Hollywood studios bought the motion-picture rights to Broadway musicals. Warner Brothers, in particular, led the way by buying up music publishing houses and the rights to their compositions. Additionally, composers and lyricists were offered very generous terms to write popular songs for films and to move from Tin Pan Alley to Hollywood. "Scouts were sent to every cabaret in New York and to every night club in a mad search for song writers," *New York Times* journalist John Flinn proclaimed in 1929, adding that "Tin Pan Alley has moved all the way from New York's West Forties right into the heart of Hollywood." One of these was Dixie songster Jack Yellen.[49]

Although composing Dixie songs became less in vogue by the late 1930s, Hollywood continued to use them in movies. There was a return to sentimentalism and a revival of nineteenth-century composers whose songs about the South had become American classics, namely Stephen Foster and Daniel Decatur Emmett.[50] Numerous films were set in the American South between 1915 and 1945, and nearly all of them, of course, incorporated songs about the region. The result was a revival of Negro spirituals as well as the music of both Daniel Decatur Emmett and Stephen Foster. "Dixie" was part of the sound track of several southern films, including *The Littlest Rebel* (1935), in which it was sung by its star, Shirley Temple; *Under Southern Stars* (1937); *Gone with the Wind* (1939); and, a few years later, *Dixie* (1943), starring Bing Crosby in the role of the composer. The latter film revived the song "Dixie" as a patriotic song with a particular resonance and currency for World War II by proclaiming it to be "the greatest war song of all time."[51] Hollywood also used Stephen Foster's music to bolster its southern films. *The Little Colonel* (1935), another vehicle for Shirley Temple, and *Jezebel* (1938), which starred Bette Davis, both included songs by Foster. Moreover, the most successful motion picture of the genre—*Gone with the Wind*—used no less than ten Stephen Foster tunes to accompany the film, including "My Old Kentucky Home" (1851) and "Massa's in de Cold Ground" (1852).

The image of the South in American popular songs written between the Civil War and World War II was consistent with ideas about the region that were visible in other areas of popular culture. The South of the composer's imagination, of the music publisher's imagination, and of American audiences was of a region still wedded to its agrarian past. It was the region where southern blacks were both happy and comic, and if they had migrated North, which was a reality with sociocultural implications, then they most assuredly wanted to return home to the South—at least in the lyrics of popular songs.

For nearly a century, the South of American popular song was the region that many of America's best-known composers relied upon to provide them with inspiration for sentimental lyrics. As Jack Yellen remarked, "Nostalgia gives a song a quality that nothing else can give it." Dixie undeniably worked well as the lyricist's muse for nostalgic songs—songs that New York and Hollywood produced and Americans consumed. The South in popular song was the region they knew from advertising, radio, and motion pictures. Dixie was a mythological region still steeped in its antebellum past where blacks were a servant race. Moreover, the region as a whole appealed to nonsoutherners as the antithesis of the modern urban-industrial world with which many of them were coming to terms. "Mammy" was in "Alabammy" where she "belonged," not in Chicago or Detroit, and the ideal America existed below the Mason-Dixon Line.[52]

CHAPTER 2

Selling Dixie

"After several months of study, a package was finally designed that stands today as one of the most striking and powerful appeals in any line of grocery products. Not only has all unnecessary type matter been removed from the package, but the head of the Southern mammy has been changed from a mere trade mark to an irresistible suggestion of Southern hospitality and good cooking." This interior report by Madison Avenue's J. Walter Thompson Agency (JWT) was intended to showcase the value of package design in their advertising campaign for Aunt Jemima pancake flour. As the agency noted, prior to the repackaged design that appeared in stores in 1916, the container was "unattractive, with little store display value, and little appeal to the consumer." Indeed, it noted that "[the name] Aunt Jemima was of no special advantage." Fortuitously, the agency secured a painting by the American artist Arthur Burdette Frost—best known for his illustrations of Joel Chandler Harris's Uncle Remus tales. The painting was of a mammy, reportedly of Nancy Green, who had portrayed the character of "Aunt Jemima" since the Chicago World's Fair of 1893. According to JWT, it was Frost's distinctive image of a southern mammy that conveyed the "appeal and glamour of the old South" and increased the sales of the pancake flour.[1]

Selling products by using the allure of the Old South is as old as the history of modern advertising and the mass production of goods. Classified ads, which promoted the sale of an item at a particular place and time, were and continue to be efficient for the sale of local goods. The emergence of national advertising during the late nineteenth century changed this sales model; it allowed for more direct communication between the manufacturer and consumers and often bypassed retailers. National ads interpreted goods for consumers. They offered a more abstract explanation of the connection between customers and the product, in effect selling both the product and the values that the product represented. Advertisements swiftly became more than a tool for selling goods; they reflected and expressed larger cultural values.[2]

From the late nineteenth century through World War II, national advertisements consistently offered a cultural narrative that reflected Ameri-

JUST ONE WAY
to get that old-time Southern flavor—

GET AUNT JEMIMA'S RECIPE READY-MIXED

Worth while? Well, a number of people evidently think so; more than 500,000,000 Aunt Jemima Pancakes were eaten last year!

PROBABLY you know how it came about that we have Aunt Jemima's famous recipe—the very one she used when she was cook in Colonel Higbee's mansion in the days "befo' de wah." If you don't, send for the folder offered below.

Yet, having that priceless recipe, it isn't easily that we retain the old-time Southern flavor for which millions buy Aunt Jemima Pancake Flour.

How we keep that flavor

Aunt Jemima never used ordinary flour in her pancakes; for them she always had on hand a special kind, an exceptionally fine grade of wheat flour.

And she added to it smaller quantities of other flours—flours that you can't buy in the stores today.

It is only by milling these flours ourselves, by mixing them *just so* with the other ingredients of her recipe that we can keep that wonderful flavor Aunt Jemima got.

It isn't that Aunt Jemima Pancake Flour is ready-mixed, that you simply add water or milk to it and have your batter ready for the griddle. Many other kinds of pancake mixtures have been produced since Aunt Jemima was first put on the market over thirty years ago.

Nor is it the tender lightness of Aunt Jemima Pancakes which makes them so distinctive today. Many women can equal that at times—with work, and luck.

Today Aunt Jemima Pancake Flour is used in some ten million homes because it makes perfect pancakes every time, quickly, economically—pancakes with that inimitable old-time Southern flavor! And it's the only way to get that flavor.

At your grocer's—or we'll send sample

If you've never tasted genuine Aunt Jemima Pancakes; or if the kind that you've been making haven't turned out *just right* every morning, then get a package of Aunt Jemima Pancake Flour from your grocer now. Or accept our special offer of a generous sample; send the coupon today.

Pancakes can be not only the most popular breakfast at your house—but the easiest to get. Aunt Jemima Pancakes *one morning* will prove that for you. Aunt Jemima Mills Company, St. Joseph, Mo.

"I'se in town, Honey!"

Today it's so easy. Aunt Jemima Pancake Flour is Aunt Jemima's famous Southern recipe ready-mixed. You simply add water or milk to it, spot your batter on a hot griddle and you have 'em—pancakes just like Aunt Jemima's!

And muffins

Waffles, too

If you've never made waffles with Aunt Jemima Pancake Flour you've missed a treat and done a lot of unnecessary work. Notice the easy recipe on the back of the next package you buy.

Delicious muffins are also made with Aunt Jemima Pancake Flour—light tender muffins that fairly melt in your mouth. The recipe is on every package just try it!

Special offer

In return for this coupon and 8c in stamps or coin (to cover cost of special packaging and mailing) we will send you a sample package of Aunt Jemima Prepared Buckwheat Flour, a sample package of Aunt Jemima Pancake Flour and an interesting folder, "The Romance of Aunt Jemima," with recipes for special pancake treats. If you want the jolly Aunt Jemima family of 4 rag dolls, too—all in bright colors, ready to cut and stuff—send 40c in stamps or coin.

MAIL THIS COUPON TODAY

Aunt Jemima Mills Company, Dept. 1-B
St. Joseph, Missouri

Enclosed find_____cents for which please send me

☐ Sample packages of Aunt Jemima Pancake Flour, Aunt Jemima Prepared Buckwheat Flour and recipe folder.

☐ Samples, recipe folder and the Aunt Jemima rag dolls.

Name_____

Street Address_____

City_____ State_____

AUNT JEMIMA PANCAKE FLOUR

Aunt Jemima advertisement showing the image developed by artist Arthur Burdette Frost in 1916. (Author's collection)

cans' shared values. Such ads often drew upon the past in order to make sense of contemporary society, by offering Americans a counterbalance to the changes brought by modernity. When that cultural narrative focused on the South, for example, "Dixie" was not simply a reference to a region; it was a brand purposefully linked to the nation's nostalgia for the antebellum South. In the period marked by the rise of mass consumption, Americans shared a "common heritage defined by goods," and in many instances that heritage was expressed through the cultural icons, traditions, and language of the Old South. Thus, while advertising sold goods, it also helped to define American identity. Moreover, it helped define southern identity for American consumers.[3]

In the early years of mass advertising, which began in the 1890s, American consumers could buy "Songs of Dixie" from S. Brainard's Sons of Chicago, the "Game of Dixie-Land" from the Fireside Game Company of Cincinnati, Confederate flags from a company in New Jersey, and any number of books about Dixie from New York publishers—from the children's primer *A B C in Dixie* to Paul Laurence Dunbar's *Folks from Dixie*—all of which were advertised in the nation's leading magazines. All of these products were sold using language that implicitly and explicitly attached them to the Old South. "Songs of Dixie" were listed as "Sunny, Southern songs, Home, Plantation and Camp songs." The "Game of Dixie-Land" depicted "Negro life in the Sunny South" and "happy sketches of a happy people." The subtitle of *A B C in Dixie* was "A Plantation Alphabet," which, in addition to using the caricature of an elderly black man, made the claim that the book would "appeal to the little folks, whether they have been to Dixie land or not." Very often, the latter was true. Finally, Dunbar's *Folks from Dixie*, which was notable because it did not caricature southern blacks, was so popular with American consumers who were enamored with the exoticism of former slaves that 5,000 copies of the book were issued for the first printing in 1898.[4]

The Old South not only provided nonsouthern companies with a useful sales tactic but it also gave national advertising agencies a treasure trove of stories and characters and an identity with which to sell products, and as advertising became more sophisticated so too did the imagery. The mammy, the southern belle, the bearded and mustachioed southern colonel, the male house servant or "uncle" figure, the "pickaninny," the opulent southern plantation, and even that hard-to-define quality known as "southern hospitality," all appeared in national advertising for products ranging from flour and coffee to cleaning supplies and liquor. The use of these stock southern characters was no accident. Advertising agencies were in the business of conveying familiar images that provided cultural meaning to products that consumers often recognized in other elements of American culture like literature, art, and film. When advertising agencies employed the image of a southern mammy or a belle, for example, that image intentionally served as a symbolic extension of the Old South that was present in and familiar to consumers from other areas of popular culture.[5]

The emergence of a mass consumer society at the end of the nineteenth century was evidence of a much broader transformation taking place in American culture. Consumer habits were revolutionized in the period between 1890 and 1940. During these years, the American landscape experienced sweeping change, both literally and figuratively, particularly in the Northeast and the Midwest. Rapid urbanization and industrialization, accompanied by mass consumption and modern advertising, heralded a modern era and forever altered the consuming habits of Americans. Between 1890 and 1920, Americans witnessed the development of brands and brand names for the first time in the country's history. As the 1920s gave way to the 1930s, the new medium of radio further altered the way companies advertised their products. In both print and early radio, national images and perceptions of the American South infused the catalog of American advertising. Indeed, throughout the first half of the twentieth century, the Old South—the land of "moonlight and magnolias" and happy blacks eager to serve—remained a frequent advertising trope.[6]

The rise of mass consumerism highlights the ambivalent relationship American society had with modernization, and advertising provides insight into how the benefits of modernity, such as mass-produced consumer goods, could be sold using people's need to connect with an uncomplicated past. The emergence and evolution of modern advertising in the early twentieth century suggests that the iconography of the antebellum South offered consumers that uncomplicated past and a way to connect with the pastoral ideal even as they consumed mass-produced goods. In doing so, they not only came to associate such goods with the South, but it was one way in which they continued to see the South as the region that maintained the values of preindustrial America and continued to represent a culture of leisure, pastoral romance, and loyal servants—a lifestyle to which many middle-class consumers aspired.[7]

The use of southern images to sell goods was both a function of the advertising agency that created the ad campaigns and the messages associated with those images. These developments were also tied to the evolution of advertising in the period from 1890 to 1940—from simple print advertisements and messages, to the creation of the social tableau advertisement of the 1920s that told a story, to the period of radio advertising, which began in earnest in the late 1920s and was in full swing by the 1930s.[8]

The earliest southern images to be employed in modern advertising were black personalities, which by any measure were the "uncle" and "mammy" figures of the Old South. The derogatory term "pickaninny" was assigned to images of black children, who were very often portrayed eating a slice of watermelon and were used to sell everything from food to detergent. Aunt Jemima, the mammy figure, was employed to sell pancake flour, and Rastus, an Uncle Tom figure, was associated with Cream of Wheat. Both personalities first appeared in the advertising of the 1890s and were the best known of an entire genre of racial stereotypes used in advertising. Historian T. J. Jackson Lears cautions not to view these figures as merely racial stereotypes, arguing that Aunt Jemima, Rastus, and, later, Uncle Ben were folk characters who represented the preindustrial world with which people were familiar and who stood in stark contrast to the new, industrial "world of abundance" of the late nineteenth century.[9] In other words, their personalities provided consumers respite from the world of rapid change because of their association with a nostalgic past.[10]

To be sure, nostalgia for preindustrial America was part and parcel of advertising campaigns that employed southern black characters. Yet there can be no doubt that these were racial stereotypes. Moreover, they were clearly southern racial stereotypes that need to be understood as part of the regional myth often associated with the plantation South. In other words, these particular racial stereotypes fit into the larger "moonlight-and-magnolias" advertising theme, which, as described earlier, included several characters from the mammy to the cavalier southern gentleman to the belle. It is also true that these images can be understood in the context of the turn-of-the-century longing for a preindustrial American past. Certainly, a quaint New England town could and sometimes did serve this purpose. The American South, however, was used to represent this nostalgic past for a much longer period of time—in part because the region remained rural and agricultural through World War II, even as the rest of the country became more urban and industrial. Thus, as a region, the South continued to serve as the pastoral ideal for Americans living in places like New York, Detroit, and Chicago. Moreover, for advertisers, these southern stereotypes represented the idealized master/servant relationships of a bygone era that was highly desired by American consumers.

The use of such stereotypes in advertising often represented the ideals of the advertising men who created them. Anglo-Saxon Protestant men from the Northeast and Midwest who were urban elites staffed the leading advertising agencies, most of which were located in New York. Not only did they live better lives than the consuming public over whom they sought influence, but they tended to see consumers as in a class beneath them—people who needed advertisers to show them how to raise their own standards of consumption. These men were very likely to employ domestic servants in their own homes, and, not ironically, they crafted advertisements that incorporated an iconography of status and leisure. When such advertisements involved the South, the narrative was about the status and leisure associated with the Old South, and very often the icons of that time and place were the uncle and the mammy. When creating advertising campaigns, these northern ad men were selling the American consumer on an idea of leisure and comfort—comfort food, comforting characters, and the ease of having something prepared effortlessly, if possible by a servant.[11] This South of plantation legend was used by ad agencies well into the 1930s. The black mammy and uncle caricatures appealed to white consumers nationwide, because the image often conveyed blacks as loyal employees who willingly took care of their white employers. Furthermore, such "faithful servants" projected the image of leisure that Madison Avenue ad men lived and to which white middle-class consumers aspired.[12]

The account history of the Aunt Jemima brand offers vivid evidence of how Madison Avenue purposely developed an advertising icon associated with the Old South. JWT, the nation's largest and most profitable ad agency, was responsible for the long-term success of the Aunt Jemima brand, yet her connection to pancake flour had a long history even before JWT made her the most recognizable icon of American advertising in the twentieth century. Although the pancake flour itself was developed by a Missouri milling company, the long-told story within the agency was that the recipe was created by a former slave named Aunt Jemima and that her recipe was bought by the R. T. Davis Milling Company of St. Joseph, Missouri. According to its internal history, JWT took over the account in 1909 and sent a representative to the mill to unearth a story that would help sell the brand. As he discovered, the best way to sell the pancake flour was to associate the story of Aunt Jemima with "the old never-to-be-forgotten South as it existed many years ago." The flour was considered to be of high quality, but with the tale of Aunt Jemima the agency believed it could gain an advantage in the marketplace by advertising the flour's "romantic origins."[13]

The man who developed the story was James Webb Young, a highly successful agent at JWT. Young, a native of Covington, Kentucky, began his advertising career in Cincinnati and used his personal acquaintance with childhood friend Helen Resor, wife of JWT president Stanley Resor, to get a job with the agency's New York office. In Young's telling of his success story as an ad man, his father worked on a Mississippi steamboat and his mother was a "southern belle," and he learned about the South firsthand as a traveling Bible salesman. These influences, he asserted, shaped his understanding of people, their habits, and their personal desires. Given this background, and with the support of his Madison Avenue employer, he created the mythology associated with Aunt Jemima.[14]

Young once asserted that "the purpose of advertising is to disturb the status quo."[15] Yet in many ways he and JWT helped preserve the racial status quo through their promotion of the Aunt Jemima brand. JWT developed the mythology surrounding the brand, which consumers in Jim Crow's America readily accepted. According to this myth, Aunt Jemima was born on a Louisiana plantation owned by one "Colonel Higbee" near the junction of the Red and Mississippi Rivers. From this plantation, she developed her flour recipe, becoming famous throughout the South for her pancakes. Following the Civil War, the R. T. Davis Milling Company sent a representative to see her, who then bought her recipe and "hired her to supervise" the production of the flour mix at the mill in St. Joseph.[16]

The idea of hiring a former slave woman to "supervise" the production of the pancake flour for a milling company was far-fetched, and the truth is that Nancy Green—a real woman and a domestic from Chicago—was hired by the milling company to appear as Aunt Jemima at the 1893 Chicago World's Fair. There, Green played the role of the southern mammy and demonstrated pancake making for thousands of people from around the world who were visiting the expo. World's fairs were important to the emerging consumer society of the late nineteenth century. There, companies with goods to sell were able to capitalize on the fair's popularity with people from around the globe, who visited the fair by the hundreds of thousands.[17] Significantly, among the many displays at this and later world's fairs were exhibits of primitive people from exotic locations like the Philippines or Egypt, but also slave cabins and former southern slaves. The Davis Milling Company first showcased its product at the Columbian

Exposition in ways that were similar. Certainly, the company had a product to sell. Yet it decided to use the primitive figure of a former slave who had lived her life as the mammy on a plantation in the exotic Old South to attract people to its exhibit and to its product. Aunt Jemima was such a big hit with fairgoers that an estimated 50,000 orders were placed for the pancake mix. Indeed, from that point forward, Nancy Green enjoyed a long career as Aunt Jemima, demonstrating the pancake mix at fairs for the next twenty years.[18]

In 1909, when JWT secured the Davis Milling Company account, it assumed responsibility for advertising the pancake mix and expanding its sale beyond immediate local markets into a product with sales throughout the Midwest. Known as a leader in market research, JWT advertised in newspapers, created billboards, and placed ads on streetcars and subways. Sales increased. By 1914, the agency convinced the mill to change its name to Aunt Jemima Mills Company and within a couple of years sought to increase sales nationally by focusing on advertising directly to the product's primary consumers—women. JWT bought and controlled much of the advertising space in American magazines, generating much of their revenue. Women's magazines were the most popular American magazines, and in 1916–17, full-page ads for Aunt Jemima pancake flour appeared in *Ladies' Home Journal*, *Woman's Home Companion*, and *Saturday Evening Post*, among others, and, once again, product sales increased. It was at this time that the company "improved" its trademark figure by incorporating the painting of Aunt Jemima by Arthur Burdette Frost.[19]

The ad agency, and particularly James Young, recognized that the appeal of the Old South, and the story of Aunt Jemima in particular, helped sell the product. Indeed, both the dramatization of a southern mammy and the story of how the recipe came into being were the hooks used to attract consumers. According to internal account histories, by incorporating the special appeal of Aunt Jemima, JWT was able to "draw upon the full resources of romance and association which lay back of this product . . . the appeal and glamour of the old South." The story encompassed a southern mammy and a Louisiana plantation, but, to pique consumer interest even further, the agency expanded on the legend of the southern cook by claiming that the log cabin in which she was born had become well known among tourists and "more famous than Uncle Tom's." Moreover, her recipe was "the despair of all Southern mammies," who felt they simply could not compete.[20]

Proof of the brand's success was in the sales figures determined by market research. JWT was on the cutting edge of such research, which by the 1920s was making advertising increasingly about lifestyle and image. In other words, how did people distinguish between brands of pancake flour? On the one hand, success and consumer choices could be measured by the competition. Several other companies tried to adopt an Aunt Jemima–like image for their products and had to be legally restrained from using the name "Aunt Jemima" or even from using an image of a southern mammy. The company's research also produced revealing figures on market share and on where, exactly, people were buying the product. JWT investigated small towns and large cities and interviewed hundreds of housewives, showing that Aunt Jemima was most popular in cities with over 100,000 inhabitants. This demographic consumed 55 percent of all the pancake flour produced by the mill. In order to gain an even larger share of the market in large cities and small towns, JWT waged an aggressive campaign on "flavor." And in the war of flavors, Aunt Jemima's flour was the best—not because it necessarily tasted better but because it was made from a "famous Southern recipe," which was not available in any cookbook.[21]

Throughout the 1920s, Aunt Jemima's pancake mix continued to be advertised in leading women's magazines. Over that period, Quaker Oats, which acquired the company in 1925, often resisted sales gimmicks like merchandise tie-ins, although ads show that much earlier in the company's history it did offer coupons for a rag doll collection of Aunt Jemima's "family," which had grown to include her husband "Uncle Mose" and her "pickaninny" children. By the latter part of the decade, however, a new medium—radio—emerged and proved to be a highly lucrative sales tool for any number of consumer goods, including pancake mix. In 1930, JWT convinced Quaker Oats to adapt its advertising to include the radio. Initially, ads for the pancake mix were run on stations on the Pacific Coast, where the agency recorded "phenomenal" sales results. By 1931, Aunt Jemima was on the air nationally, and the story of Colonel Higbee, his mammy cook, and the Old South literally came to life.[22]

JWT's own market research and its advertising plans reveal even more than just how the agency sought to best the competition, also offering evidence that the story of Aunt Jemima sold best *outside* of Dixie. The South was not a region of large cities—there were only seven with 100,000 or more residents in 1920. Therefore, the primary consumers for this southern brand were not native southerners. Several years later, in 1945, the agency produced another report that confirmed the brand's recognition in larger cities and areas outside of the South. Aunt Jemima was "one of the best known trademarks in America," but the research showed that "public familiarity with Aunt Jemima's picture [was] highest in the Midwest and lowest in the South." Perhaps most revealing was that even though the majority of consumers associated the image of Aunt Jemima with the pancake mix, as late as 1945 some people also related the mammy image to *Gone with the Wind* and a laundry chain, exposing the nation's larger cultural association of black women with servitude.[23]

African Americans had known for years the negative effects of "Aunt Jemima" on the progress of their race. In 1937, the *Cleveland Call and Post*, an African American newspaper, endorsed a "drive to take the bandanna off 'Aunt Jemima's' head." Noting that the image was one of many "insulting caricatures," the paper argued that the bandanna was "no longer acceptable in good society," adding that "it would be much better if Aunt Jemima removed this headpiece and revealed to the world her croqui[g] nole waves." In other words, a more realistic image of a black woman in contemporary society would be one who wore the latest hairstyle and cultivated racial pride.[24]

National advertisements suggestive of "southern-ness" were not limited to black stereotypes alone. *Life* magazine included a number of national advertisements beckoning consumers with all manner of things reminiscent of the Old South. Gorham, a company that manufactured table silver, advertised in *Life* in 1928 that its Colfax line of silverware was "a delightful reflection of southern hospitality" much like that used by the "charming hostesses of the Colonial South." A Philadelphia distillery ad campaign for Dixie Belle Gin promoted an image of upper-class leisure often associated with the planter South. J. P. Lippincott, a book publisher also located in Philadelphia, carried a large inventory of romance novels in which northern men married southern women, the literary symbol of sectional reconciliation.[25]

An important advancement in advertising during the 1920s and 1930s was the development of the social tableau. Advertisements of this type, described by one historian as "atmospheric advertising," usually depicted a "slice of life," which was intended to give the impression of quality and prestige. Although advertisers remained focused on profits, these tableaux depicted scenes reflective of contemporary cultural values so as to make a product synonymous with that culture. These ads' messages were not simply slogans but entire stories created by the scenes. The advertised item served as a memory trigger, transporting the consumer back through time.

This was done to great effect by JWT with Aunt Jemima and other brands it represented.[26]

Social tableaux were particularly useful for advertising the South, becoming, in effect, southern tableaux. The southern tableau was most often some scene set in the Old South, generally a plantation but not always. It might include belles in hoopskirts, cavalier southern gentlemen, and, of course, ready-to-please servants. One example of a southern tableau that employed the Old South theme was an advertisement for Crab Orchard whiskey, distilled in Louisville, Kentucky. The slice of life was a scene of the old Crab Orchard Springs Hotel, where people were fed such "Southern delicacies as barbequed squirrel" or "roast 'possum and candied yams," washed down, of course, with bourbon whiskey, "a flavor which even the flower of old-time Kentucky's gentility praised." Crab Orchard whiskey, in this case, was branded as "old-fashioned" Dixie, with the accompanying value of being associated with southern gentility, and it became, according to the advertisement's claim, "America's fastest-selling whiskey."[27]

One of the most effective uses of the southern tableau was done for Maxwell House coffee, a brand also represented by JWT and also developed by James Webb Young. In a 1928 advertisement that appeared in *Ladies' Home Journal*, the tableau told the story of the company's founder, Joel Cheek, who, the ad claimed, had traveled by horseback distributing the coffee he had created. The copy for the ad describes him as a "Southerner of the old South" and suggests that "long ago" his coffee "became the first choice of all Dixie." The image that accompanies the story shows a man, purportedly Joel Cheek, sitting astride his horse gazing upon an idyllic plantation complete with the "big house." He strikes a figure very similar to that of Robert E. Lee—the romantic Lee, who sits tall and straight in his saddle and looks ahead with a sense of purpose. It is a popular image, often used to summon the antebellum past. The advertisement used this southern tableau to tell Cheek's story and associate the product with the romance of the southern past. The caption reads: "Through the old SOUTH he rode . . . spreading the news of his discovery." The truth is, Cheek had come into the wholesale grocery business *after* the Civil War and had not asked the owner of the Maxwell House hotel in Nashville to use his coffee until 1887—long after the Old South had ceased to exist. Yet it was the agency's strategy to advertise the coffee and entice buyers with a narrative linked to the Old South.[28]

Although the product's brand was connected to the Nashville hotel of the same name, the Old South association was a creation of the agency.

Years ago Joel Cheek set out from Nashville on horseback, carrying samples of his new famous coffee blend

Through the old SOUTH he rode . . .
spreading the news of his discovery

In his saddle-bags, Joel Cheek carried the first samples of that special blend which has now captured America—

Where the great folk of the old South gathered for banquets and balls—at the old Maxwell House in Nashville—Joel Cheek's blend was served for years

HE was a Southerner of the old South, born with an unusual sense for flavor.

Down in old Tennessee, he dreamed of a special richness in coffee—of a taste no single coffee grown could yield. To please the critical families of old Dixie he set out years ago to create a totally new shade of flavor.

For months he worked patiently and skillfully, blending coffee with coffee, joining taste with taste. Through trial after trial he persisted until he discovered it—a particular way of blending many coffees, a new, full-bodied goodness.

Soon it became the favorite coffee of the South

On horseback, Joel Cheek started out from Nashville to sell his blend. With samples in his saddle-bags, he carried the news of it through that land of good living.

From the first, his coffee won approval among the great Southern families. Long ago it became the first choice of all Dixie.

Today that extra touch of richness in Maxwell House Coffee has captured the entire country. The blend that Joel Cheek sold on horseback long ago is now pleasing more people than any other coffee ever offered for sale.

Known to the South alone until recently, Maxwell House is now by far the largest selling coffee in the United States. Seven great plants are needed to supply it fresh-roasted to millions of homes from coast to coast.

A new experience in good living awaits you in the smooth, full-bodied liquor of this blend. Your grocer has it

in sealed blue tins. Maxwell House Products Company, Inc., Nashville, Houston, Jacksonville, Richmond, New York, Los Angeles, Chicago.

Radio listeners—tune in! Noted artists every Thursday—Maxwell House Coffee Radio Hour—9:30 p.m. Eastern Standard Time, 8:30 p.m. Central Standard Time: WSL, WBZ, WSEA, WHAM, KSEA, WJR, KYW, WTMJ, WOC, WHO, WLW, WOCO, WEBC, KSD, WDAF, KVOO, WBAP, KFRC, WSM, WSM, WMC, WHAS, WLW, WBAL, WJAX, WBT. Mountain Standard Time, 7:30 p. m.: KOA. For stations west of the Rockies, see local announcements.

"Good to the last drop"

MAXWELL HOUSE COFFEE
It is pleasing more people than any other coffee ever offered for sale

Maxwell House coffee advertisement representing the coffee as a product of the Old South, 1928.

In fact, JWT's account history confirms that its advertisements "sold, not coffee, but the fashionable, gay social life of the old Maxwell House, and, finally, the place our coffee played in those aristocratic functions of the Old South." They were selling status and leisure. Based on its own market research, the agency determined that it had to distinguish its brand from all the other brands that advertised in the highly competitive coffee market. As its research revealed, "So far as the housewife was concerned, the net result of all this advertising had been confusion, with no single brand of coffee standing out clearly in her mind." What, then, did the agency determine was important to female consumers? The conclusion was that women would buy a brand because of the ideas with which it was associated. Beauty, romance, and social prestige were the key ingredients to the successful formula JWT associated with other products it represented, and the agency decided that "the most effective copy appeal would be the romantic history of the old southern Maxwell House, after which the coffee was named."[29]

Despite the fact that the Maxwell House did not even operate as a hotel until after the Civil War, the agency created a series of advertisements intended to dramatize the leisure and status associated with patrons of the Maxwell House and link this narrative to the Old South. To accomplish this task, JWT once again sought out one of America's best illustrators to create and invent scenes for the advertisements, which would make Maxwell House coffee the best-selling coffee in America. Henry Raleigh, a well-known illustrator of society and aristocracy, was hired for the campaign. William Randolph Hearst took notice of Raleigh's illustrations while he was working for the *San Francisco Examiner* and moved him across the country to become an illustrator for his *New York Journal*. While in New York, Raleigh created illustrations for several leading magazines, including *Harper's Bazaar*, *Cosmopolitan*, and *Ladies' Home Journal*—many of which focused on elite society. Once Raleigh was hired for the Maxwell House campaign, he was sent to Nashville to develop sketches for the illustrations that would accompany the stories included in the full-page and full-color advertisements placed in the leading women's magazines.[30]

Henry Raleigh's illustrations were part of a campaign that began in earnest in 1926. The company's founder, Joel Cheek, also secured the services of John Trotman Moore, described as an "old and distinguished Tennessean" and the president of the Tennessee State Historical Society, to help uncover the "personal historical events" to be used in the ad copy. Many of Raleigh's illustrations included mustachioed men in topcoats and vests, ladies wearing beautiful frocks, and elderly black men in the role of servants. In a 1927 ad for *McCall's* magazine, Raleigh's illustration included a man arriving at the Maxwell House who, having just stepped out of a horse-drawn carriage, is greeted by an elderly black servant, there to carry his bags. Entitled "Distinguished travelers . . . spread its fame," the ad copy describes how at the old hotel "the great folk of Dixie gathered for their most brilliant balls and banquets." "Over its coffee were made the greatest speeches the old South ever heard—over that special coffee which has now won lasting and nation-wide fame." The ad even suggests that the coffee was vetted in the homes of the South's "critical" (meaning "elite") families.[31]

JWT employed various advertising tableaux that associated Maxwell House coffee with status and leisure—at a hunting lodge, for example, or at a yacht club. However, well into the 1940s, the coffee's association with the Old South helped to present a particular theme of status and leisure, accompanied by servants and perpetuating the myth that this southern antebellum ideal was only a cup of coffee away. The southern association with Maxwell House coffee, combined with Henry Raleigh's illustrations, proved to be a highly successful ad campaign. In 1927, JWT reported significant increases in coffee sales in the first year of its taking over the account. During the months of May and June, for example, sales of Maxwell House increased by 108 percent and 129 percent, respectively, over those same months in the previous year.[32]

The southern identity of Maxwell House coffee continued as a marketing ploy even after the account was taken over by the Benton & Bowles Agency. In a 1941 advertisement for the brand, the Maxwell House was again the setting dramatized by another of Henry Raleigh's illustrations, which included John Philip Sousa, who "found a coffee as heart-warming as his marches." In this tableau, Sousa's 1899 visit to the hotel was described as a place where he "enjoyed Southern hospitality at its bountiful best." The ubiquitous theme of "southern hospitality" helped to make and maintain the product's association with elite taste.[33]

The Old South obviously had cachet in both print and radio advertising throughout the 1930s, even before Margaret Mitchell's epic novel, *Gone with the Wind*, was published. It proved to be a boon to advertisers, who used this mythic imagery to great effect. Maxwell House coffee, in particular, entered into the realm of radio advertising as a sponsor of one of the most popular radio shows of the 1930s, the *Maxwell House Show Boat*. The program reached a national audience from its home in New York, and

Maxwell House coffee advertisement showcasing the illustrations of artist Henry Raleigh, 1930. (Author's collection)

it not only perpetuated white southern stereotypes but it engaged in what scholars call "radio minstrelsy," in which whites, the case with *Show Boat* and *Amos 'n' Andy*, portrayed black characters who spoke in dialect. Of course, listeners never saw the characters, but the dialect they used made it clear they were performing in blackface. As the print advertisements for *Show Boat* made clear, the program's two black characters were portrayed by white men in blackface but were known to listeners as "Molasses" and "January." These full-page color ads appeared in the most popular magazines of the day, including *Ladies' Home Journal* and *Saturday Evening Post*.[34]

Despite the fact that advertisers found the mass audience that listened to radio even more "unsophisticated and ignorant" than they had before the medium existed, they also recognized that the power of radio to sell their goods was even better than print advertisements. Radio's middle-class audience was their target audience, and radio achieved what a print ad could not—it provided a more intimate link between the consumer and goods because the human voice was selling the goods. With that in mind, Benton & Bowles, another Madison Avenue advertising agency, which took over the Maxwell House coffee account from JWT, created the *Maxwell House Show Boat* in 1931 as a vehicle for promoting the coffee brand.[35]

In the fall of 1933, *Radioland* published an article about the development of the show with a lengthy title: "How Radio Programs Are Built: The Story of How the Showboat Hour Came to Be Created and How the Imaginary Cruise of Cap'n Henry Up and Down the Mississippi River Has Grown into a National Institution." Its author, Edward Sammis, explained that although the Maxwell House name was based on an actual Nashville hotel, Benton & Bowles found a hotel hard to dramatize. As they developed ideas for sponsorship, one of the agency's representatives recalled that a Cincinnati radio station broadcast a program using a steamboat as its setting and recommended the same for Maxwell House. "*Here* was a setting for the musical comedy of your dreams rich with southern glamour," he recalled. It was a "showboat of illusions," and southern ones at that.[36]

Maxwell House Show Boat was a spin-off of the Broadway musical based on Edna Ferber's 1927 novel of the same name and was set on a paddle wheel steamboat that traveled along the Mississippi River. The program was essentially a variety show of skits, songs, and comedy, with guest appearances by some of the best-known entertainers of the day, including Bob Hope, Mae West, and even Hattie McDaniel, who immortalized the role of "Mammy" in the film version of *Gone with the Wind*. The Old South associations of Maxwell House were brought to radio, with southern characters that came to life, and were a marketing success. In 1935, *Radio Guide* conducted a poll of over 1.25 million people and found that *Maxwell House Show Boat* was the most popular musical program on radio, and one of its star cast members, the tenor Lanny Ross, was just second in popularity to Jack Benny among individual radio performers. Such recognition meant that not only was radio good for sales of Maxwell House coffee but employing the theme of Old South was also extremely effective.[37]

The links among forms of popular culture altered what was simply a market for goods into a mass market for goods with a national consumer base. What Americans saw in magazines or heard on radio, they might also be reading about in popular literature or seeing in the movies. The Old South provided a lucrative narrative for advertisers in both print and on early radio. Yet that effort was enhanced by the success of films set in the Old South, which had become a genre unto itself, but also by popular books about the South, not the least of which was the publishing phenomenon of Margaret Mitchell's *Gone with the Wind*.

Gone with the Wind's popularity as a book affirmed that "moonlight and magnolias" sold well. The sales of Mitchell's novel exceeded 1 million copies within its first six months of publication, and advertisers, as well as anyone with something to sell, swiftly capitalized on its success by associating their products with the book. Mitchell and her publisher, Macmillan, were inundated with requests for commercial rights related to the book and its characters. Today, commercial tie-ins to films are common, and *Gone with the Wind* as a book initiated that process, actually causing some minor conflict between Margaret Mitchell and David O. Selznick, the film's producer, who believed he should have the commercial rights to products sold with a *Gone with the Wind* affiliation.[38]

There were so many commercial requests for permission to use *Gone with the Wind* characters or themes that Macmillan maintained an internal account of the requests. In November 1936, for example, the Stehli Company asked for permission to use the name "Gone with the Wind" for a printed fabric. Winter-Drittel, a New York dress manufacturer, wrote to the publisher in early February 1937 asking to use the name "Gone with the Wind" on a cotton dress and to reproduce the jacket design from the book on the hangtag label for each garment. In March, the Merrell Schwarz Music Company asked Macmillan about publishing a song to be titled 'Gone with the Wind.' Ethel Wallenstein, who represented another merchandising corporation, requested permission for use of the title in connection with hat styles. S. Wieder Company received permission to make girls' dresses called "Gone with the Wind." The Alexander Doll Company of New York City asked for, but was refused, permission to create a "Scarlett" doll, primarily because Margaret Mitchell did not want any dolls or toys made in affiliation with the book.[39]

Pepperell Manufacturing requested and received permission to produce "Gone with the Wind" chintz, perhaps because the company had a sales office in Atlanta and a plant in Lindale, Georgia. The chintz pattern incorporated six scenes inspired by the book, including images of Tara, a plantation field with slaves picking cotton, a battle scene outside of Atlanta, a blockade runner sitting in front of Fort Sumter, the Civil War railroad engine known as "The General," and a scene re-created from the book of "Mrs. Tarleton driving [the carriage] with the colored Mammy sitting beside her holding the boxes containing the gowns the four daughters, seated in the carriage[,]were to wear at the Barbecue at Twelve Oaks."[40]

Lois Cole, an associate editor for Macmillan who was most responsible for getting Margaret Mitchell to submit her work to the publisher, also handled some of the commercial requests. The Parker Pen Company of Chicago asked to sell pens that used both the book title and Mitchell's name. Cole forwarded the request to John Marsh, Mitchell's husband, and his reply was less than enthusiastic. Marsh wrote to Cole that he refused to even forward her note to his wife, saying, "She has been bombarded with requests for endorsements of all kinds and varieties . . . and I am confident I know what her answer would be. To begin with, she has never used a Parker fountain pen. . . . On top of that her policy from the beginning has been that she did not intend to commercialize her name or permit anybody else to commercialize it. As she has turned down endorsements into the thousands . . . she would not break her rule now for a product she knows nothing about."[41]

Still, products abounded, and in 1939, Macy's department store in New York decided to turn several floors of its store over to products associated with the film version of *Gone with the Wind*. The theme of the store displays was "The Old South Comes North," which appeared in several windows. Macy's decided to do the displays after *House & Garden* magazine published a special issue on *Gone with the Wind*. Macy's ads quoted the magazine as saying that the film "will influence fashion and decorations. We foresee new trends in textures and colors as a result of this film." The department store created displays of "Rhett Butler's Dressing Room" and

Macy's newspaper advertisement for its *Gone with the Wind*–inspired windows, ca. 1939.

"Scarlett's Bedroom," with "elegant 'Old South' displays on 7 floors," all of which it claimed was "as good as a [Broadway] show."[42]

The book also inspired individual entrepreneurs, like Helen Sohl, a housewife from Cleveland, who wrote to the Macmillan Company for permission to submit her idea for a "Gone with the Wind" quiz game to a woman's magazine for publication. Sohl wrote to the publisher that she had "planned an evening devoted entirely to the story for [her] friends." The party was such a great success, "both from the entertainment and intellectual standpoint," that she wanted to sell her idea for publication. There is no record whether Macmillan approved her request, but the fact that a woman in Cleveland was so taken by the book that she developed a party game offers a small glimpse into the impact the book had on readers outside of the South.[43]

Companies of all kinds sought to capitalize on the Old South craze that erupted after the film version of *Gone with the Wind* debuted. The Boston grocery chain S. S. Pierce advertised its biscuits as the "Aristocrat of Southern Delicacies." Claiming that theirs was an original recipe from the "deep" South, S. S. Pierce told its customers that they would enjoy the biscuits, "just as [they] enjoyed the 'Old South' in *Gone with the Wind*." The New York distributors for Southern Comfort whiskey, known as "The Grand

THE GRAND OLD DRINK
OF THE SOUTH

An American Specialty...not a
whiskey, but 100 Proof...Some like
it straight...some, in a highball
...or—try it in a
SCARLETT O'HARA COCKTAIL
but no more than 2, lest you be
GONE WITH THE WIND

SOUTHERN
COMFORT

R. C. WILLIAMS & CO., Inc. • Distributors • New York

Advertisement for Southern
Comfort's New York distributors,
ca. 1940. (Courtesy of Southern
Comfort Properties, Inc.)

Old Drink of the South," prepared a catchy ad that recommended to customers that they "try it in a Scarlett O'Hara Cocktail," warning, "No more than 2 lest you be Gone with the Wind."[44]

The "moonlight-and-magnolias" theme continued to appear in national and regional advertising during and after World War II, especially the iconic southern belle. Such advertising was not simply about the continuing influence of *Gone with the Wind*; it reflected the broader cultural message to American women about maintaining their femininity during the war and, once the war was over, returning to their homes as standard bearers of femininity and keepers of the hearth. The southern belle was employed not only to sell products to female consumers but to further an ideal of femininity that was southern in origin. This image of the southern belle was not simply a reflection on a southern type; she was also used to model feminine behavior for *all* American women.

In 1942, Avon cosmetics ran advertisements for their products in leading women's magazines. One *McCall's* ad, entitled "Romantic Mississippi Days Inspired This Coiffure," suggested that the woman's hairstyle was inspired by the "romance," "suave gallantry," and "gentle charm" of an America that no longer existed. Then, in the next instant, Avon claimed it was similarly inspired by "modern, smart America." In this one ad, the message of a femininity that was both southern and American becomes conflated. An Avon ad for colognes that appeared in *Cosmopolitan* was much more explicit in its message of southern women as models of femininity for American women. The ad copy reads, "Our Southland, famed for its charming contributions to the art of dressing for cool comfort, inspired this flowered cotton dinner gown by Tappé, noted designer." Avon's colognes, the ad continued, would help women "meet daintily the challenge of the sultriest summer evening." To refer to the region as "Our Southland" conveys ownership for a region that was considered both distinct and yet American; moreover, through the image of the southern belle, Avon was able to illustrate one of the region's "contributions" to American society, which was that its women were skilled in maintaining their femininity as well as their personal cool, even during the extreme heat of summer. In other words, American women who bought Avon products should follow the example set by their southern sisters.[45]

Following the war, Old South Perfumers, a New York company located on Fifth Avenue, created a series of advertisements for leading women's magazines that employed the moonlight-and-magnolia image for its line of toiletries. The full-color ads are reminiscent of more modern book covers for romance novels. They included men in Confederate gray uniforms holding hands with or whispering into the ears of women in hoopskirted gowns that Scarlett O'Hara herself might envy. With ad copy that declared that the products symbolized the "rare beauty, the serene, gay, gracious living of a land, a time," the perfumers advertised an entire line of products in fragrances "as lovely as the Old South itself," with names like "Plantation Garden Bouquet," "Natchez Rose," and "Cotton Blossom." The company combined products into sets named the "Virginia Reel Trio," the "Romance Box," and the "Charleston Box." These ads may reflect the long-term influence of *Gone with the Wind* in American advertising, but they also reveal the values of immediate postwar America for men and women to return to traditional gender roles, and in these ads the desired result was symbolized by the antebellum South.[46]

The success with which northern ad agencies employed Old South imagery to brand products in the twentieth century offers evidence that the long reconciliation between North and South had achieved a resonance within popular culture. Northern and midwestern consumers had developed a level of comfort with southern racial stereotypes, which allowed them to make Aunt Jemima pancake mix and Maxwell House coffee top-selling national brands. They not only bought the consumer goods but

Avon Cosmetics
advertisement, 1942.
(Author's collection)

Refreshing Summer Coolness
AS PRESENTED BY TAPPE AND AVON

Our Southland, famed for its charming contributions
to the art of dressing for cool comfort, inspired this
flowered cotton dinner gown by Tappe, noted designer.

With crisp, fragrant coolness, Avon Toilet Waters
and Colognes, too, help you meet daintily the challenge
of the sultriest summer evening.

In your own comfortable living-room, you may
choose from many delightful summertime fragrances
the Toilet Water and Cologne which you find most
appealing. Your Representative will acquaint you,
also, with new Atom-Blown Face Powder...and with
the season's most fashionable shades in lipstick, rouge,
and nail polish, which Avon has created to give you
new and refreshed summertime loveliness.

LOOK FOR A FRIENDLY VISIT FROM YOUR AVON REPRESENTATIVE

AVON
Cosmetics
RADIO CITY, NEW YORK

Old South Toiletries
advertisement, 1946.
(Author's collection)

also the ideas about the region that were couched in stereotypes. They did so, in part, because nonsoutherners accepted the South as the region that best represented America as it was before the advent of modernity. Here, in the land of moonlight and magnolias, perhaps, Americans could envision themselves living a life of leisure and comfort, away from the noisy city and the rush of modern life, and, if they were lucky, they could have their coffee and pancakes served to them with a smile.

CHAPTER 3

Dixie on Early Radio

Beginning in 1926, Chicago radio station WGN and its owner, the *Chicago Tribune*, introduced midwestern listeners to *Sam 'n' Henry*, a show developed by two blackface performers, Charles Correll and Freeman Gosden. The primary characters of the show were based on two black men who, according to the official story, had migrated to the Windy City, where they had construction jobs building skyscrapers. The two began their journey in Alabama on a mule-driven wagon, which took them to the train depot in "Bummin'ham," where they caught the train that took them north. Once there, the pair got into all sorts of mishaps, much of it due to their naïveté, creating the basis for a serial comedy. *Sam 'n' Henry* became so successful in its two years on radio that Correll and Gosden became celebrities and were wooed by a new national network to continue to perform their minstrel act, to the delight of listeners across the country. The new network was the National Broadcasting Company (NBC), and for contractual reasons the show was renamed *Amos 'n' Andy*. In the years that followed, it became the most listened-to radio program of all time.[1]

One can discern in *Sam 'n' Henry* and, later, in *Amos 'n' Andy* the story of the Great Migration of southern blacks to northern cities and the difficulties of that adjustment. Yet the radio program itself was a blackface performance, and in that performance one also recognizes the stereotypes that were part of the minstrel tradition and, more specifically, about southern blacks. According to an early history of minstrelsy, there had long been a "Negro type," which was identified by characteristics that ranged from being shiftless to loving watermelons to having a fondness for gambling and mispronouncing words. Many of these traits were employed in the development of Sam and Henry as characters for radio and were specifically based on southern blacks. Indeed, when white audiences tuned in to listen to the characters developed by Gosden and Correll, they consumed long-held ideas about race and region, and any stereotypes they may have had about the South, and about southern blacks in particular, were reinforced. Perhaps it is not surprising that white midwesterners often held such stereotypes, given the large migration of southern blacks to Chicago. Yet the audience for the more successful *Amos 'n' Andy* was na-

Charles Correll and Freeman Gosden as Amos and Andy, 1930s. (Courtesy of the Library of American Broadcasting, University of Maryland at College Park)

tionwide, with an estimated 40 million listeners—53 percent of the radio audience—at its peak. Moreover, the show inspired a spate of minstrel acts on radio, and the medium kept blackface performers employed well into the 1940s, to the enjoyment of audiences in every region of the country.[2]

Radio minstrelsy was not the only form of radio entertainment with the ability to shape perceptions of Dixie and its people. Hillbillies, too, represented a southern type that appeared not only on radio but also in film and syndicated cartoons. Hillbilly acts might perform music or comedy, and although scholars of the medium argue that such performers represented rural America, most often they were identified on radio as having come from the southern mountain regions, either the Appalachians or the Ozarks, often conflated as one single place. Still other performers, some of them native southerners, were driven by this new mass medium and its advertisers to maintain and perform other stereotypes based on the region's history, particularly the mythological Old South. Singing groups, like the Pickens Sisters from Macon, Georgia, or the Boswell Sisters from New Orleans, were pegged in radio fan magazines as modern-day southern belles. Radio, with the influence of the national networks, quickly proved its ability to shape listeners' perceptions of the South. More often than not, those perceptions were based on stereotypes with a long history on the vaude-ville stage, now being brought to life for a radio audience that was national in scope.[3]

The Golden Age of radio, from the late 1920s to World War II, represented a period in American history in which a new technology, the wireless set, gripped the American public, who tuned in daily for music, comedy, and variety programming, which offered listeners some relief, and release, from the effects of the Great Depression. Throughout this period, radio emerged as an important form of mass media, with the ability to communicate simultaneously to millions of listeners. It was also an important medium for advertising agencies, which swiftly developed radio marketing departments, instrumental in shaping content and employing talent to sell their clients' products. In fact, networks controlled only about 10 to 12 percent of radio programming. Therefore, agencies and their advertising clients determined the type of program, its content, who performed, and the time the show aired. Major firms like J. Walter Thompson, Benton & Bowles, and N. W. Ayer & Sons ruled the airwaves and were instrumental in shaping Americans' listening habits.[4]

Radio as a form of popular culture influenced widely held perceptions about the South and about southerners themselves, because what minstrel and hillbilly radio shows, as well as programs that promoted an Old South ideal, had in common was not only southern characters but characters whose popularity allowed them to shape a recognizable southern identity for mass consumption.[5] Significantly, the majority of national programs that employed southern stereotypes were developed in Chicago, New York, and Los Angeles, and even the shows with native southerner performers portrayed southerners according to the biases of advertisers and the national networks, if these performers wanted to continue to earn a living as radio entertainers. Thus, nonsoutherners were far more invested in creating perceptions of the South and its people than were native southerners themselves.[6]

The fact that these stereotypes found a welcome audience in the 1930s was no fluke. As cultural historian Warren Susman has argued, the Great Depression caused an identity crisis among Americans, who were well versed in the rhetoric of optimism and boundless opportunity. The Depression shook that foundation, and the result was a herculean effort to describe the American character, through documentaries, photojournalism, psychology, and sociology—all part of a greater quest to *know* who Americans were and to define the "American Way of Life." Even radio, because of its rapid rise in popularity, inspired studies of its place in American life. One of those studies, *The Psychology of Radio*, by Ivy League professors Gordon Allport and Hadley Cantril, delved into how radio was affecting the lives and minds of the listening audience. Among their findings—findings that may seem obvious today—was that radio listeners had to create their own imagery and aural perceptions since they could not see for themselves what was happening. And, because thousands of people listened to the same programs, individuals felt a sense of community with other listeners. Cantril and Allport's conclusions are particularly useful for understanding how Americans developed their perceptions of the South, which they shared with a national community of listeners.[7]

Hearing the "marked" speech used by individual radio performers, such as accents, dialect, or stereotypical statements, helped listeners create opinions about race, class, gender, ethnicity, and even region. Like other forms of popular entertainment, radio served as a vehicle through which class and cultural tensions were expressed. It was such a powerful medium that it helped to reshape language, to the extent that people across the country might repeat catchphrases heard on popular shows like *Amos 'n' Andy* or *Lum and Abner*, while also identifying those characters as southern in origin. Radio also acted as a medium where frustrations about the larger issues of the day—unemployment, economic despair, and the failure of American capitalism—could be addressed through radio comedy and the "verbal dueling" that ensued when characters hurled insults or told jokes. Moreover, the use of improper English—used by both minstrel and hillbilly performers—allowed many white listeners from other sections to privately identify with the trials and tribulations of those characters while also feeling a sense of racial, class, and regional superiority.[8]

By the mid-1930s, the radio audience and network programming already had a regional hue. The percentage of homes with radios in 1935 was highest in the Northeast, where 80 percent of homes had a radio, compared to the Southeast, where that percentage was 48 percent, including Mississippi, where radios were owned by just 24 percent. In addition, 93 percent of homes in urban areas owned radios, compared to just 34 percent in rural areas. The majority of the radio audience was middle class, followed by poorer classes. The least likely listeners were the well-to-do, who, when they listened to radio, were tuned into opera or symphony orchestras.[9]

Given these statistics, a general determination can be made that the majority of radio listeners lived in the North and were white, middle-class urban dwellers, and they (more than rural and poor southerners) made up the primary audience for shows that employed southern stereotypes. Indeed, that reality was reflected by radio programming in both regional and national markets. Cantril and Allport's study on the psychology of radio found that broadcasters were mindful of sectional differences and therefore did not play songs like "Marching through Georgia" or "John Brown's Body" below the Mason-Dixon Line, for example, because they celebrated individuals hated in the former Confederate states.[10] At the same time, minstrel and hillbilly shows were successful with national audiences and were heard by more listeners outside of the South than within the region itself.

Serial comedies were some of the most popular programs on radio, and the most successful of all was *Amos 'n' Andy*, which first aired on March 19, 1928. Freeman Gosden and Charles Correll, who portrayed Amos and Andy, were two of hundreds of former vaudeville minstrel performers who found success in this new mass medium. Radio scholars agree that the debut of *Amos 'n' Andy* on NBC's national network in 1928 marked a major shift in radio as a shaping force in American popular culture. The story of this program is well known: Freeman Gosden, a native of Richmond, Virginia, and Charles Correll, from Peoria, Illinois, both stage performers, met in Durham, North Carolina, and eventually joined forces in Chicago, where they were signed to perform the radio minstrel act known as *Sam 'n' Henry*, about two black men from Birmingham, Alabama. The show, described as a comic strip brought to life, was highly successful. After performing on *Sam 'n' Henry* on Chicago station WGN for two years, the pair contracted with another station, WMAQ, owned by the *Chicago Daily*, which allowed them to perform their act on the new national network—NBC.[11]

Sam and Henry became Amos and Andy, also two fictitious black southerners, described in an official telling of the program as "two ignorant, struggling colored boys." The version of their story changed only slightly. The two now hailed from Atlanta, Georgia, and had migrated to Chicago, where they were the proprietors of the "Fresh Air Taxi Company, Incorpulated." Gosden's dialect was considered authentic because he was raised in the South by a mammy and had a black playmate (named Snowball) from childhood, who was said to have inspired several of the show's characters. Correll's considerable experience on the minstrel stage was given as the reason for his authenticity. The program hit its peak in 1931, when *Amos 'n' Andy* had an estimated audience of 40 million, representing more than half of all American homes. The success of *Amos 'n' Andy* led to copycat minstrel duos and a minstrel formula, which radio readily adopted.[12]

Scholars have carefully addressed the subject of whites as blackface performers, as well as the minstrel tradition in vaudeville, from which this form of "racial ventriloquism" emerged. Yet, aside from noting that these minstrel figures may have been southern in origin, these same scholars have not examined the significance of this regional connection and its meaning for the listening audience. Melvin Ely, whose social history of *Amos 'n' Andy* stands as the exception, rightly places the program's black characters within the context of the Great Migration. He further examines the show's reception among northern black leaders and journalists, who either applauded or decried the portrayals of African Americans by Correll and Gosden.[13]

Robert Vann, editor of the black newspaper the *Philadelphia Courier*, for example, criticized the show for perpetuating "the stereotyped Negro of the Old South."[14] Black responses to *Amos 'n' Andy* certainly varied— there were blacks who enjoyed the show. However, the response of black journalists like Vann suggests there was a heightened awareness of the specific stereotype of southern blacks that was harmful to the larger African American community. Indeed, radio minstrelsy shaped the ways in which American audiences consumed ideas about southern blacks.[15] Moreover, northern ad agencies insisted that radio programs, as vehicles for advertising products to a primarily middle-class white audience, maintain the minstrel image. That image, to be sure, had a direct relationship to images of the South and southern blacks. There is no doubt that minstrelsy was derogatory and that it sustained racist portrayals of African Americans. Yet there remain important historical distinctions that suggest that it was the perpetuation of what Vann called the "stereotypical Negro of the Old South" that shaped a particular black southern identity in early radio. That identity, according to one historian, made it difficult for southern blacks to be taken seriously for jobs in the North, and it "may have exacerbated regional tensions within the black community." Moreover, such images hurt the efforts of southern blacks seeking to rid themselves of an identity that continued to link them to the institution of slavery.[16]

Blackface performance by radio personalities was part of a long minstrel tradition dating to the 1840s in the United States, where it was first performed on theatrical stages in the Northeast and swiftly became a popular form of entertainment throughout the United States. Over the course of the nineteenth century, minstrels were primarily white performers who entertained white audiences in blackface. In 1916, a journalist for the *San Francisco Chronicle* described minstrelsy's history: "It was supposed to depict life of the slave section of a plantation in the Sunny South or on the Mississippi levees," he explained. "There was much rolling and tumbling about, plunkety plunketing of banjoes and shuffling of feet in hoedowns and whooping of voices in plantation glees and choruses," he continued, "with perhaps a touch of sentiment centering around old Black Joe with his wig of white wool."[17] Carl Wittke, who wrote an early history of American minstrelsy entitled *Tambo and Bones* (1930), agreed: "The origin of American minstrelsy may be found in the singing and dancing of the slaves of the Southern plantations of antebellum days; at least this may be considered its prototype."[18]

The historical context of minstrelsy's beginnings holds answers for better understanding how radio minstrelsy carried not simply black stereotypes to a popular audience but also specifically southern stereotypes. Indeed, throughout the nineteenth century, minstrel acts performed as black stereotypes—the plantation Negro or the more urban and nattily dressed black dandy, whose command of the English language was to take words and "[twist] the syllables in the most ludicrous fashion."[19] These same traditions were carried into vaudeville performances and can be easily identified on early radio. The character of Amos Jones, for example, was described as "trusting, simple, and unsophisticated." He was the more easygoing of the two and served as the modern-day version of the happy-go-lucky plantation Negro. Andy, on the other hand, was the bellicose dandy who was lazy and known to mispronounce words, his most famous phrase being "I'se regusted."[20]

Vaudeville minstrel acts found radio an easy transition and were often paired with variety shows. The most prolific teams were Mack and Moran, who appeared as The Two Black Crows, and Pick Malone and Pat Padgett, who, in addition to having their own radio program, *Pick and Pat*, often used different names to perform as minstrel acts on other radio programs. Inevitably, the minstrel pairs portrayed stereotypical southern blacks, as was the case with Honey and Alexander. They were characterized as the "first citizens of Shanty Town," who, among other activities, edited the "*Southern Breeze*," their fictional town's local paper. Honey and Alexander "interviewed" each other for the fan magazine *Radio Varieties* in 1940. The article was accompanied by a photograph of the pair in blackface surrounded by paper strewn across their office. The entire piece was written in black dialect, which signaled that the pair was from the South—in this case, Texas and Alabama. As with other minstrel acts, the two men were depicted as two foolish southern blacks who were often caught in predicaments in which they were easily outwitted.[21]

Pick Malone and Pat Padgett appeared on the Maxwell House–sponsored *Show Boat*, one of the most successful radio programs of the 1930s. All the action takes place on a Mississippi steamboat, and the show's evolution to radio was made possible by Benton & Bowles, the agency responsible for advertising Maxwell House coffee. There were several southern characters on the show, including Molasses and January, played by Malone and Padgett, who spoke in black dialect and provided comic interludes. Despite being described by *Life* magazine as "perhaps the worst blackface team in existence," they remained on the air through the 1940s—a testament to the longevity of radio minstrelsy.[22]

Black women performers were not allowed on radio during its early years, but the medium consistently indulged in long-held stereotypes about black women, which can be traced back to slavery. As historian Deborah Gray White has shown, slave women were often categorized by whites based on their station on a plantation or to justify how they were treated. Thus, some slave women fit the role of "mammy"—the nurturing house slave who cooked for the white family and cared for its children. Still other slave women were categorized as "jezebels" because they were considered sexually promiscuous. Often, slave owners used the latter term as justification for having forced sexual relationships with their female slaves. On the minstrel stage of the nineteenth century, white men in blackface also introduced the "Negro wench," and these so-called wench acts became increasingly popular over the course of the nineteenth century. All of these minstrel types can be found in the "coon songs" of the late nineteenth century, which employed the racially derogatory term "coon" and were performed by vaudevillians. Such songs continued to be written and performed during the early decades of the twentieth century. Eventually, these black female stereotypes found their way into several programs during radio's Golden Age.[23]

"Aunt Jemima" was the most obvious of the mammy figures. Nancy Green, an African American, first appeared as Aunt Jemima at the 1893 Columbian Exposition in Chicago. Later, the image of a heavyset black woman in apron and kerchief appeared in print advertisements, and eventually the character of Aunt Jemima found success on early radio, where she advertised pancake flour. In both mediums, her character was clearly a representation of the southern mammy in her role as a cook and house servant. The J. Walter Thompson Agency of New York, which was responsible for the Quaker Oats brand and spearheaded a number of minstrel acts for its sponsored radio programs, created a serial drama starring Aunt Jemima, which was based on the "old Higbee Plantation," where she supposedly got her start as a cook. On the show, the plantation was located somewhere in "Dixie," Negro spirituals were performed, and listeners were invited to imagine the carefree days of the Old South and life on a southern plantation.[24]

The character of Aunt Jemima was a minstrel performance, pure and simple. Although white women were not generally known as minstrel performers, the Aunt Jemima of radio was played by a series of white women, beginning with the vaudevillian Tess Gardella. Gardella, an Italian American stage actress, began playing Aunt Jemima in 1921, and throughout her career made her living as a blackface performer. Her appearance as Queenie in the 1929 stage version of *Show Boat* established her as a blackface actress who could be called on to do similar roles. She was tapped for the role in the original Aunt Jemima radio program, very likely due to her stage experience playing the southern mammy, and there was a series of other white women in the role through the late 1940s.[25] The Aunt Jemima radio character did not change with time. In 1943, Harriett Widmer, another white actress, took up the role. The show began with the singing of "Dixie," followed by the white announcer's introduction of "smiling, happy, Aunt Jemima," who then asked her, "What is your happy thought for today?" Once it was offered, the "Jemima Chorus" broke into a Tin Pan Alley song about Dixie, such as "Alabammy Bound." Surprisingly, Widmer, a native of Mississippi who grew up in Little Rock, Arkansas, won praise from African American audiences for her dialect.[26]

J. Walter Thompson was single-minded in its efforts to make the connection between the South and the goods it helped to sell by employing this stereotype. As internal account records note, the goal was to associate pancake flour with good southern cooking, with Aunt Jemima as the "old southern cook."[27] Aunt Jemima pancake mix became one of the most recognizable American brands of the twentieth century and, more important, helped to sell middle-class Americans on the idea of leisure, in which having an easy-to-make pancake mix was akin to having a servant do the work. Moreover, it also perpetuated the mammy stereotype of the southern black woman whose primary role was to serve whites—the target audience for the product.

The black woman as jezebel was also evident in early radio shows. One

Tess Gardella performed as Aunt Jemima on radio and in the film short
Aunt Jemima: The Original Fun Flour Maker (1927). (Courtesy Photofest)

of the most noticeable characterizations of that type was Beulah, played
by a white man, Marlin Hurt. Hurt introduced Beulah, a black maid, on
the *Fibber McGee & Molly* show, on which he also appeared as himself. The
success of the character afforded Hurt an opportunity to continue to
perform as Beulah on another iteration of *Show Boat* in 1940, sponsored
by Brown and Williamson Tobacco Corporation. As with many minstrel
acts, there was the role of the interlocutor—the straight man who main-
tains the show's pace through questions and conversation with the minstrel character. Hurt plays both the interlocutor and Beulah. Beulah was
cast as simple-minded and man-crazy, whose catchphrase "Love dat man!"
was fodder for laughs, given her penchant for having a steady stream of
boyfriends.

Like the jezebel of the Old South, Beulah had a series of love interests. In her case, one could say she had a man in every port. Each week,
the showboat figuratively made stops in different cities throughout the
United States, where Hunt would ask Beulah about the men she had dated
in that locale. In one episode, the showboat stopped in "beautiful, spar-

kling, Asheville, North Carolina," where Marlin Hurt asks, "By the way . . . what happened to your Asheville boyfriend?" "Oh, you mean Asheville Ashley," Beulah responds and then proceeds to tell the story of his demise. This same exchange was repeated weekly, as she explained the whereabouts of Cincy Quincy, Charleston Charles, and others. Through a constant succession of men, Beulah became the living stereotype of black female promiscuity, whose Old South antecedents were clearly evident.[28]

White female blackface performers, like Tess Gardella, might perform black female characters, but more often white men portrayed them, as was the case for Marlin Hurt's Beulah. Most of the female characters from *Amos 'n' Andy* were never voiced characters but were often included in the program through the dialogue. Gosden and Correll were uncomfortable with manufacturing female voices, so the writers created characters who "spoke" with Amos and Andy on the telephone or through letters. As historian Melvin Ely argues, Gosden and Correll's black female characters were far more progressive than the mammy type. They were sophisticated and well-to-do, and when there were negative associations they were more likely aimed at their gender rather than their race. For example, during several episodes in the show, Andy was involved in a breach-of-promise suit with the Widow Parker, who sued him for backing out of his marriage proposal. The Widow Parker was portrayed as a gold-digging woman—an insult frequently made about white women as well.[29]

Minstrelsy extended to singing acts that also performed comedy, and one of the more successful was the Sinclair Minstrels act, which appeared on WENR in Chicago. Sponsored by Sinclair Oil, these minstrels sang and told jokes, most of which were solicited from listeners. They, too, had an interlocutor—Gene Arnold—who guided the action. The Sinclair Minstrels were very popular during their time on radio in the 1930s. They held their show in front of a live audience at the Chicago Merchandise Mart in a studio that held 500 people. The show, which often sold out, began with the singing of Stephen Foster's minstrel song "I Love the Land of Old Black Joe." Following intermission, the Sinclair Minstrels performed the famous Tin Pan Alley song "Are You from Dixie?" The four white men, though they did not appear in blackface, were introduced as black characters. Cliff Soubier was Little Chocolate Drop; Mac MacDonald was Mamma's Little Red Hot; Fritz Clark was known as "that sentimental son of the South," who interjected with "Mah mammy calls me t-bone;" and Big Bill Child was introduced as "radio's gift to the ladies."[30] The jokes were often about one of the minstrels and were often designed to make these "black" men appear foolish.

African American cultural identity as found on early radio was defined by the absence of black performers and by the stereotypes through which they were represented to white audiences. Significantly, many of these shows originated in Chicago, to which thousands of southern blacks migrated in the years surrounding World War I. Aside from jazz and blues musicians or gospel quartets like the successful Southernaires, there were no programs with an entirely black cast, the one exception being the program *John Henry—Black River Giant*, a dramatic series on the CBS network. In 1933, the fan magazine *Radio Stars* told its readers: "To those of you who don't know the South, and its folk legends, this must mean nothing. To Southerners whose roots are deep in the history of slavery and emancipation, it means a fresh and startling program to take the ragged edge off today's hi-de-ho and vo-de-o-do 'scat' singing that has been, up to now, the Negro's principal contribution to entertainment. . . . John Henry is a person, a legendary giant of prodigious powers conjured up in the minds of many generations of black folk." Even though the show won recognition from the magazine for distinguished excellence, it was a true rarity for its time because advertisers preferred minstrelsy. Radio obliged by allowing minstrelsy to continue long after it had become passé on the professional stage, because northern ad agencies determined that if race were being performed it would be done so as a minstrel act—thus, they preferred comical southern stereotypes to a black folk hero like John Henry.[31] And in the days of early radio, a program's survival often depended on corporate sponsorship. Shows without sponsors, known as sustained programs, either found success and a sponsor or did not survive.

Although minstrelsy was the most common way to represent the South on radio during the 1930s, there were other acts whose success helped to define southern identity in popular culture, for both good and ill. In May 1935, the fan magazine *Radioland* reported on its audience poll of favorite radio shows and performers. That year, the *Maxwell House Show Boat* was the number one show, and Lanny Ross, its star, was America's favorite radio performer, just ahead of Bing Crosby. The ad agency for *Show Boat* had capitalized on the Broadway show of the same name by creating a radio program whose characters were instantly recognizable. Within a few short years, the program, with its southern setting and themes, proved to be a successful formula for radio, just as it had been on Broadway.

Cast of the *Maxwell House Show Boat*, 1933. (Author's collection)

The *Maxwell House Show Boat* premiered on October 6, 1932, and was fictitiously launched from Biloxi, Mississippi. In reality, the program was performed in NBC's Fifth Avenue Studios, where a "mellow southern atmosphere [was] deftly blended with the background of the advertised product."[32] Charles Winninger, who played the lead, had also played the role of Captain Henry in Florenz Ziegfeld's Broadway version of *Show Boat*. Although he was born in Wisconsin, *Radioland* described him as a "silvery-tongued Southerner," to give his character the mark of authenticity. For those who saw the show being performed in person, Winninger apparently looked the part. Indeed, an early study of radio audiences reported that "parents were glad to see that Captain Henry really looks like a kindly old southern gentleman."[33]

This "showboat of illusions" proved so successful that fans were convinced the program was real. Sound effects transported listeners to the Mississippi River. They could hear the whistle of the steamboat and a crowd cheering as it paddled into dock. Once, when it was announced that the *Maxwell House Show Boat* was going to visit Erie, Pennsylvania, several hundred people—who were convinced that the show was real—showed up on the waterfront to greet the cast and crew. People visiting New York sought out the studio to catch the show live, but did so at the risk of having their illusion destroyed. "We came to New York intent on seeing the *Show Boat* broadcast," said one man. "What we imagined was all wrong. We had a delightful picture of the showboat in our minds, and each one in the family envisioned the entertainers to suit themselves. . . . We regret we peeked behind the radio scenes," he lamented. Still, few people went behind the scenes, and many believed in the show's authenticity and that the actors were real people—even when they were southern stereotypes like Captain Henry or the blackface duo of the show, Molasses and January.[34]

The moonlight-and-magnolias image of the South created and sustained by *Show Boat* was well known to most listeners in the 1930s. Fans of Tin Pan Alley music were familiar with songs set in the Dixie of the Old South; millions more read Margaret Mitchell's *Gone with the Wind* when it came out in 1936; and films with an Old South setting belonged to a genre unto itself. This fascination with moonlight and magnolias—of a region wedded to its antebellum past where blacks loyally served whites—was realized on radio not only through minstrel acts and variety shows but also through musical acts that hailed from the South, specifically sister singing acts, which were presented to the public as southern belles.

A publicity scout for NBC discovered the Pickens Sisters, from Macon, Georgia. Their specialty was singing Negro spirituals, and they appeared on a variety of radio programs throughout the 1930s. Like the Boswell Sisters from New Orleans, an extremely successful jazz trio that performed on the Bing Crosby show and eventually had its own show in Los Angeles, the Pickens Sisters' southern roots were often the subject of articles published by radio fan magazines. In a *Radio Stars* article that was also intended to advertise makeup, writer Mary Biddle commented that, upon meeting the Pickens Sisters, she found them to be "true products of the Old South and that gracious femininity which we Northerners have long admired, and, I think, faintly envied." Although she interviewed the women in their Park Avenue apartment in New York, Biddle noted that from a practical standpoint they were not far removed from the "sleepy plantation on which they were born, 'way down in Georgia." She found them to be "picturesque" and concluded that "Southern women are the only ones left who are wise enough to capitalize on women's greatest asset of femininity." *Radioland* also perpetuated this image of the sisters when it emphasized that the "girls" had been brought up on a plantation in Georgia and that "every day fried chicken and hot biscuits [were] served in the Pickens home" in New York City.[35]

The Pickens Sisters, 1930s. (Courtesy Library of American Broadcasting, University of Maryland at College Park)

Mary Biddle often used southern women as models of femininity in her articles. In one article about the singer Linda Lee, "a charmer from the South," Biddle employed moonlight and magnolias to great effect. She asserted that on the Louisiana plantation where Lee was born and where her "crinoline-frocked ancestors" once lived, Lee had the "perfect background for Southern beauty," as if beauty was absorbed from the "sweeping lawns and stately trees" that Biddle described. Linda Lee not only embodied "southern charm," she also offered tips for staying calm, since one of the lessons she learned growing up in the South was to "take life leisurely." In effect, Linda Lee embodied many of the qualities associated with the belles of the Old South in her femininity and charm. She also embodied the characteristic most northerners associated with the region, which was the unhurried pace with which southerners approached life—a quality valued by many living in the nation's urban-industrial centers. All of these qualities were, in the 1930s, still clearly admired by northerners like Mary Biddle and promoted in national fan magazines.[36]

The *New York Times* also participated in maintaining the perception that southern women radio performers were belles. In an article entitled

"Dixie Sent Irene Beasley and the Pickens Sisters to the Northern Microphone," the newspaper played up the southern roots of these female radio acts. Irene Beasley, known on radio as the "long, tall gal from Dixie," was described as a southern woman who could not be contained by the "quiet contentment and shaded trees" of her birthplace "below the Mason-Dixon line," and so she eventually made her way to New York. The Pickens Sisters were also associated with their plantation roots. Their singing was cast as authentic, because they had learned the Negro spirituals from the source, having lived their entire lives listening to "Negroes sing in the singularly simple and unusual style that is peculiarly their own." "Quiet contentment and shaded trees" and listening to Negro spirituals was coded language for an Old South image of leisure and black servitude, which northern writers helped to maintain in popular culture.[37]

The other enduring image of southerners was of the rural hick, more commonly known to Americans as "the hillbilly." Hillbillies became a popular cultural stereotype in the 1930s, appearing in comic strips and movies and through their ties to country music, then called "hillbilly music." The popular image of the hillbilly—as poor, working-class, southern, barefoot, and ignorant—was so pervasive that Americans had a difficult time discerning the difference between perception and reality. In his study of the hillbilly as cultural icon, Anthony Harkins argues that hillbillies were more defined by cultural traits than geography, citing evidence of the term being used outside of the South. Yet the enduring image of hillbillies was that of southern mountain people who were caricatures of the region and a separate "race" of people and who represented the last vestiges of a premodern society.[38]

The migration of southerners to the West and Midwest between the world wars certainly contributed to the development of the hillbilly stereotype. The number of southern whites who migrated to the midwestern cities of Detroit and Chicago was even larger than the number of southern blacks who moved to those places. Despite this fact, the national media paid little attention to this element of the southern diaspora until the mid-1930s. Important changes in politics and journalism, as well as the rise of radio and film, signaled changes in the way white southern migrants were perceived and treated. Politicians and journalists, for example, focused their concern on the homeless and transient, while publishers found a new market for novels on the primitive and exotic. Moreover, within the popular media, rural white southerners proved to be a rich source of comedy. Caricatures and stereotypes of white southerners, like those of black southerners, were employed in film and radio for the amusement of non-southern audiences everywhere.[39]

Radio's depiction of white southerners, especially those who lived beyond the haze of moonlight and magnolias, was as a rural, mountain people who were at best primitive and exotic and at worst backward and dim-witted. "Hillbilly" was a label applied to these southerners, and although it generally conveyed rural, it more often conveyed southern—especially Appalachia and the Ozarks. The term had been used in print since 1893 to describe backwoods southern inhabitants but was not commonly used as a term for southern country music until 1925, when Okeh Records, a New York record label, named one of the first country groups it recorded "The Hill Billies." Even though many performers considered the term a pejorative, it was used widely by country musicians and enthusiasts, though eventually recording companies backed away from the term and employed phrases like "old-time tunes" or "hill country tunes" when describing the music they produced.[40]

Radio reshaped the hillbilly icon into one that was both rural and humorous. Both hillbilly music and hillbilly comics became part of the radio landscape as early as 1924 when Chicago radio station WLS presented *National Barn Dance*—a weekly program featuring music and comedy. WLS, whose call letters were an acronym for World's Largest Store (a nod to its first corporate sponsor, Sears Roebuck), was home to *National Barn Dance* through the mid-1950s. Radio barn dances were popular on stations throughout the South and the Midwest and could be heard on southern stations like WSB in Atlanta, Georgia, and WBT in Charlotte, North Carolina. The *Grand Ole Opry* premiered on Nashville station WSM in 1925 as the *WSM Barn Dance*. It had a large regional following but did not overtake the more successful *National Barn Dance* until World War II, when it became part of the NBC national network.[41]

Throughout the 1930s, *National Barn Dance* and its panoply of hillbilly performers created an audience, as well as a stage, for both regional musicians and cornpone humor. Despite being on radio, the image of the performers was well crafted to suit the live audience. Many, though not all, musicians performed in overalls, straw hats, checked shirts, and gingham dresses. The show was broadcast every Saturday evening from Chicago's Eighth Street Theater, which had 1,200 seats and was always filled to capacity for two shows. Although *National Barn Dance* contained more representations of the South than just hillbillies, several musicians came from the mountain South, like the popular Cumberland Ridge Runners or the novelty act of Walter Peterson, known as "The Kentucky Wonder Bean." Singing partners and North Carolinians Myrtle Cooper and Scott Wiseman, who performed as Lulu Belle and Scotty, were an extremely popular act; in a 1936 poll, Cooper was voted "Queen of the Radio." Rustic comics were a vital part of the show as well. Missourian Luther Ossiebrink, who performed as Arkie, the Arkansas Chopper, and Kansan Ezra Hawkins, who portrayed Uncle Ezra, were regular fixtures on the show. Pat Buttram, who had a long film career and earned television fame as Mr. Haney on *Green Acres*, got his start on the show as the Winston County Flash. Originally from Addison, Alabama, Buttram was the son of a Methodist circuit minister and was discovered while in Chicago for the 1933 World's Fair. In an audience participation interview, his voice stood out as distinctively southern, and he became a regular cast member of *National Barn Dance*, where he performed hillbilly comedy for thirteen years.[42]

Southern music and comedy was also promoted regionally. In 1939, talent manager John Lair, who was instrumental in developing talent for WLS in Chicago, decided to create a unique settlement in Renfro Valley in the Cumberland foothills of Kentucky, where the show *Renfro Valley Folks* was broadcast on NBC's southern network. After taking musicians from the area to give them their start in Chicago, he felt that many of them had lost what made them and their music unique, because of the influences of the big city. Rather than continue to take the talent to Chicago, he decided to establish a settlement in Renfro Valley and broadcast the music of the region from there. Lair literally built a settlement, which included a lodge that served local fare to visitors, a grist mill, and cabins for tourists from the Midwest, who had a direct route to Renfro Valley on the Dixie Highway. The old log schoolhouse that Lair attended as a young boy was also brought to the site and served as the studio for radio broadcasts of "hillbilly life and music of long ago." From that cabin, Lair launched the careers of several local musicians—the most famous were the Coon Creek Girls, tapped by Eleanor Roosevelt to play for the king and queen of England during their visit to the White House in 1939.[43]

Radio was a cheap form of entertainment and particularly valued by poorer audiences, most of which were located in the South. But radio also transformed America's popular tastes, even when it came to hillbilly music. Although country music's audience remained primarily rural and southern throughout the 1930s, the genre did meet with success in urban communities in the Northeast, Midwest, and West, and, as the Great Depression deepened, hillbilly acts became increasingly popular throughout the country, in part because they harked back to an easier, more self-sufficient way of living. Just as the Old South represented the ideal of preindustrial America, so too did the rural South. These images of the South served as a form of escapism for Americans, who were suffering economically and dealing with the challenges of modern civilization.

For some critics, the increasing success of hillbilly performers represented a devastating blow to American culture.[44] In 1935, Weldon Melick, a writer for *Radioland* magazine, wrote a scathing critique of such acts, entitled "The Hill Billy Menace." Melick's focus was on KMPC, a station in Beverly Hills, California. To Melick's dismay, "mountain singers were such an instant and terrific hit on the air" that the station manager, Glen Rice, "had to increase the supply [and] went to the heart of the Ozarks, where spinning wheels are in common use today." His "new discoveries were lionized by film society where they were entertained at parties given by Mary Pickford" and other Hollywood stars, and, Melick seethed, "the women practically mobbed them." "There is something about a rat's nest haircut, a dirty shirt, and rawhide boots that Valentinos simply can't compete with," Melick ranted. "Moreover, the depression seems only to have encouraged the hill billy business."[45]

Interestingly, Glen Rice created the Beverly Hill Billies from local musicians he hired to perform as a hillbilly band. Still, as Melick's tirade made evident, critics of this new "hillbilly business" regarded it as degrading to American culture. Melick had no compunction about making stereotypical swipes at rural southerners, describing them as dirty and unkempt and a century behind the rest of modern civilization by virtue of the fact that spinning wheels were still in use. On the other hand, the success of hillbilly music hinted at America's growing interest in country music, especially in the nation's urban areas. Yet Melick's criticism also reflected another regional stereotype, though one commonly used by hillbilly comics, the "rube in the city," when he suggested that hillbilly musicians who had come to California were stupid with their money and in navigating the urban landscape of Los Angeles.[46]

There was some truth to the stereotypes that Melick used. Many hillbilly acts contained genuinely fine musicians, but there was often an element of caricature to these performances. Pie Plant Pete or the Coon Creek Girls, for example, were recognized as talented musicians. Pete, who grew up on a farm in southern Illinois, sang Scottish ballads, many of which, the *New York Times* commented, were still "sung in the cabins of the South." Yet there was an element of "aw shucks" in his performance that was common to many hillbilly acts. The Coon Creek Girls were equally talented musicians from eastern Kentucky, and yet the fact that they hailed from "Pinch 'Em Tight Holler" and wore gingham dresses also shaped their persona as hillbilly characters.[47]

There were native southerners who willingly portrayed the southern hillbilly for comedic effect and with great success, despite the negative associations of the term. Native Arkansan Bob Burns appeared for several years as the Arkansas Traveler, on radio and in film, offering less flattering portrayals of rural southerners, especially of ones from his native state.[48] He was briefly married to Judy Canova, a native of Florida, who also had a hillbilly act, which Burns was said to have influenced. Canova, once described as the "nation's preeminent hillbilly comedienne," was a talented singer with a well-trained voice who went to New York with her sister Anne and brother Zeke in an effort to have a legitimate career as a singer. Believing, in part, that she was not attractive enough to succeed as a traditional entertainer, she joined her brother and sister to form a musical group, the Three Georgia Crackers. Individually, Canova appeared as a guest on the *Rudy Vallee Show*, where she first had success playing a hillbilly character, which she embellished by wearing gingham dresses with oversized boots and putting her hair in braided pigtails. Eventually, she parlayed her hillbilly act into a successful radio program for the CBS network, as well as into film, again playing the hillbilly rube.[49]

Not all hillbilly acts perpetuated southern stereotypes. One of the best-known hillbilly comic duos was Lum and Abner, played by two natives of Arkansas, who portrayed southerners who were civic-minded and entrepreneurial—two qualities that appealed to listeners in the throes of the Great Depression. Chester Lauck and Norris Goff had known each other growing up in small towns in Arkansas. Both were experienced minstrel performers, but as Lum and Abner they offered listeners two southerners who were funny but also progressive in their outlook—not simply stupid hillbillies. In fact, the pair never liked the term "hillbilly" because of its negative connotations and sought to portray Arkansans as genuine and resourceful. The show's broad appeal was that Lum and Abner offered their listeners entertainment that dealt with Americans' shared concerns about the poverty and unemployment that accompanied the Great Depression. The duo provided a different image of the South and southerners in popular culture by "using a rural, overtly southern setting." As Randal Hall argues, Lauck and Goff "recast the hillbilly as a likeable, forward-looking, still authentic, yet recognizably American icon."[50]

Judy Canova, 1930s. (Courtesy Library of American Broadcasting, University of Maryland at College Park)

Chester Lauck and Norris Goff as Lum and Abner, 1930s. (Courtesy Library of American Broadcasting, University of Maryland at College Park)

Prior to becoming a show on NBC's national network, *Lum and Abner* achieved early success on WTAM in Cleveland, where the pair was sponsored by the local Ford dealership. According to *Radio Stars*, "People in northern Ohio liked their characters, who were somewhere between Tennessee hillbillies and Down East Seth Parkers"—the latter a reference to another show with rural characters from Maine.[51] They became so popular that once NBC purchased the show the network was able to convince several other Ford dealers in other cities to continue to sponsor *Lum and Abner*, and the show soon carried the tagline "Ford Dealers on the Air." Eventually the show was moved to Chicago, and although it was always popular with midwestern and southern listeners it gained a national following by virtue of its airing on the NBC network.[52]

Much of the appeal of *Lum and Abner* was its rural setting—the fictional town of Pine Ridge, Arkansas—and characters in situations that offered a sharp contrast to the modern and urban environment. Indeed, whether it was film or radio or even literature that gave nonsoutherners an image of the South, that image was, more often than not, the antimodern, the rustic, the primitive, the exotic. It was an image fixed in the American imagination, and it served as the source of Americans' attraction to the South—or perhaps the very thing that repulsed them about the region. Radio represented just one aspect of American popular culture, but one that was consistent with other forms in the way it represented southerners. Black southerners, even those who had migrated away from the region and lived in places like Chicago and Detroit, were presented in popular culture as iconic figures that listeners easily recognized as being from the South—in roles as servants and entertainers for white audiences. White southerners, too, were presented in radio and other forms of popular culture in this period as either part of the "moonlight-and-magnolias" genre or as rural southerners who were increasingly being represented as hillbillies. Nonsoutherners, especially those who worked on Madison Avenue, pursued these images of the South and shaped the region's identity for mass consumption—an identity that was readily consumed by radio's listeners. The negative implications were obvious to African Americans in the North as well as in the South, and to those rural southerners everywhere who sought respectability.

CHAPTER 4

Dixie on Film

"As all cinema observers knew, it was time for a cycle to come along. Another is here—the Deep South cycle, you might call it. Producers and writers alike have turned their attention to the aspects of Dixie, and there's scarcely a studio in Hollywood that hasn't a story of the South in production." Thus began a 1936 editorial in the *New York Times* entitled "Sowing the South Forty." Of course, *Gone with the Wind*, Margaret Mitchell's bestselling novel about the Civil War, was credited with starting the cycle. By the time of this December editorial the book had sold more than 1 million copies—less than seven months after its publication. To capitalize on the book's success, there were several films about the Old South in production. Mitchell's story, and especially its protagonist, so resonated with the American public that *New York Times* film critic Frank Nugent observed that "casting Scarlett became a game the entire nation played." German-born director Kurt Neumann, who later made *The Fly* (1958), was interviewed for the *New York Times'* piece. "Call it a cycle," Neumann said, but "the fact is the South is one of the best subjects Hollywood has ever had for sustained interest." Neumann, director of *Rainbow on the River* (1936), a film set in New Orleans, predicted that "some of the greatest pictures of the future will be placed in a Southern setting," adding that "we are just beginning to understand the South."[1]

Although the *New York Times* may have regarded the emphasis on southern films coming out of Hollywood as a cycle, the fact was there had been numerous films set in the South prior to the publication of Mitchell's novel. It is true that *Gone with the Wind* set off this frenzy, but the region's antebellum past had long been a fascinating topic for both the reading public and moviegoers. Yet there can be no doubt that the film version of Mitchell's Civil War epic cemented a nostalgic image of the South in American popular culture that still resonates with the American public. In the book and most certainly in the film, the cultural mythology of the Old South was in full flower. As early as World War I, there was already a consensus of opinion that favored the dominant southern narrative of the Civil War, and that opinion was further influenced by the story that emerged from Mitchell's pen and from David O. Selznick's vision as a filmmaker. It was an image that remained stable well into the 1950s, when the southern civil rights movement, and its coverage by the more popular medium of television, pulled back the curtain to reveal an image of the South that was far more complicated.[2]

Before television, motion pictures were arguably the most popular and influential medium of culture in the United States. From the time Thomas Edison introduced "moving pictures" on his kinetoscope at the Chicago World's Fair in 1893, movies swiftly became America's first mass amusement. This new technology to entertain the masses helped signal that the United States had entered the modern era, and motion pictures very rapidly became part of the urban-industrial landscape. In their infancy, motion pictures were a cheap form of entertainment with a working-class consumer base, especially in the large urban centers of the North and on the West Coast. Entrepreneurs were quick to capitalize on society's fascination with film by building literally thousands of nickelodeons in urban working-class neighborhoods where Americans could, for the cost of a nickel, watch a film lasting ten to fifteen minutes.[3]

Middle- and upper-class audiences initially saw films as depraved and nickelodeons as corrupt and immoral venues, but the movie industry sought to turn a large profit by creating motion pictures with mass appeal, regardless of class. By World War I, American filmmakers—influenced by their European counterparts—began making feature films that were longer and thus more costly to make (and to see), in an effort to appeal to middle- and upper-class audiences. This formula worked, and it also did not deter the working classes from spending an additional five to ten cents to see a longer and better-produced film. In a very short span of time, motion pictures developed a mass audience that traversed class lines. As a result, movies not only became America's most influential mass medium but also its most profitable.[4]

Most scholars of film agree that motion pictures, from their inception, have had a critical impact on American society. Movies revolutionized how different communities of Americans perceived one another and influenced their opinions on race, class, ethnicity, and even different regions of the country. Early on, movies became an influential form of cultural expression that helped to reinforce as well as reflect the deep-rooted values and attitudes held by larger society. Films set in the South or ones that featured southern characters were most certainly expressions of the nation's perception of the region and were in line with other forms of popular culture in their construction of various images of the South.[5]

Ironically, although movies were made possible by modern technology and were symbolic of modern life, the actual motion pictures made between 1915 and 1945 often consciously reflected America's nostalgia for its preindustrial past, including the American frontier. This longing for America's utopian ideals became more pronounced in the 1930s during the Great Depression but was evident in the feature films produced since the beginning of World War I. The American frontier, without a doubt, was most often represented in Westerns, which were the most popular films of the 1920s and 1930s. Yet, in these decades, the South also served as an exotic and preindustrial location in the American imagination, as evidenced by the stereotypes of hillbillies, belles, and African Americans, who were used to define the South in radio, literature, advertising, cartoons, and even music. Motion pictures magnified these southern stereotypes and brought them to life on the big screen.[6]

The American South was certainly not the most popular setting for motion pictures. Movies set in New York City and the American West were far more common. The number of films set in the American South, however, increased over time, and Hollywood's interpretation of the South and southerners consistently relied on stock images of the region and its people. A survey of motion pictures made between 1915 and 1945 shows that the Old South served as the primary setting for the majority of films set in the region during those years. As a rule, the films set in the South were engaged in some form of cultural or historical mythmaking, from D. W. Griffith's *The Birth of a Nation* (1915) to Walt Disney's *Song of the South* (1946). When the South was represented on film, it was usually based around plantations, southern belles, and loyal slaves. Then, in the late 1930s and early 1940s, when several hillbilly films were made, Hollywood added yet another regional stereotype to its catalog of films set in the region.[7]

D. W. Griffith's *The Birth of a Nation* (1915) was the most profitable and most watched silent movie ever produced, and there is no shortage of analysis on Griffith as an innovative filmmaker or on the film's influence in helping to revise America's memory of the Civil War and Reconstruction. Historians have also rightly noted the influence of Thomas Dixon Jr. on the production and distribution of the film, as the visual expression of his Reconstruction novel *The Clansman* (1905). As historian John Hope Franklin has argued, *The Birth of a Nation* was "Dixon, all Dixon," in its promotion of racist propaganda as historical truth. Perhaps most important, because it was the most successful film of its kind, it helped perpetuate racial

The Birth of a Nation, 1915. (Courtesy Photofest)

stereotypes that, while southern in origin, found a receptive national audience and signaled the direction Hollywood would take for the next three decades in its films about the South.[8]

W. E. B. Du Bois called the film "Tom Dixon's latest attack on colored people" and, along with other black intellectuals, wrote to Dixon condemning his novels, but the uproar against the film was much more significant than the criticism leveled at the book, largely because of the impact of seeing racism dramatized on screen. Although there was considerable criticism from both black and white Americans that *Birth of a Nation* was "a travesty against truth as well as an insult to an entire race of people," Thomas Dixon Jr. weathered the storm and in the end proved to be a formidable adversary when it came to promoting and defending the film.[9]

Dixon went to his old friend Woodrow Wilson, whom he had met while attending Johns Hopkins University some years earlier, in an effort to quash the criticism of the film. If Wilson, now president of the United States, supported the film, Dixon believed, the criticism would subside. It has been well documented that Wilson did lend the prestige of his office and showed the film at the White House. Less known, and even more impressive, was that Dixon influenced members of Congress, as well as sitting judges of the U.S. Supreme Court, to attend a viewing of the film at the Raleigh Hotel in Washington, D.C. Once this became common knowledge, censors in New York City, who had previously objected to showing the film, allowed it to open in the city's Liberty Theatre in March 1915, where it ran for forty-seven weeks.[10]

The social and political milieu into which the film was "born" is important to understanding its reception, both positive and negative. The South was expanding its system of Jim Crow, several race riots had taken place in both the North and the South, and African Americans saw Woodrow Wilson's presidency as yet another instrument to defend the "southern way of life." Moreover, the success of Dixon's novels, as well as that of D. W. Griffith's film, helped to fuel racial prejudice and incite fear among northern whites, who were concerned about the migration of southern blacks into northern cities, as well as the influx of eastern European immigrants.[11]

Despite the NAACP's lobbying efforts to sink the film due to its racist portrayals of African Americans and negative impact on racial progress, and despite heated protests of the film in cities like Boston, *The Birth of a Nation* succeeded in spreading Dixon's racist message. As the most financially successful and widely acclaimed film of the silent era, it had grossed $18 million by 1931, and by 1946 it was estimated that more than 200 million people had seen the film. It was also the film that African American leaders often pointed to as being one of the most damaging to race relations and to their morale as a people.[12]

The social impact of the film and its negative impact on race relations were made possible because of how well it was received far beyond the boundaries of Dixie. Moreover, although the novel was authored by a white southerner and made into a film by another white southerner, the publisher was northern and a Hollywood studio distributed it and profited handsomely. The fact was that nonsoutherners had a far greater interest in the film's financial success and nonsoutherners made up the film's primary audience. Thus, for all the vitriol spewed by Dixon through his novels and Griffith's achievement in dramatizing it on film, they were undoubtedly assisted in their efforts by the marketing and consumption of their ideas nationally.

Motion pictures that dramatized the Old South began in earnest during the 1920s and were common fare by the end of the decade. In 1929 alone, Hollywood made half a dozen such films, ranging from an adaptation of the Broadway play *Show Boat* to the film *Coquette*, in which Mary Pickford played the "heartless belle of a southern town." Even when a film was set in the contemporary South, the region was still portrayed as being ensconced in the past. One such film, entitled *Crinoline and Romance* (1923), was set in North Carolina. Its protagonist, Emmy Lou, lives on a secluded plantation and still wears crinolines with her dress in the style of the Old South. When she visits the home of a family friend, she "quickly takes to the jazz ways of the young people" living there. The film implies that southerners were still wedded to their antebellum past and lived in isolation from the changes that were taking place outside of the region. In other words, the region remained provincial, even in the Jazz Age.[13]

The Deep South and southern plantations provided the most common film settings for motion pictures about the region in the two decades prior to 1945. One estimate suggests that there were nearly seventy-five films set in the pre–Civil War South in the decade leading up to World War II, with Louisiana and Mississippi Hollywood's favorite locales. In the 1920s, thirty-four films were set in those two states, and during the 1930s, twenty films were set in Mississippi alone. New Orleans, antebellum plantations, and the Mississippi River offered romantic backdrops for films about the Old South, the planter elite, riverboat gamblers, and showboats.[14]

River of Romance (1929) was typical of the southern fare offered to American film audiences. The film, set in the river port town of Natchez, Mississippi, during the 1840s, is a story about Tom Rumford, the son of a plantation owner and "southern general," who returns to his father's home in Natchez from Philadelphia, where he had been raised by Quaker relatives. When Tom gets challenged to a duel, he scoffs at the idea of this southern ritual and is subsequently banished from his father's home for this breach of honor. The Mississippi River, the old southern town of Natchez, a plantation, a duel, and southern honor were all used to create a specific image of the region.[15]

One of the most successful films of the 1920s was *Show Boat* (1929). Like many of the early films produced by Hollywood, the film was based on a successful Broadway play. Florenz Ziegfeld, who produced *Show Boat*, the play, brought to life the Edna Ferber novel of the same name and worked with Hollywood on the film's production. The movie was directed by Carl Laemmle, who incorporated a prologue that showcased some of the featured players from the original play, including the plantation singers and Queenie, the mammy character played on stage in blackface by white actress Tess Gardella. The story was already familiar to American audiences who had read the novel and to many more who had enjoyed the play. The title character, Magnolia Hawkes, the star of her family's riverboat revue,

River of Romance, 1929. (Courtesy Photofest)

marries a "charming, river gambler" named Gaylord Ravenal, who squanders the family's money and is asked to leave by Magnolia's mother. This forces Magnolia to support herself and her child by going back on stage, where, in blackface, she sings Negro spirituals. *Show Boat* proved to be such a successful southern formula that Hollywood decided to remake the film in 1936 and again in 1951. For the 1936 remake, the roles of the black characters were played by two leading African American actors of the time—Hattie McDaniel as Queenie and Paul Robeson as Joe. Both roles were southern stereotypes—the black mammy and the lazy darky. In fact, in one scene, Queenie tells Joe, "I believe you're the laziest man that ever lived on this [Mississippi] river." Irene Dunne played the lead female role of Magnolia, performing Negro spirituals in blackface, accompanied by a banjo, in what is clearly a minstrel sequence.[16]

Films about the South in the 1930s may have increased in number, but the story of the region remained the same. The musical costume drama *Dixiana* (1930) began the decade with a story set in New Orleans and also featured a plantation, members of the southern aristocracy, a "powerful riverboat gambler," and a duel. The year 1935 was an especially productive year for Hollywood films about the South, which became some of the

Hattie McDaniel and Paul Robeson in *Show Boat*, 1936. (Courtesy Photofest)

most successful the industry produced that year. In addition to the remake of *Show Boat*, Paramount Pictures produced *Mississippi*, based on the Booth Tarkington play *Magnolia*, and *So Red the Rose*, drawn from the best-selling Civil War novel by Stark Young, whose setting was the Portobello plantation in Natchez, Mississippi. That same year, Twentieth-Century Fox produced *The Little Colonel* and *The Littlest Rebel*, both of which were vehicles for America's favorite child star, Shirley Temple.[17]

The Little Colonel was based on the children's novel of the same name written by Annie Fellows Johnston. Johnston's story, originally published in 1895, tells the story of a young and feisty girl from Kentucky, Lloyd Sherman, whose name was a combination of her southern mother's maiden name and her Yankee father's last name—a name both familiar to, and despised by, white southerners. The little girl's mother, Elizabeth, had married a "New York man" and for doing so was disowned by her father, the colonel, who "hate[d] Yankees like poison." Elizabeth and her husband move back to Kentucky, and the old colonel unwittingly meets his granddaughter (now his neighbor), who, in temperament, turns out to be much like her grandfather, thus earning the nickname, Little Colonel.[18]

In both the novel and the film, the Little Colonel is surrounded by

The Littlest Rebel, 1935, starring Shirley Temple and Bill Robinson.
(Courtesy Photofest)

the stock characters one would find in a southern plantation setting. The old Confederate colonel and his daughter Elizabeth, a southern belle, are present. There is also the mammy figure, in this case the family cook, Mom Beck, played by Hattie McDaniel, whose career was filled with such roles. Lloyd Sherman's playmates are Mom Beck's children, who are referred to as "little darkies" and "picknaninnies" in Johnston's book. In the film, the black actor Bill "Bojangles" Robinson plays the uncle figure, Walker, another household servant, with whom Shirley Temple sings and dances. Finally, the music for the film includes minstrel songs by Stephen Foster and Daniel Decatur Emmett's "Dixie."[19]

The Littlest Rebel likewise cast Temple with Robinson in a story set in the Civil War South. The film begins with a scene of a slave cabin sitting in the middle of a cotton field in full bloom and quickly moves to a white-columned antebellum mansion where Virginia Cary (Shirley Temple) is having a children's party, at which Uncle Billy (Bill Robinson) and a fellow male house servant, James Henry, attend to the children. Temple asks Uncle Billy to dance for the children, and with a smile he loyally complies. The film is replete with southern racial stereotypes—from Uncle Billy, the dancing, happy slave, to James Henry, the slow-shuffling oaf who provides comic relief, to the mammy and the pickaninnies. Temple's character also gets in the act when she hides from the Yankees and is discovered in black-face dressed like a miniature mammy, including kerchief. The combination of America's little sweetheart playing the part of a precocious "little rebel" and a plantation setting with happy and loyal slaves sold well with American audiences nationwide, who made *The Little Colonel* and *The Littlest Rebel* two of the highest-grossing films of the year.[20]

The terrific success of *Gone with the Wind* only increased Hollywood's desire to produce films set in the Old South, and publishers were definitely in on the act. Several Hollywood studios maintained offices in New York, where they kept close tabs on successful novels as well as Broadway plays. Novels and plays about the Civil War and the Old South were popular in the 1930s, but no book at the time grabbed the attention of Hollywood as much as did *Gone with the Wind*. The book's tremendous sales meant a readymade audience for its film treatment. The American Institute of Public Opinion, founded by George Gallup, known today as the Gallup Poll, estimated that 14 million people had read the novel in whole or in part by 1938. Based on that evidence, the institute estimated that there was a "better-than-even chance" that almost two-thirds of the moviegoing public planned to see the film. As *New York Times* movie critic Bosley Crowther wrote, "Perhaps no cinematic consummation has been so devoutly wished by the American movie-going public" as *Gone with the Wind*.[21]

Before the book was even published, nearly every studio in Hollywood was in contact with Macmillan for an advance copy of the novel. Paramount, Metro-Goldwyn-Mayer, Twentieth-Century Fox, Columbia, Universal, and Selznick, International—all were interested in making a bid on the movie rights. Warner Brothers initially wanted the film for its star, Bette Davis. Likewise, RKO Radio Pictures expressed an interest in the story for Katharine Hepburn. Margaret Mitchell eventually signed a contract giving Macmillan the right to sell her book to a movie studio, and one month after its publication it was announced that David O. Selznick had bought the film rights to the novel for $50,000.[22]

Mitchell was relieved to hand over the task of selling the film rights to Macmillan and wanted no part in the production. She knew that an adaptation of her 1,037-page novel would be difficult, at best, although she expressed to her editor, Harold Latham, that she "wouldn't put it beyond Hollywood to have General Hood win the Battle of Jonesboro, Scarlett seduce General Sherman and a set of negroes with Harlem accents play the

Clark Gable and Vivien Leigh on the set of *Gone with the Wind*, 1939.
(Courtesy Photofest)

back woods darkies." Mitchell's concern for historical accuracies and for scenes that would set most white southerners' teeth on edge were genuine, as motion pictures had taken liberties with both.[23]

Before the ink was dry on the contract, Hollywood was abuzz with excitement about the picture, and actors and actresses were angling to be selected to play the film's principals. Kirtley Baskette, a columnist for *Photoplay* magazine, described the phenomenon as a "grade-A tornado" sweeping the country and Tinseltown. "Actors and actresses who have never been South of the Slot in San Francisco or below Twenty-third Street in Manhattan, whose closest tie to Dixie in fact, is a faint resemblance to a Virginia ham, wander around calling people 'Honey' in a languid, molasses manner," adding that "even the high yellows down on Central Avenue are brushing up on their southern accents." *Gone with the Wind* was being touted as the "greatest film" to ever be made.[24]

Even before David Selznick began production on his magnum opus, Hollywood rushed to cash in on the novel's mass appeal. The most successful effort was Warner Brothers *Jezebel* (1938), based on the 1933 play by Owen Davis. Margaret Mitchell, who saw the film, discerned no similarities between it and her book, and she told a friend that she did not "have a copyright on hoop skirts or hot-blooded Southerners."[25] Selznick, however, did notice the similarities and sent a letter to studio head Jack Warner letting him know as much. "The picture throughout is permeated with characterizations, attitudes and scenes which unfortunately resemble 'Gone With the Wind,'" he wrote, and cautioned that "it would be a pity . . . if so distinguished a picture as 'Jezebel' should be damned by the millions of readers and lovers" of Mitchell's book.[26]

The similarities between *Jezebel* and Selznick's as-yet-uncompleted film were not lost on critics. Nor was Hollywood's attempt to cash in on the success of *Gone with the Wind*. Frank Nugent, writing for the *New York Times*, remarked that "since a Southern cycle is in the offing, where it has been since Mr. Selznick started looking for Scarlett, it is probably for the best that Owen Davis's 'Jezebel' should have got in the first licks. Being heavy in melodrama with the intense Miss Bette Davis as its heroine, the [film] should clear the air, prepare us for the gentler things to come." Even the trailer for the film did not attempt to hide a connection with *Gone with the Wind*, proclaiming that the story was "a scarlet portrait of a gorgeous spit-fire." Despite Selznick's fear that *Jezebel* would be "damned" by fans of Mitchell's work, the reverse was true, and Davis won the Oscar for Best Actress. If anything, the film whetted the appetite of American audiences, which were eager to see the most celebrated romantic epic of the Old South ever made for the large screen.[27]

The cinematic expression of Margaret Mitchell's novel undoubtedly did more to promote a nostalgic image of the Old South than the novel itself. A few years after the film premiered, Mitchell wrote to her friend Virginius Dabney, editor of the *Richmond Times-Dispatch*, and expressed her embarrassment that she was "included among writers who pictured the South as a land of white-columned mansions whose wealthy owners had thousands of slaves and drank thousands of juleps." The reality was that the film had done more to influence that perception of the book; even Mitchell recognized the impact of the film on people's understanding of southern history. "Southerners could write the truth about the ante-bellum South," she wrote, but "everyone would go on believing in the Hollywood version." She had resigned herself to the fact that "people believe what they like to believe and the mythical Old South has too strong a hold on their imaginations to be altered by the mere reading of [my] book."[28]

Mitchell clearly did not place her own work in the context of Lost Cause literature, and yet all the elements of the Lost Cause were there—belles and loyal slaves, plantations and Confederate heroes, and a vindication of the Ku Klux Klan. The Hollywood version, to be sure, embellished the myth. After learning from fellow Georgians Susan Myrick and Wilbur Kurtz, technical advisers Selznick hired to ensure regional and historical authenticity, that Tara was going to have columns and Twelve Oaks would have two staircases, Mitchell admitted she "did not know whether to laugh or to throw up." She confessed she was "mortally afraid" that Tara would resemble the Natchez homes that were seen in the film *So Red the Rose* (1935), adding that she feared that Hollywood might add columns "on the smokehouse, too," rather than portraying the more modest Georgia plantation she described in her book.[29]

Mitchell's concerns about how the South might appear in film were not unfounded. Motion pictures about the region often represented its antebellum history by showcasing a southern plantation with a white-columned mansion. George Cukor, the original director for *Gone with the Wind*, spent several scouting trips—none of which were in middle Georgia where the novel was set—in search of the perfect antebellum mansion. He visited the James River plantations in Virginia, as well as plantations around Charleston and Savannah. Northern film critics revealed their preconceived, and yet commonly held, notions about the South when they reported on the film's progress. They used Cukor's trips to the region, for example, to describe the South as a place where the director had enjoyed "the lazy life." Even those who worked on the film were accused of being swept away by the "Southern *dolce far niente*," which translates as "pleasant idleness." Thus, although *Gone with the Wind* was a nostalgic take on the antebellum past, the South's national reputation in the late 1930s remained one of a region where people went about their lives at a slow pace and with a carefree attitude.[30]

For white southerners, the most important element in the film, aside from adhering to Margaret Mitchell's narrative, was that the actors and actresses not sully the southern accent. Southerners everywhere expressed their concerns to Mitchell personally on this point, and thousands of others wrote to David Selznick himself. As Lucille Pratt, a woman from Shreveport, Louisiana, explained to the producer, "Having had our nerves frayed every time we hear the 'Southern drawl' in a motion picture, we are not hankering at this time for an overdose of it in 'Gone With the Wind.'" Selznick apparently got the message. "We got thousands of signatures on petitions from the South, urging us not to put the northern version of the southern accent in the picture," he explained, and he hired Atlantan Susan Myrick to advise the actors in the film to avoid that pitfall.[31]

The selection of the actress to play Scarlett O'Hara was a national obsession, but in the South it played out in the cultural politics of the Lost Cause. A United Daughters of the Confederacy (UDC) chapter in Ocala, Florida, passed a resolution to "secede" from Selznick International in protest for choosing anyone other than a native-born, southern woman to play the role. Once Vivien Leigh was chosen, however, the president-general of the entire organization praised her selection, preventing any further uproar by the membership. Getting approval from the UDC was important, given that the organization still wielded influence in the region. After the film's premier in Atlanta, the predecessor of the UDC, the Ladies' Memorial Association, made Vivien Leigh an honorary member of its organization and passed a resolution commending David Selznick "for making the picture conform to the facts of history." This stamp of approval was noteworthy, because it validated the film as staying in step with the *southern* version of history, which was steeped in the mythology of the Lost Cause.[32]

Gone with the Wind's achievement in reinforcing the Lost Cause myth in American culture was matched only by its financial success. On the one hand, American audiences readily consumed the film's ideas about the southern past, the idealized race relations presented on the screen, and the image of the South as a place locked in time. Yet Americans also literally consumed the myth, through the film's commercial tie-ins and by spending their tourist dollars to see the Dixie they witnessed on film, in the hope of seeing blacks working in the cotton fields next to grand, white-columned mansions.

If Hollywood was anything, it was a business, and merchants considered movies to be their greatest salesmen. Metro-Goldwyn-Mayer and David Selznick, in fact, were singled out for "taking advantage of this newly developed form of exploitation." The studio and the film's producer signed agreements with nearly seventy-five manufacturers to create and market items associated with *Gone with the Wind*, including "jewelry, slippers, house coats, pajamas, hats, snoods, ladies' suits and fur jacket ensembles." Entrepreneurs around the country were quick to capitalize on clothing and jewelry linked to the film or its primary characters—extending the mythology of the South into the marketplace. Atlanta's business community was no exception. F. J. Coolidge & Sons advertised wallpapers that were "expressive of the influence we have come to know and cherish in the Deep South." Interior designers Lang and Fritz, Inc., had a window display in their store "emphasizing the Southern Aristocratic Charm of the 'Gone With the Wind' days."[33]

Writing about the film a few years after it debuted, Mitchell's friend Virginius Dabney offered his own assessment of how the film version of *Gone with the Wind* helped to create a false impression of the South. He decried the prologue of the film, which described the South as a "land of Cavaliers and cotton," as "grotesque" and argued that "many of the misconceptions concerning the New South [stemmed] from earlier misconceptions of the Old South." Dabney may have been concerned with historical inaccuracies presented in the film, but the essence of his statement was true. That is to say, most Americans in the 1930s did not have an image of a "New South." Rather, they were content with their image of the region as a place still immersed in the culture of the Old South.[34]

Dabney may have been offended by misconceptions concerning southern whites, but stereotypes of southern blacks were far more offensive in the eyes of contemporary black leaders. One writer contended that *Gone with the Wind* was a "worthy successor to the other rotten output, *The Birth of a Nation*" in its portrayal of blacks.[35] Religious and labor leaders in Chicago protested the film as "anti-Negro" and one that incited hate and lynching. Their appeal to the Chicago Board of Censors to ban the showing of *Gone with the Wind*, although it failed, highlighted their concern about the film's potential to provoke racial violence.[36] Andy Razaf, a writer for the Associated Negro Press, offered a creative and pointed criticism of the film with his poem entitled "Gone with the Wind." Razaf's lament is a larger critique of the nation's racial prejudice as revealed in the poem's final stanza:

What of the black man's liberty?
Today, he's half slave, half free,
Denied his rights on every side,
Jim crowed, lynched and crucified
He's even barred in Washington—
Gone with the wind? You're wrong, my son.[37]

Hollywood's romantic vision of the South and of southerners, black and white, illustrated what was inherently insidious about films set in the region in the early decades of filmmaking, especially for African Americans. Before hillbillies emerged as a regional type, Hollywood offered American consumers a South in which whites were portrayed as elites and African Americans were there to serve or entertain them. For moviegoing audiences in the urban North, in cities to which southern blacks had migrated, motion pictures provided an ideal of race relations that was modeled on the Old South. These films also perpetuated a romantic version of the region that northern consumers of the genre assumed they might still find in the modern South, and they toured the region expecting to see plantations and blacks working in cotton fields. Such films perpetuated an image of the region—an image that in many ways kept it locked in the antebellum past, hindering racial progress not only in the South but in the nation as a whole.

Indeed, African Americans across the nation who longed for racial progress were thwarted in their efforts at reform by the perpetuation of stereotypes that were wedded to the mythology of the Old South. Hollywood helped maintain this state of affairs through numerous motion pictures set in the region, the majority of which were based on stories set in the pre–Civil War South. In a speech before the Hollywood Writers' Congress in 1943, American screenwriter Dalton Trumbo commented that "the most gigantic milestones of [Hollywood's] appeal to public patronage have been the anti-Negro pictures *The Birth of a Nation* and *Gone with the Wind*." Trumbo's larger argument was that Hollywood had done very little to help end racial prejudice and, to some degree, had helped perpetuate it through motion pictures. Significantly, he pointed to the two most successful films set in the American South to make his point.[38]

In 1946, film critic John McManus and theater critic Louis Kronenberger reflected on the role motion pictures had played in race relations in the period between *The Birth of a Nation* and *Gone with the Wind* and, like Dalton Trumbo, criticized Hollywood for "never [accepting] as its responsibility the function of helping to destroy race and group prejudice." McManus and Kronenberger argued that, because Americans were three times as likely to see a film as to read a newspaper or magazine, the motion picture industry had a responsibility to produce films that might help improve race relations. They acknowledged that racial prejudice was "virtually national in extent" and was "built into American custom," but they encouraged Hollywood to make films that exposed racial prejudice, even though such films would be "in advance of national policy." To be sure, film audiences were familiar with several talented black entertainers on film, including Lena Horne, Duke Ellington, Paul Robeson, Katherine Dunham, and Fats Waller. Yet most African American artists were in what were known as "all-Negro" films, or performed in a segregated scene, or continued to play stereotypical roles—many of which were based on southern stereotypes.[39]

In 1942, Wendell Willkie, chairman of the board of Twentieth-Century Fox and former Republican candidate for president, gave the keynote address at the annual meeting of the NAACP in which he spoke of providing a "new deal" for African Americans in films and implored Hollywood to offer films that did not limit black actors to playing menial or comic roles. He reiterated this message later that year at a meeting with motion picture industry executives and producers, who promised to offer films with more realistic portrayals of African American life. Still, Hollywood was a business, and in that regard the industry was careful not to take this experiment too quickly and too far, lest it offend southern theater owners, who were essential to the financial success of a film.[40]

Willkie's comments about the types of roles offered to black actors— either menial or comic—reflected the long history of Hollywood films set in the South and the portrayal of African Americans in roles that were clearly southern in origin. Most black actors only appeared in films as extras or to provide a racial "atmosphere." However, when African Americans appeared on film, they generally appeared in what were known as "bit parts" and they nearly always portrayed domestic servants. Even when they were offered actual film roles, they were usually defined as "mammy roles," like those played by Hattie McDaniel in several films, including *Show Boat*, *The Little Colonel*, *Gone with the Wind*, and *Song of the South*. With few exceptions, Hollywood offered black actors few alternatives to these servant roles until the late 1940s.[41]

What did this emphasis on southern racial stereotypes in films mean for African Americans nationally? Claude Barnett, founder of the Associated Negro Press, argued that the popular press and media, including radio and films, influenced national morale and that when popular mediums dealt with issues of race they played an important role in shaping the morale of African Americans. He observed that, although there was "plenty of work" for black actors and actresses in Hollywood, the roles offered to them had not changed substantially in two decades. It is telling that when Margaret Mitchell received the cast list for *Gone with the Wind*, she admitted that she had "never seen . . . any of the Negro characters except Hattie McDaniel." Barnett lamented that black actors and actresses were still being offered parts as "servants, comedians, chicken thieves, razor wielders, believers in ghosts and the supernatural, and [characters that possess] a simple, child-like religion." And, he argued, such stereotypes in film, the nation's most influential form of popular culture, were particularly damaging to black morale because they sustained an image of African Americans as inferior.[42]

Not surprisingly, Barnett also criticized *The Birth of a Nation* — as a film that not only incited racism but pitted "race against race." Even when Hollywood produced feature films with a black cast, such as *Hearts in Dixie* (1929) and *Hallelujah* (1929), the real interest was to showcase slave spirituals and to depict African Americans in nostalgic settings generally linked to the Old South. *Hearts in Dixie*, for example, was initially applauded for offering black performers an opportunity to work in motion pictures. The characters, however, included stereotypical roles with character names like Nappus and Gummy, the latter described as "lazy and shiftless." The only benefit Barnett saw in having increasing numbers of African Americans in motion pictures was that even though these films invoked such southern mythology, at least the black roles were less likely to be played by whites in blackface.[43]

Hollywood persisted in producing films that typecast the region and its people throughout the period of World War II. Hillbilly pictures became the favorite of smaller movie studios, especially Republic Pictures, which saw an opportunity to capitalize on the cornpone humor that was increasingly popular on radio. But many of the actors chosen to play the roles were from places far removed from the Ozarks or Appalachia. A *New York*

Hearts in Dixie, 1929, the first film to have an all-black cast. (Courtesy Photofest)

Times movie critic noted that, since "the people of the Southern mountains resolutely refuse to leave their homeplaces for Hollywood," the industry resorted to hiring actors from places like New York, Maine, and Indiana. The fact was that hillbilly films, too, were profitable. "There continues to be gold in them thar hillbillies," he wrote, "and so long as that happy state of affairs exists, what difference does it make who does the mining?"[44]

There were native southerners whose radio popularity playing hillbilly characters translated into film careers. Radio personalities Chester Lauck and Norris Goff, who played the roles of Lum and Abner from the fictitious town of Pine Ridge, Arkansas, were featured in no less than six movies. Another Arkansas native, Bob Burns, known on radio as the Arkansas Traveler, also turned his radio fame into a Hollywood career.[45]

Perhaps no other radio star had as successful a run in hillbilly movies as did Judy Canova. Born in Stark, Florida, into a relatively affluent family, Judy and her siblings, Anne and Zeke, began their careers as a hillbilly trio called Three Georgia Crackers. They sang and acted, as well as performed comedy. Judy eventually became a solo performer, playing hillbilly roles on Broadway and on the radio, where she further developed her role as a hillbilly comic. Eventually, she signed with Republic Pictures to star in films in which she played a simpleminded country girl often caught up in situations that pitted her against scheming city folk who tried to take advantage of her naïveté. In 1941, she starred in the films *Puddin' Head*, as Judy Goober, and *Sis Hopkins*, in which she played the "naïve but good-hearted hillbilly." Canova's wardrobe for these films included calico or gingham dresses, and her hair was styled in her trademark braided pigtails. One of Canova's films, like other movies of the genre, also integrated contemporary themes of war. In *Joan of Ozark* (1942), Canova played Judy Hull, an Arkansas native who, while hunting quail, accidentally shoots a carrier pigeon being used by Axis spies, which earned her the nickname Hillbilly Mata Hari.[46]

Prior to World War II, hillbilly films were mildly successful with American audiences, but they also influenced the nation's image of the mountain South as a place where there lived an unsophisticated and fecund population, which carried shotguns, feuded, and went shoeless and whose rural isolation kept them ignorant. During the war, stereotypes remained, but a new type of southern hillbilly emerged. As Anthony Harkins has noted in his cultural history of the hillbilly image, this genre of films in the 1940s was more likely to celebrate the "goodness of the 'plain folk'" as a means to critique "the evils of modern urban America," often represented in these films as corrupt businessmen or aristocratic snobs.[47]

Southern stereotypes like the hillbilly and the "old-time Negro" finally came under fire in the years following the conclusion of World War II. Thousands of men and women from Appalachia and the Ozarks who took war-production jobs in largely northern cities like Detroit, Chicago, and Baltimore, along with the thousands of others who enlisted in the armed forces, influenced a change in attitude—at least among movie critics, who ramped up their attacks on Hollywood for promoting ethnic and racial stereotypes in the movies. Nonetheless, movie studios continued to produce films that perpetuated images of the South as a region still wedded to its agrarian roots. Was Hollywood hard of hearing or was it keenly aware that many Americans were still enamored with the Old South? In the case of *Song of the South* (1946), the answer was a little of both.

Walt Disney made plans to produce an animated version of Joel Chandler Harris's Uncle Remus tales before the end of the war, and in 1944 the studio sent its consultants to Georgia to gather background for the movie. They visited Turnwold, the Eatonton plantation of Joseph Addison Turner, where Harris honed his writing skills, and Disney hired Wilbur Kurtz—the historian and technical adviser for *Gone with the Wind*—and

Judy Canova in *Scatterbrain*, 1940. Canova made several hillbilly films during World War II. (Courtesy Photofest)

James Baskett as Uncle Remus in *Song of the South*, 1946. (Courtesy Photofest)

his wife, Annie, to serve as consultants for *Song of the South*. The couple was hired to advise on costumes, architecture, and dialect. According to the *Atlanta Constitution*, Annie Kurtz, who "reared her own five children on Uncle Remus stories and poems . . . [was] an authority on southern dialects." One of the Disney artists who traveled to Georgia told the paper that she, too, had been "brought up on Uncle Remus stories" and was eager to see a Georgia cotton field firsthand and to learn "all about the briar patch."[48]

Song of the South, like *Gone with the Wind* before it, had an Atlanta premier. The film debuted in the city's Fox Theater on November 13, 1946, and, not surprisingly, was well received. The only criticism that Wright Bryan could summon in his editorial in the *Atlanta Journal* was that the film's title should have included the name of Uncle Remus. "To those of us who were brought up on bedtime readings of Uncle Remus stories, the change in the name seems to border on sacrilege," Bryan complained, adding that "[the title] *Song of the South* could do for any picture with a scene below the Mason Dixon Line," an observation that speaks volumes about how Hollywood portrayed the region. Critics writing for newspapers above that line, however, had far more to say about Disney's film.[49]

Bosley Crowther of the *New York Times* lambasted the film in his review, which was appropriately titled "Spanking Disney." Prior to World War II, characters like Uncle Remus were common in motion pictures set in the South and managed to slip through unnoticed by white critics. But, in the postwar era, Crowther's review signaled a change. He began with an assault on the character of Uncle Remus, played by James Baskett, who appeared as the "sweetest and most wistful darky slave that ever stepped out of a sublimely unreconstructed fancy of the Old South." Crowther's description of Disney's vision as "unreconstructed" was significant, even though several critics did not agree, because it was an "unreconstructed" vision shared by a broad cross section of the American public, who turned out to see the film in droves.[50]

Crowther was troubled by what he saw in *Song of the South* and its meaning for race relations, and he chastised Walt Disney directly. "The master-and-slave relationship is so lovingly regarded in your yarn, with the Negroes bowing and scraping and singing spirituals in the night," he wrote, "[that one] might almost imagine that you figure that Abe Lincoln made a mistake." He added, "Put down that mint julep, Mr. Disney!" Not surprisingly, the NAACP joined Crowther in his disdain for the film. The organization had consistently protested negative portrayals of African Americans in the movies since *The Birth of a Nation* had premiered more than two decades earlier. Walter White, executive secretary of the organization, issued a statement saying that, although the group recognized the "artistic merit" of the film, specifically its music, it was disappointed that "in an effort not to offend the South, the production [helped] to perpetuate a dangerously glorified picture of slavery."[51]

The National Negro Congress protested by picketing the Palace Theatre in New York when the film opened in December. In a show of interracial cooperation, several whites joined with African Americans to picket the theater, with placards reading, "We fought for Uncle Sam, not Uncle Tom"—a clear reference to the recent war, in which thousands of African Americans had served. The group brought an effigy of "Jim Crow" in a wooden coffin, which it placed in front of the theater, and, to the tune of "Jingle Bells," the protestors marched with their placards, singing, "Disney tells, Disney tells, lies about the South. We've heard those lies before, right out of Bilbo's mouth"—alluding to the race-baiting senator, Theodore Bilbo, of Mississippi. They also gave handouts to the theatergoers, on which they criticized the film as "an insult to the Negro people because it uses offensive dialect; it portrays the Negro as a low inferior servant; it glorifies slavery"; and, not insignificant, "it damages the fight for equal representation."[52]

Two weeks after the protest, a subcommittee of the National Board of Review—the organization that monitored the motion picture industry—recommended *Song of the South* as a suitable film for children. Known as the Schools Motion Picture Committee, the group, made up of teachers and parents in the New York area, with its stamp of approval essentially promoted the film and its message to another generation of Americans. Therein lay the problem being protested by the National Negro Congress, which saw a correlation between the continued presence and support for such images on the big screen and their negative impact on African Americans' struggle for equal representation under the law.[53]

It took both social and political change, as well as a new mass medium, to shake up Hollywood's stale approach to its stories about the South. African American veterans came home from World War II and assumed leadership roles in the southern civil rights movement, and President Harry Truman's executive order ending segregation in the armed forces signaled an important change in national policy. Such changes meant that Hollywood's image of African Americans, an image that was modeled on a southern narrative of blacks as loyal servants, would soon no longer be tenable. Moreover, the new medium of television increasingly replaced motion pictures as the form of entertainment sought out by most Americans. Ten years after *Song of the South* was made, television had replaced motion pictures as the most influential form of mass media. During those years, Hollywood turned its attention toward making films that might draw Americans away from their television sets, and, as a rule, movies set on a southern plantation with happy-go-lucky slaves were no longer desirable nor profitable. Despite all these changes, Hollywood's representation of the South in motion pictures, both grand and ordinary, continued to influence how the South was perceived in the American imagination—and this reality had consequences for the region and the nation.

CHAPTER 5

Dixie in Literature

Writing to her editor, Harold Latham, Margaret Mitchell recalled how she had once worried that the Macmillan Company "would be stuck with at least 5,000, if not more," of the first edition of *Gone with the Wind*. She was now able to laugh about that, she told Latham, especially as the book had sold just more than 1 million copies. What was personally difficult for her, however, was the loss of privacy. Telegrams, special deliveries, and phone calls were a daily nuisance, and a constant stream of visitors came to her home. Even though her fellow Atlantans and local newspapers "begged" people not to bother Mitchell, it was all for naught, and it made her feel like a spectacle. "The out of town visitors and tourists . . . seem to feel that I am like the Dionne quintuplets and should be on view twenty-four hours a day."[1]

Peggy Mitchell, as she was known to those closest to her, found herself pleased to be slipping off the best-seller list if it meant less scrutiny of her personal life. "I do not mean that I am unhappy over the marvelous success of the book. That is something I will never get over," she wrote. "But the public interest in me as a person has been unendurable for some months. I cannot buy a new car or a new hat or pay a fine for improper parking or send a modest wedding present without it getting into the papers." *Gone with the Wind* was a publishing phenomenon, and Mitchell's frustrations about the loss of privacy were very real. The nation, not just the American South, was taken by her epic on the Civil War. The 1,037-page novel exceeded the success of previous novels set in the South. Her epic of the Lost Cause reached an enormous audience—the publisher estimated that 10 million people had read it by 1937—which extended far beyond the borders of the former Confederacy. This was accomplished with the help of a northern publisher, Macmillan, a company that promoted and sold the novel as not only a great story but an authentic portrayal of life in the Civil War South.[2]

The North had long been the center of publishing, and books about the South and the Civil War, as well as the region's antebellum past, were a mainstay for publishing houses in New York, Boston, and Philadelphia during the late nineteenth and early twentieth centuries. By contrast, as

Margaret Mitchell, author of *Gone with the Wind*, 1936. (Courtesy Kenan Research Center at the Atlanta History Center)

literary critic and historian Archibald Henderson put it, not only was the southern public the "poorest field for national publishing firms" but the region itself was culturally stunted by the "absence of publishing houses or even [an] influential magazine of national significance."[3] There were southern publishing firms, to be sure, but they tended to offer books and novels that justified the South's role in the Civil War or promoted the concept of southern exceptionalism. Moreover, southern publishers did not have the marketing reach of firms like Macmillan & Company of New York or the J. B. Lippincott Company of Philadelphia. What northern publishers did was to provide the broader American reading public with books about the South on a grander scale, because they had the means to market and distribute books to a larger audience. Joel Chandler Harris's Uncle Remus stories, Thomas Nelson Page's books about the plantation South, and Thomas Dixon's enormously successful trilogy on the Ku Klux Klan were printed and marketed by New York publishers. These books appealed to readers across the United States, and their success, as Henderson argued, did not depend on a southern audience. By the time *Gone with the Wind* came out, in fact, the American reading public was already primed for an epic tale set in the South, because such stories had long been part of their reading diet.

Scholars have written extensively about southern literature and its place in the American literary landscape, as a regional literature that has contributed to southern identity and memory and helped to define the South as a "place."[4] Yet it is significant that literature about the South and the definition of southern identity has often emerged from outside of the region, particularly from the North. Northern publishers marketed the writing of southern authors as authentic portrayals of the region, even when those portrayals included racist caricatures. Northern writers, too, have long held a fascination with Dixie and have helped to define the region for nonsoutherners, profiting handsomely from doing so.

In the period following the Civil War and extending well into the twentieth century, there was an entire genre of travel literature that described the region to the American reading public, whose curiosity about the South provided a niche market for northern publishers. After four years of war, many northerners—veterans, entrepreneurs, wealthy travelers—wanted to see the South for themselves, and they toured the region in droves. Certainly, Americans traveled to other parts of the United States during the second half of the nineteenth century, but, as Cindy Aron points out, the West "remained primarily accessible to those with sub-stantial wealth."[5] Americans fantasized about what could be found on the national landscape, and tourism provided an opportunity to fulfill those fantasies. Moreover, tourism helped people to define "America as a place," freeing them from their everyday constraints. This was especially true of tourists from the urban-industrial North, who ventured south in search of the nation's historical and pastoral landscapes.[6]

Domestic tourism and vacationing increased steadily throughout the nineteenth century, especially by members of the emerging northern mid-dle class, who had the leisure time and the means to travel.[7] The South offered a place to unwind from the physical and psychological stresses that accompanied living in cities. Many northern tourists went south for health reasons, to seashores, mountains, and "watering places" (that is, hot and cold springs). Indeed, there were several popular health resorts in the region—from Aiken, South Carolina, to Hot Springs, Arkansas. Many be-lieved disease could be prevented or cured at these places. Natural springs remained popular through the 1880s, but by the end of the century there was a movement toward visiting "natural wonders, historic places, and the numerous cultural attractions of cities."[8] Improved and additional rail lines, as well as the advent of steamships, meant increased travel to the re-gion. The South was a cultural commodity, and travel literature helped to sell it as such.[9]

Northern tourists came to the South in part because they were, as historian Tom Selwyn argues, "chasing myths" about the American past. Tourist destinations tend to have their own "spirit of place," and local peo-ple, especially in rural settings, serve as representatives of this "imagined world," which is both premodern and preindustrial. For northern travelers of the late nineteenth and early twentieth centuries, the South was that imagined world. In Dixie, they went in search of pastoral America and convinced themselves that when they traveled south they had exchanged the modern for the authentic.[10]

Throughout the late nineteenth century and well into the twentieth, journalists and travel writers published their views of the region in widely read magazines like *Century*, *Scribner's Monthly*, and *Harper's Weekly*, and northern firms published books giving the American traveling public firsthand accounts of the region and its people. This literature helped de-fine the region and encouraged northern tourism to the South. And for southern entrepreneurs who sought to capitalize on the tourist market, northern travel literature helped them determine and develop the types of attractions that northern tourists hoped to see when they ventured below the Mason-Dixon Line.

In some ways, all types of literature about the South between the Civil War and World War II can be regarded as travel literature. Joel Chandler Harris's stories of Uncle Remus not only offered readers descriptions of the Old South and what was commonly referred to as the "old-time southern negro" but also enticed travelers from the North and Midwest to visit the South in the hope of seeing a southern plantation and people like Uncle Remus. Margaret Mitchell's complaints about visitors and tourists coming to her door in Atlanta also offer evidence that *Gone with the Wind*, published fifty-six years later, was more than a successful novel. It was a powerful piece of travel literature, which drew thousands of people to her hometown and to the state of Georgia.

Northern tourism to Dixie was certainly not a new phenomenon in the late nineteenth century; thousands of northerners traveled south prior to the Civil War. Historian Eric Plaag has argued in his research on northern travelers to the South in the antebellum period that the northern press was responsible for the creation of the national narrative about the region in the period leading up to the war—a narrative that attracted wealthy tourists to Dixie. That trend continued in the war's aftermath. The southern press did not wield such influence nationally, and though the Lost Cause narrative took hold in the former Confederacy soon after defeat, it did not have the same traction in the North. Thus, the *national* narrative of the South in American culture continued to be defined by nonsoutherners, specifically by the northern press.[11]

Nineteenth-century tourists, most of whom were well-to-do and had the leisure to spend anywhere from a few days to a few months traveling, had to look no further than popular magazines to learn more about the South. Articles describing life in the region after the Civil War appeared with frequency in northern magazines. In 1874, for example, *Scribner's Monthly* offered its readers an entire series on the former Confederacy. Journalist Edward King and artist J. Wells Champney wrote and illustrated the articles, all of which were eventually published as *The Great South* (1874). The record of their journey is almost 800 pages and covers the expanse of the former Confederacy from Texas and Louisiana in the west to Florida and Maryland along the East Coast. King's travels took him to rice plantations in South Carolina and cotton plantations in Mississippi and from the French Quarter of New Orleans to the summit of North Carolina's Mount Mitchell. Along the way, he spoke with various southerners, whom he placed in different categories of the "southern type"—for example, the planter, the Negro, and the poor white. Champney provided illustrations of each. King also observed what he regarded as the failure of Reconstruction in Georgia and of "negroes in absolute power" in South Carolina.[12]

Throughout, King's observations provide a relatively impartial examination of the South, though he is not immune to stereotypical references. For example, he offers a poignant and sympathetic description of black field hands on a Louisiana plantation, who, because they were illiterate, had no choice but to go to the plantation owner with hat in hand to request that he read the letters they received. Later, King links the adjective "lazy" to "negro" in describing some black workers and writes with some surprise about an "intelligent-looking" black woman. Yet *The Great South* in its entirety offered a realistic portrait of the region in the years prior to sectional reconciliation.[13]

Philadelphia publisher J. B. Lippincott followed, in 1876, with the book *Florida: Its Scenery, Climate and History*, a volume that provided descriptions of Charleston and Aiken, South Carolina, as well as Augusta and Savannah, Georgia. Sidney Lanier, best known for his poetry and literary criticism, was the author. Although he was a Georgia native, Lanier's descriptions of the South helped define what northerners could expect from the region. Like most nineteenth-century tourist accounts, the book focused on the landscape, health benefits of the region, flora and fauna, commerce and agriculture, and escape from northern winters. In Aiken, for example, "a considerable number of persons from the North [found] the climate so grateful" that they bought land and built homes, only to have to think about "those unhappy persons whom one has left in the Northern winter." Charleston offered its visitors "genial old-time dignity," and Savannah was awash in its "lavish adornment of grasses, flowers and magnificent trees" hung with Spanish moss. In a section on resort towns, Lanier emphasized the health benefits of the South in towns where even those tourists who were not sick sought "to flee from the rigors of the northern climate."[14]

Books about the South did not simply make for good reading. They were also useful to northern travelers headed to Dixie. In fact, one of the preconditions for significant tourism to occur, according to historian Patricia Mooney-Melvin, is that enough information exists "to excite the imagination and encourage people to leave home for sites unknown." Another is that there be a sufficient number of people with the disposable income and the leisure time needed to travel.[15] In the immediate post–Civil War era, mostly only wealthy northern industrialists could afford to travel. But, as the century wore on, tourism in the United States became more affordable and a mass phenomenon. This trend continued in the twentieth century with the mass production of automobiles, beginning in 1908 with Henry Ford's Model T, which forever changed tourism and who could tour. Thus, books about the South—whether fiction or travel literature—served an important function in promoting tourism to the former Confederacy.

Florida was considered the most exotic of southern landscapes and often the destination of many northern tourists, especially the wealthy, who early on wintered at the lavish hotels of St. Augustine, later abandoning them, in the early twentieth century, for the newly created resort of Miami. "We are soon en route for Florida," one northern tourist exclaimed, "which is the kind of Mecca of our hearts' desires. Florida! The very name is suggestive of sunshine and flowers, orange groves, and the sweet-scented air of 'Araby the blest.'"[16] Still, there were many destinations for northern tourists to explore along the way to Florida, and their descriptions offer insight into how they defined the South for the American traveling public.

In the years following Reconstruction, both northern and European travel writers explored the South, largely in an effort to describe how the region was recovering from four years of civil war. Richmond received considerable attention by travel writers in the 1880s. Virginia was the first state northern tourists saw of the South, and Richmond seemed to be particularly southern, as the former capital of the Confederacy. The city was a place of economic revival but one that was still battle worn. *Scribner's Monthly* described Richmond's rebound from the war as seen through its tobacco and iron industries, and Matthew Arnold described the "rather ragged streets of Richmond . . . which suffered terribly in the war."[17]

More often, however, travel writers were struck by the differences between North and South. C. B. Berry, writing for New York publisher E. P. Dutton, described the South as "more homelike than farther north, if less luxurious." For Berry, the hotels seemed quainter than those in the North, as they had fireplaces instead of steam pipes to heat the rooms. Lady Duffus Hardy, who toured the South in 1883, was more enamored with the southern people—white and black. Her observations, although insightful about white southerners, were racist when depicting African Americans. "It is at Richmond we get our first view of the South and the Southern people. Although we are only twelve hours from the booming, bustling city of New York . . . we feel we have entered a strange land," Hardy wrote of Virginia. In this strange land, she swiftly sensed the spirit of the Lost Cause, noting that "it impregnates the very air we breathe." In essence, Richmond's whites lived as though "it is ever yesterday." Richmond's blacks, like other southern blacks described by travel writers, come across as exotic and pathetic creatures in Hardy's account. The group of black men she saw whittling sticks while sitting on a fence were to her a "gathering of black crows," and she likened them to "lazy cattle basking in the sunshine in supreme idleness." As offensive as these comments are to the modern reader, it was these types of observations that furthered the idea of an exotic South and attracted tourists to the region.[18]

Lady Hardy's fellow Englishman, Matthew Arnold, toured the United States two years later, and he, too, visited Richmond. In his letters to his sister back in England, Arnold's observations were reminiscent of Hardy's. He remarked on the vivid reminders of suffering caused by the Civil War and made a point to visit Hollywood Cemetery. Like Hardy, he wrote with curiosity about seeing "coloured children" and referred to them as "dem little things." Before leaving Richmond, he remarked wistfully, "If I ever come back to America, it will be to see more of the South."[19]

New York native and Anglophile Henry James saw little that was different in "melancholy Richmond" when he visited the city in 1907 and described it as "simply blank and void." He was pointed in his criticism of the institution of slavery, calling it the "absurdity [that] had once flourished there." The "old Southerners" of the Confederate generation were nothing more than "pathetic victims of fate." Yet James's criticisms of the city no doubt contributed to the romantic image of the Confederacy, a tragic romance to be sure. On his tour of Richmond, James visited what had quickly become an important tourist destination in the city—the Confederate Museum, founded in 1896 by the women of the Confederate Memorial and Literary Society. In describing his tour of the museum, he referred to it as an exhibit of "sorry objects" that told of a "heritage of woe and glory" and yet found that the old woman who greeted him at the museum embodied a certain southern charm. Clearly taken by her southern accent and fine manners, James wrote, "No little old lady of the North could, for the high tone and the right manner, have touched her." His descriptions, even his critiques, likely aroused northerners' curiosity and contributed to the increasing number of tourists that traveled to Virginia and the rest of the South.[20]

Southern writers, too, helped to shape an image of the South for popular consumption. Thomas Nelson Page and Thomas Dixon, for example, wrote novels that revived a mythological South. Dixon was successful, in fact, in helping the nation reconstruct its views about race and the region's "Negro problem." Page's books were also profitable releases. *In Ole Virginia* (1887) and *Social Life in Old Virginia* (1897), both published and marketed by New York's Charles Scribner's Sons, offered readers an idyllic image of the plantation South. Dixon, a popular evangelist in Boston and New York well before Doubleday Press published *The Leopard's Spots* (1902), was already considered by northerners and the northern press to be an expert on all things southern prior to the release of his Reconstruction trilogy, which assured its success in the marketplace. Even though Dixon's work was intended to highlight the perceived threat of black men, which northern and southern whites shared, what his writing made clear was that the South had control of its "Negro problem" and thus was a safe place for the northern tourist to observe the black man in his exotic and "natural" environment.[21]

Savannah was a frequent stop for tourists on their way to Florida. As early as 1874, Sidney Lanier noted that the city was "much frequented by Northern and Western people during the winter and spring."[22] Bonaventure Cemetery was already a tourist attraction, as was Forsyth Park. In 1878, Philadelphia publisher J. B. Lippincott produced *Georgia: A Guide to Its Cities, Towns, Scenery, and Resources*, which claimed that Savannah was "well calculated to charm the stranger" and that it had become a favorite destination for northern tourists because it offered them the chance to "retreat from the din and confusion of larger and more bustling cities."[23] Indeed, escaping the modern city for one that was less congested was one of the appeals for tourists traveling south.

Lady Duffus Hardy, who was struck by the way in which Richmond lived and breathed its Confederate past, liked Savannah well enough but found "little architectural beauty in the city or its surroundings." And although she complained that Forsyth Park was so diminutive that it would fit into a small corner of Kensington Gardens, it was balanced by the "warm southern breeze, and the oleander, orange, lemon, and magnolia."[24] The Reverend Timothy Harley, who toured Savannah a few years later, in 1886, sought to describe the city's residents, whom he found to be representative of the heterogeneous nature of the United States. Harley noted that northerners had adopted the city as home for purposes of trade and observed that "the Hebrews are a numerous and wealthy class

Postcard of the Hotel DeSoto, 1911. The hotel was a favorite of northern tourists, described by one as "the 5th Avenue hotel of the South." (Author's collection)

of residents." He did not observe African Americans as exotic creatures; rather, he offered insight on the city's race relations, commenting that "the coloured people are not treated there [Savannah] as equals." Significantly, he noted that neither were they treated as such in the North.[25]

Tourists traveling from the North and Midwest found Savannah particularly southern—for its landscape and for its tourist attractions. Northern travelers admired the city's Spanish moss and regarded it as "the mainstay of the Southern landscape."[26] Even more interesting to northern travelers was the opportunity to visit and see in person a true southern plantation—the Hermitage—and its former slave quarters. John Martin Hammond, a travel writer from Germantown, Pennsylvania, referred to the Hermitage as a place that survived as an example of life "befo' da wa.'" The slave quarters had a "picturesque quality," although they appeared to him to be "more like habitations for pigs than for human beings of any color or condition of servitude."[27]

The Hotel DeSoto, which catered to northern tourists, billed itself and Savannah as a "natural resting place" for the traveler headed to the "extreme South" (that is, Florida). For the 1896–97 tourist season, the DeSoto published a brochure designed for the northern tourist, which emphasized the city's "enticing scenery and balmy climate." The brochure also included photographs of the slave quarters of the Hermitage plantation, as well as of a "negro cabin on Bonaventure Drive." The cabin was a dilapi-dated wooden structure chinked with mud, and a black woman and her children were pictured sitting at the front door. Including photographs of such a cabin or the slave quarters of a plantation in a brochure to attract northern travelers indicates that the proprietors knew that this particular group of tourists had expressed an interest in seeing images of the "Old South."[28]

Southern literature and travel accounts changed markedly in the sec-ond half of the nineteenth century, especially after the publication of Joel Chandler Harris's Uncle Remus stories. Certainly, Harris did not invent the style of writing in black dialect—it had long been a part of Ameri-can literature. However, Harris's influence was pervasive and long lasting. He was respected by contemporary folklorists and inspired other writers to incorporate dialect, among them Mark Twain, but also lesser-known writers, who employed black dialect with much less success. Moreover, although ethnic dialects were often used as a device to portray other non–Anglo-Saxon people, especially German and Irish, the use of black dialect in portraying African Americans was the most common use of a non–Anglo-Saxon dialect.[29]

Harris's folktales were a phenomenal success, attracting an interna-tional audience. The stories were highly regarded by folklorists for their dialect, and they appealed to adults and children alike. Moreover, one cannot underestimate the impact of Harris's stories on the South's tourist industry. There is no doubt that readers in the North and Midwest—the two regions that produced the greatest number of tourists for the South in the late nineteenth and early twentieth centuries—were fans of the sto-ries. In 1917, a travel writer who defined herself as a "true provincial New Yorker" described her impending trip to the South as going to "a place of sun, chivalry, romance and Uncle Remus."[30] What was it about these folktales that entertained readers and then motivated them to visit the region?[31]

Joel Chandler Harris re-created scenes from an antebellum southern plantation, and, although the stories were set in the post-Reconstruction South, his purpose was to open for readers a window onto the world of the "old-time negro" who had lived under slavery. Harris originally wrote the tales for publication in the *Atlanta Constitution*, and they were eventu-ally published by New York's D. Appleton & Company. As Harris wrote in his introduction to *Uncle Remus: His Songs and His Sayings* (1880), "I have endeavored to give to the whole a genuine flavor of the old plantation."

UNCLE REMUS

HIS SONGS AND HIS SAYINGS

THE FOLK-LORE OF THE OLD PLANTATION

By JOEL CHANDLER HARRIS

*WITH ILLUSTRATIONS BY FREDERICK S. CHURCH AND
JAMES H. MOSER*

NEW YORK
D. APPLETON AND COMPANY
1, 3, AND 5 BOND STREET
1881

Title page from Joel Chandler Harris's *Uncle Remus: His Songs and His Sayings*, 1881.
(Courtesy Special Collections, J. Murrey Atkins Library, University of North
Carolina at Charlotte)

He also intended his stories to serve as a counterpoint to Harriet Beecher Stowe's *Uncle Tom's Cabin*. Stowe, in his estimation, "attacked the possibilities of slavery," but Uncle Remus portrayed former slaves who had lived under the system and who, according to Harris, had "nothing but pleasant memories of the discipline of slavery."[32]

Harris's use of dialect gave the stories a perceived authenticity, and, in the wake of *Uncle Remus*'s success, the use of dialect appeared with even greater frequency in articles, essays, novels, and travel accounts in which the South was the setting. That success had as much to do with the political and social landscape as it did with Harris's talent for writing. Following the war, African Americans became players on the national stage of politics, challenging the Anglo-Saxon status quo. Immigration from southern and eastern Europe steadily increased throughout the nineteenth century and contributed to the size and diversity of America's cities. Thus, Harris's stories, like those of Thomas Nelson Page and others, offered readers a retreat from the anxiety of all that change by focusing on a time and place—the plantation South—where life was simpler and the "race question" was not a question at all.

Against this backdrop, scientists pursued Darwin's theory of "survival of the fittest," and white men, North and South, became brothers in the cult of white supremacy that emerged in the late nineteenth century. This Anglo-Saxon brotherhood was buoyed, in part, by sectional reconciliation—a reconciliation that celebrated white manhood while ignoring the most significant outcome of the Civil War—emancipation. In the South, moreover, the social and political backdrop to the bucolic imagery of plantation literature was an increasingly violent racism. Lynching escalated dramatically in the 1890s and was soon accompanied by race riots. Yet, through the culture of reconciliation, in which Confederate veterans were redefined as patriots, northerners turned a blind eye to that violence and left white southerners to their own devices to deal with "the Negro." Veterans' reunions were organized, and wealthy northerners spent their money touring the South to see the plantations described by Page and Harris and to meet any number of southern "types," but most especially the happy-go-lucky blacks of literature.[33]

Southern authors undeniably contributed to this bucolic image of the South, which northerners bought into, but they were not alone. Northern travel writers complemented those works by describing the southern landscape and its people in a way that perpetuated stereotypes. Significantly, the northern publishing industry was most responsible for carrying out the construction of southern identity for American audiences. D. Appleton, of New York, sold and marketed the tales of Uncle Remus; and Charles Scribner's Sons sold and marketed the stories of Thomas Nelson Page, including *The Negro: The Southerners' Problem*. Without the support of the northern publishing industry, the circulation of these stories would have been severely limited.

What did the travel literature to the South say about the region? What was it that northerners and midwesterners hoped to see and experience while below the Mason-Dixon Line? In part, what attracted northerners were the differences between the two regions—urban versus rural, industrial versus agricultural, modern versus antimodern. During the late nineteenth century and well into the twentieth, the reasons for traveling south were clear. Cold northern temperatures were certainly a motivation. Rapid industrialization and urbanization, as well as immigration from southern and eastern Europe, produced feelings of anxiety among residents in northern cities and motivated people to travel to the South, where they might experience a preindustrial America. It was the same reason tourists traveled to the West. But the rural South, with its ties to the agricultural past, its slower pace of life, and its pliant servant class, was more easily reached from the East. The South offered northern tourists the antithesis of modernity, and the region served as the embodiment of the nation's rural ideals well into the twentieth century.[34]

The South remained largely agricultural in the early twentieth century, except for some cities like Richmond and Atlanta, and visitors remarked on those differences in their travel accounts. "Everything is done with leisurely dignity and quietude in the South; there is no bustle or confusion, no general rush, even at the [train] depots," noted Lady Duffus Hardy in 1883. Near the end of the century, Julian Ralph, a native New Yorker and longtime journalist for the *New York Sun*, offered a similar description in his book *Dixie; or Southern Scenes and Sketches*. Speaking of the South, Ralph wrote, "I could cast my lines off from the general world of today and float back into a past era, there to loaf away a week of utter rest." He contrasted the urban-industrial North and Dixie by explaining that in the South he could while away the hours, "undisturbed by telegraph or telephone, a hotel elevator or clanging cable car, surrounded by comfort . . . and at liberty to forget the rush and bustle of that raging monster which the French call the *fin de siècle*."[35] New Yorker Mildred Cram, who in 1939 achieved fame for her screenplay *Love Affair*, later remade as *An Affair to Remember* (1957), noted these differences in her trip to seaport towns in 1917.

"Charleston is perhaps the only city in America that has slammed its front door in Progress's face and resisted the modern with fiery determination," she wrote.[36]

Much of what made travelers to the South feel at ease was its rural landscapes, although it was not without its critics. Henry James caustically remarked that in the South "illiteracy seemed to hover in the air like a queer smell."[37] Most writers were much more generous than Henry James, and they tended to see a South he clearly was not looking for. John Henry Hammond traveled to and wrote about the South that intrigued many northern travelers, in *Winter Journeys in the South* (1916). "The 'Old South' has been clearly defined by sentimental historians and in works of popular fiction," Hammond wrote. "According to this definition," he continued, "the 'Old South' is a place of perpetual sunshine, large blooming, fresh-hued flowers, a balmy atmosphere, gardens, quaint walks hedges, big white houses embowered, and leisurely men."[38] Although Hammond appeared to acknowledge that the South was an imagined place, he still claimed to have found, in Camden, South Carolina, "more of the atmosphere of the 'Old South' than in any other place in the Southern States."[39]

The South was often described as "romantic," and what made it romantic was its landscape and, very often, the region's history. During the nineteenth century, Americans were motivated to tour by their need to define America as a place, and, although tourists were attracted to a picturesque countryside, historic sites ranked high on their list of places to visit. Moreover, northern tourists sought to experience a way of life that was no longer contemporary. This proved to be especially true in the South, where, as historian Rebecca McIntyre has argued, the "old world landscape [of] crumbling plantations . . . turned southern losses into tourist attractions."[40]

Since the early nineteenth century, plantation literature had drawn on descriptions of the region as a place where visitors could expect "romance, hospitality, and beauty."[41] This romantic image of the South in literature remained constant well into the twentieth century, as northern tourists sought to come face-to-face with antebellum mansions, where they might imagine chivalrous planters, beautiful belles, and faithful Negroes.[42] New Yorker Mildred Cram's descriptions of the Hermitage, a Savannah plantation frequented by northern tourists, provide evidence of how fiction about the South influenced her thinking. "The Hermitage seemed to us the realisation of a literary dream," she mused. "[It] satisfied our longings, stirred up memories of dreams we had ever dreamed of the South, [and] filled us with satisfactions," she continued, "as if the chimera we had been pursuing all the way from New York were captured at last. . . . It was all that a plantation should be."[43]

A black driver, whom Cram referred to as her "chocolate chauffeur," took her to see the Hermitage. What she did not seem to recognize was that the driver, as well as a former slave she met while at the Hermitage, understood their role in the tourist trade that came through Savannah and played it up for economic benefit. The driver, who was paid, took Cram to the old plantation, where he stopped and called out for a woman named Molly. "Who is she?" Cram asked. As he lit a cigarette, the driver responded, "She was a slave," and then turned to Molly and said, "Molly, tell us about the ole times—befo' the wah." At first, Molly feigned illness, but then the driver said she always gave that response. Then he told Cram, "Give her a qua'tah and *she'll* find her tongue." Later, a group of young children came running over and shouted that they would dance for ten cents. Thus, the driver, the former slave with her stories of life on the plantation before the Civil War, and the children willing to dance for white people all provide evidence that African Americans, too, were keenly aware of being part of the South's exotic tourist trade and used it to support themselves.[44]

Significantly, the driver wanted Mildred and her husband to also see the progress of his race and took them to see the homes and community that African Americans had created since the end of slavery. As she described it, "He wanted us to see what freedom and ambition had done for him and others like him." Frame houses, women in white shoes, and children in sailor suits were a source of pride. The Crams were initially disappointed with this part of the tour, since it was the "martyrdom of his race" that had struck their imagination. "We had been demanding an eternal raggedness and poverty and picturesque ignorance for our own purely aesthetic enjoyment," she admitted. And, indeed, she was not alone, as other northern travelers were in search of a similar experience.[45]

In addition to the romance of the South, northern travel writers seemed fascinated by southern blacks, and northern tourists expected them to be part of their southern tour. To that end, publishers like J. B. Lippincott offered readers what had long been a staple of literature about the South—descriptions of the "southern Negro." From the "darkies" in South Carolina to the Florida Negro who had a "primitive" ear for music, southern blacks increasingly became stock characters in the travel literature of the South because they appeared markedly different from African Americans living in the North; southern blacks behaved more like the ser-

"Cotton Picking in the South," postcard, 1930s. Northern travelers frequently commented on their desire to see blacks working in the cotton fields. (Author's collection)

vant class that northerners expected them to be. Indeed, they were often described in terms of their labor and work habits, with the accompanying statement that the South "knows the Negro" and how best to supervise him.[46]

Post–Civil War travelers of the nineteenth century wrote about seeing blacks on southern plantations, and this trend continued into the twentieth century, even though southern blacks were now generations removed from the plantation. New Yorker Mildred Cram, who had expectations of being in the land of "Uncle Remus," went so far as to proffer observations of southern blacks on a state-by-state basis as she visited the seaports of the South. "It seemed to us that the negroes were shabbiest in Baltimore and Charleston, that they were most likeable in Norfolk, that they were most offensive in Savannah and most picturesque in New Orleans and St. Augustine," Cram wrote. "The upstart type [in the North] has crept further and further into the South to the great disadvantage of the self-respecting, infinitely better class that has not forgotten how to say 'Yessah' and 'Yes'm.'" As if she were an authority on southern race relations, Cram further remarked that she "[knew] that the jaunty, overdressed, impudent and self-assertive negro cannot possibly be the result of paternal [that is, white] authority."[47]

In a 1921 article for *Century* magazine, entitled "Quaint Old Richmond," Mary Newton Stanard described the city as one in which the Old South could still be seen in the New. What she found "quaint" were members of Richmond's black community. She found the "negro janitor" of Virginia's Medical College to be "one of the most picturesque characters in Richmond." She told readers that should the tourist "hear the singing of the negro 'stemmers' [from the tobacco factories], men and women, boys and girls, he might well wonder if he is not approaching a plantation instead of a factory." Black women street vendors appeared equally exotic to Stanard, who described their "ebon skins and snow-white sparkling teeth," as well as how they would "croon old melodies as they shell black-eyed peas or make up nosegays that charm coin from the most canny of purses." The cover illustration for this article included a slave cabin superimposed on the front lawn of the Confederate Women's Home.[48]

Even children's literature about travel to the South included romantic descriptions of the region as well as caricatures of southern blacks. An excellent example comes from the series *Bunny Brown and His Sister Sue*. The Stratemeyer Syndicate, formed by New Jersey native Edward Stratemeyer, published the series. The syndicate was also responsible for such famous series as the *Bobbsey Twins*, *Nancy Drew*, and the *Hardy Boys*. In 1921, the syndicate published *Bunny Brown and His Sister Sue in the Sunny South* by Laura Lee Hope—a pseudonym for any number of authors who wrote for the Stratemeyers, including Stratemeyer himself.[49] The premise of the story is that Bunny Brown's father has business to do in Florida and takes the entire family on his trip to the South; as they travel, the characters comment on the landscape and the southerners they meet.

Throughout the story, Mrs. Brown communicates her desire—and the desire of many northern tourists to the South—to see a cotton plantation and blacks working in the fields. Even before the trip commences, she asks her husband if she will be able to see cotton growing, adding, "I have always wanted to see a cotton field with the darkies singing and picking the white, fluffy stuff."[50] The Brown family does visit a cotton plantation in Georgia, and there Bunny Brown and his sister Sue meet the children of the plantation owner. They go out into the fields, where "they could hear darkies singing." Upon hearing them sing, Bunny exclaims, "It's jolly!" The planter's son Sam concurs: "Yes, the darkies always seem to be happy."[51]

Later, they witness black men, women, and children dancing to the music of a banjo, perpetuating the myth of a happy-go-lucky race. The use of black dialect is employed to establish southern blacks as exotic and

Cover for Laura Lee Hope's *Bunny Brown and His Sister Sue in the Sunny South*, 1921.
(Author's collection)

simple. "Golly dat suah mek me want to shuffle mah feet!" proclaims one black character, while the other chimes in: "Why doan you shuffle 'em den, Rastus? . . . Show de white folks how you kin cut de pigeon wing!"[52] Here the author uses the name Rastus, commonly used as a name for black servants. Moreover, southern blacks who speak in dialect and dance for "white folks" serve as entertainment—not only through literature, but through children's literature at that. Indeed, the thousands of northern tourists who ventured south traveled in the hope that they, too, might see blacks working, singing, and dancing for their benefit.[53]

Many authors writing about the South sought to emulate Joel Chandler Harris and attempted to write dialect for southern black characters— generally not to good effect. Travel writers and journalists used dialect, as did novelists, for local color. To black intellectuals, the use of dialect had a detrimental impact on the African American community. Sterling Brown, longtime professor at Howard University, said as much in an article entitled "Negro Character as Seen by White Authors." Brown listed seven different stereotypes in literature perpetuated by white authors—many of which were southern, but certainly not all. "Authors are too anxious to have it said 'Here is *the* Negro,' rather than here are a few Negroes whom I have seen," he argued. Of the several stereotypes he identified, the two most frequently used in travel accounts and popular literature were the Contented Slave and the Local Color Negro. The contented slave was the stereotype that appeared in the sentimental literature of Thomas Nelson Page. Like Harris, Page was a local colorist because he employed dialect. Even writers who were not southern, as in the case of Edward Stratemeyer, used dialect as local color, which Brown argued "stresses the quaint, the odd, the picturesque, the different."[54]

Earl Conrad, a white author who wrote reams of material on race relations in the United States and who was a critic of Jim Crow, concurred with Brown in his assessment of the use of dialect. Conrad, as had Brown before him, even referred to southern writers of dialect as "neo-Confederates." Not only did they use dialect to infer inferiority, Conrad argued, but "the neo-Confederate writer Jim Crows the Negro in his writing" and tries to maintain the status quo through speech. He accused Margaret Mitchell of being one of the worst offenders, because she employed black dialect but never used any nuances of language to illustrate a white southern drawl. Conrad found that northern writers were no better in their use of dialect. They, too, used words like "nigger" and "pickaninny" to describe southern blacks, "in the name of realism." The result, according to Conrad, was that

Negro dialect gave to blacks the "onus of inferiority."[55] Such valid criticism did not deter northern magazines or publishers from publishing books whose descriptions of the South were distinguished by their use of Negro dialect well into the 1930s.

By the mid-1920s, the genre of travel literature based on automobile travel by the upper classes had gone out of fashion. Middle-class Americans could afford their own cars and preferred to experience "motoring" for themselves. Rather than read travel accounts, the American reading public's interest in the South was piqued by the work of novelists. The antebellum South continued to serve as a popular setting for both fiction and plays, which helped to perpetuate the "moonlight-and-magnolias" image of the region. Although not travel literature, per se, these books were important to perpetuating the fantasies that northern travelers had about the South and continued to draw them to the region. Indeed, as Stephanie Yuhl has shown, southern writers, like those in Charleston, South Carolina, "cultivated relationships with New York publishers," which in turn were useful in promoting tourism to the region, even if this was not the authors' intent.[56]

DuBose Heyward's *Porgy* (1924) and Stark Young's *So Red the Rose* (1934) were not simply successful novels—they were also instrumental in drawing tourists to Charleston, South Carolina, and to Natchez, Mississippi, respectively. Heyward's story of southern blacks on Catfish Row, although considered racially progressive for its time, still appealed to nonsoutherners' fascination with the exotic South. Similarly, Young's portrayal of the Civil War South through the lens of the Portobello plantation was a publishing success, before *Gone with the Wind* eclipsed it in sales and popularity. Nonetheless, Young's novel was made into a film and no doubt contributed to the success of the Natchez Pilgrimage, which, during the 1930s, attracted thousands of tourists to Mississippi to see its antebellum mansions.[57]

The Southern Literary Renaissance that emerged in the 1920s and 1930s certainly offered a new and even critical perspective on the region by native southerners, and their poetry and fiction represented a departure from the romance of the Lost Cause.[58] Enter Margaret Mitchell, whose historical and romantic epic about the Old South and the Civil War refocused the nation's attention on the "moonlight-and-magnolias" South. Significantly, *Gone with the Wind* was sought out by the most successful New York publishing firm of its day—Macmillan. Lois Cole, an associate editor for Macmillan in its Atlanta office, was aware that Mitchell had long been at work on a novel about the Civil War. Yet it was Harold Latham, Macmillan's editor in chief, who convinced Mitchell to submit her manuscript. It is an oft-told story that Latham came to Atlanta in 1935 in search of southern authors and met Mitchell, who at their first meeting claimed she did not have a manuscript. Yet Latham's persistence paid off, when Mitchell showed up at his hotel before he left town and gave him the manuscript of what would become *Gone with the Wind*. According to Latham, the "pile of sheets reached to her shoulders," and he had to buy an extra suitcase to carry it back to New York.[59]

Margaret Mitchell was grateful to Harold Latham not only for her personal success but for pursuing the work of other southern authors. Writing in 1938, she told Latham, "You have done so very much for writing people here in the South." It was not simply that he had published her manuscript, she told Latham. "For so long people in the South believed that a Southern writer did not have a chance without pull," she wrote, adding that "now they know differently and it's due to you."[60] These sentiments were confirmed in Mitchell's correspondence with Thomas Palmer, president of the New York Southern Society—a group of southerners living in New York City. "As you know," she wrote Palmer, "the South is not always fortunate in her visitors from other places. Many strangers come to our section with remarkable misconceptions about the South and Southerners. . . . When they go away they spread erroneous stories about us." Mitchell's reference to "strangers" and "erroneous stories" was a common complaint among southerners, who felt that since the Civil War northerners had defined the South for the nation's readers—and poorly, at that. Latham, she assured Palmer, was different. He was in "sympathy" with the South, and she was impressed that "the editor of a great publishing house like The Macmillan Company [took] the trouble to come South twice a year hunting for manuscripts by new authors!"[61]

Gone with the Wind, more than any other novel of the early twentieth century, did much to encourage tourists from the North and Midwest to venture south, although the book had its detractors. A reader from Oak Park, Illinois, wrote Macmillan that much of what was to be found between the covers of the book was "coarse, vulgar, revolting and obnoxious to decency and refinement." Another writer from East Pembroke, New York, concurred, saying that "it can only cause disgust and condemnation and a source of shame to both author and publisher." The letter was signed "Yours for cleaner literature."[62] Even John Marsh, Mitchell's husband, warned Macmillan that, because his wife had portrayed the South "with considerable frankness" and with a "heroine [who] is a hellion," he might expect trouble from the United Daughters of the Confederacy. "The UDC ladies are a force to be reckoned with in these parts," Marsh wrote. "If they should take out after Peggy, you wouldn't have to worry about getting publicity, but it might not all be the kind you want."[63]

African American journalists, undeniably, had different issues with Mitchell's novel, especially after it won the Pulitzer Prize for literature. Frank Marshall Davis, in an editorial for the *Kansas City Plaindealer*, was incensed that the Pulitzer committee gave a prize to an author who "went out of her way to support the institution of human slavery [and] praise the Uncle Toms of that period." Elizabeth Lawson, writing for the *Cleveland Gazette*, also condemned giving the award "to a novel which chooses Klansmen for its heroes, which describes its 'Negro' characters as 'drunken black bucks' and 'monkeys out of the jungle' [and] whose climax is the attempted rape of a heroine by a 'black ape.'" As she saw it, Margaret Mitchell had done nothing more than to follow in the "rotten" footsteps of "Dixon's odoriferous novel," *The Leopard's Spots*.[64]

Critics of *Gone with the Wind*, however, were certainly outnumbered by the millions who loved it. The book became a best-selling novel and arguably one of the best pieces of promotional literature the South could have ever imagined. According to a review in the *New Yorker* magazine, the book was a "masterpiece of pure escapism."[65] In fact, northern tourists, most of whom had read the book, traveled in search of the Old South of Mitchell's imagination, in the hope of seeing plantations, southern belles in hoopskirts, contented and loyal blacks, and romantic landscapes. Mitchell had provided readers with a modern tale set in a premodern world. Constance Lindsay Skinner, a critic and writer from Canada, wrote as much to Lois Cole, Macmillan's associate editor: "It is so very *modern*—and yet it is set in the most romantic period of America's past."[66]

Harold Latham once told Margaret Mitchell that she could expect "half the population of North America" to camp at her doorstep, a prospect Mitchell laughed at. She later wrote to Latham to apologize and to ask how long "all this" (the tourists coming to her home) would last. "For months I have been aroused every morning at five by telegrams and special deliverys [sic] and long distance phone calls," she complained, and "there are usually visitors sitting in our living room waiting for us to get through our meals." Mitchell learned that several "Taras" had emerged in Clayton County, Georgia, to satisfy the curiosity of northern tourists. The county served as the setting for her novel, but, as Mitchell was quick to tell anyone, Tara was not a real place. She also discovered that in Atlanta a sightseeing bus was taking out-of-town visitors on a tour that "pointed out the store where Frank Kennedy got his start, the site of Scarlett's Victorian home, Miss Pitty Pat's house, et cetera," even though there were "monthly statements in the newspapers that no such places ever existed except in my mind." Mitchell told her husband that she thought of taking the tour, and, when a site was pointed out as being from the novel, she would take the "megaphone in [her] hand and shout, 'That's a lie!'" He replied that the tourists would probably pay her a salary to do so on a regular basis.[67] In a 1941 interview, Mitchell commented that the tourist invasion of her life in Atlanta had calmed down to the point where "the sightseeing bus now only comes to the corner of the block and children get out and pull up some shrubbery and leaves of one of my neighbors." She added, "I live in an apartment and it isn't my shrubbery."[68]

Nineteenth-century tourists to the South relied on travel literature and fictional accounts to inform them about the region's offerings—from health resorts in the mountain South to trees draped in Spanish moss in the Lowcountry to the factories in the emerging urban South. The elite tourists of the nineteenth century gave way to the middle-class tourists of the twentieth, just as train travel gave way to automobile travel. The increasing numbers of tourists to the South contributed to the expansion of the South's tourist trade. Very few southern states committed resources to tourism in the nineteenth century, but by the twentieth century it was obvious to more than a few entrepreneurs that travelers from the Northeast and the Midwest represented a boon to the southern economy. By the 1920s, southern states were much more likely to invest in tourism and the roads and highways needed for travel. Moreover, southerners recognized what nonsoutherners expected to see of the South and were more than willing to give it to them. It is no surprise that the black driver in Savannah who took Mildred Cram to see the Hermitage plantation recognized that he was part of the South's tourist trade, just as the hucksters in Atlanta sold out of towners tours of the sites found in *Gone with the Wind*. The South and southerners recognized that the region and its people were a cultural commodity—a commodity from which they intended to profit.

CHAPTER 6

Welcome to Dixie

It was a crisp and cool afternoon in October 1881, as the little steamer *Gratitude* made its way up the James River to Richmond, Virginia. On board were 150 men, all from Trenton, New Jersey, who had chartered the boat on behalf of Post 23 of the Grand Army of the Republic (GAR). They slept as best they could on the straw mattresses that lined the deck of the boat, whose sparse accommodations meant that not even the general had a room. It had been sixteen years since the Civil War ended, and the New Jersey veterans were curious about their southern counterparts, which was the reason for their trip. "Who were these men we had fought? How did they feel about the Union? How did they feel toward us?"[1]

As the *Gratitude* sailed closer to the docks, its flags were run up the pole, and, as the city came into clear view, the men from New Jersey saw large crowds of Richmond's black citizens and bunting on the ships in dock, as well as on the homes and factories that lined the river. A group of Confederate veterans were front and center waiting to greet their former foes. The mayor offered members of the GAR the keys to the city, and they responded by shouting, "Richmond is ours!" Yet they swiftly realized that indeed they were the captives in this fraternal gathering. There at the dock, as they listened to the words of welcome offered by Richmond's mayor, tears trickled down their cheeks.[2]

The gathering of the Blue and the Gray in Richmond in 1881 was one of the first of its kind, predating the large reunions that would follow later in the century. It marked an important step on the road to reconciliation between the North and the South following the Civil War and Reconstruction. Such meetings were part of a larger culture of reconciliation, which manifested itself in a variety of ways, not the least of which was through the touring of the South. Indeed, the veterans from New Jersey joined a growing number of northern tourists to visit the South in the post-Reconstruction era. In addition to their tours of Richmond's colonial and Revolutionary War past, they returned to the battlefields where they had once fought, and they dug bullets from the trees as souvenirs of their trip down south. Thousands of northerners followed in the footsteps of those New Jersey veterans to learn firsthand about the American South, a region that remained shrouded in mystery to most nonsoutherners, who felt they knew the South and its people from popular literature and music and, later, from radio shows and motion pictures.[3]

Nineteenth-century travelers were often people who had both the means and the leisure time to travel, which was true of most of the South's visitors. Travel to the South in the nineteenth century was generally made in one of two ways—by steamship or by railroads; roads were nearly impassable, and tours to places like the Natural Bridge were often harrowing stagecoach rides. Leisure travelers preferred places that were more easily reached. Wealthy travelers during the latter part of the century often bypassed most of the region and took steamships directly to Florida. More and more, middle-class tourists were also likely to take trains, which managed to get tourists to the region's health resorts in the mountains, as well as to its increasingly popular beaches. Urban tourism expanded exponentially in the twentieth century, but even during the nineteenth century a distinct tourist trade had begun to develop in southern cities like Richmond, Savannah, and New Orleans.

Tourism has played an important role in the development of the South's cultural identity.[4] It has helped both outsiders and native southerners to define the region. Nineteenth-century writers often linked southern culture to its landscape, especially its plantations, but also to its flora and fauna and other natural features. During the late nineteenth century, Civil War battlefields, the majority of which existed in the southern states, also became tourist attractions and served an important purpose in the culture of reconciliation. As James Sears has argued, "Tourist attractions are the sacred places of a nation or people," and, by that definition, battlefields were especially sacred places because they "provided points of mythic and national unity."[5] In sum, even as tourism contributed to a national identity, it was also important to defining regional culture.[6]

The South's tourist trade during the late nineteenth and early twentieth centuries was made possible by improvements in transportation and the development of a travel industry spawned by the region's entrepreneurs. Certainly, they recognized that tourism represented an opportunity to make money, but they also saw that tourism could boost the regional economy. Owners of steamships, railroads, and local companies that took tourists on local outings via an omnibus or horse and buggy reached out to northern tourists through advertising and brochures. These southern entrepreneurs also recognized that the South itself was a cultural commodity and emphasized those regional features and characteristics that enamored northern writers and magazines. As a number of scholars have pointed out, the South represented the picturesque and the antimodern—and Yankee tourists could enjoy in the South an exotic location and a pastoral America that seemed to be absent in the big cities of the North and Midwest where they lived.[7]

Tourism was a commodity and tourist attractions were consumer products, and both northern and southern businesses got in on the act. Well into the twentieth century, for example, the Virginia Navigation Company offered James River tours between Richmond and Norfolk aboard a steamer, the *Pocahontas*. Significantly, the tour was advertised as a "golden historic link in the chain of communication between the northern and southern sections of the country." In addition, the company considered its tours of Jamestown, Old Point Comfort, and Fort Monroe as more than simply southern tours; they were *American* tours.[8]

Viewing northern tourism in the South as an important link connecting the sections is significant. Indeed, by the late nineteenth century, and certainly through the first few decades of the twentieth, northern tourism to the South was an important component of the cultural reconciliation that took place. Virginia, especially, was able to showcase American patriotism—an important tactic in political reconciliation—without denying its Confederate or antebellum past, including slavery. Moreover, it was this very legacy that fascinated and attracted northern tourists as heritage tourism came into vogue.

Northern companies, too, facilitated travel to the region and encouraged tourism to Dixie. In 1887, Raymond's Vacation Excursions, a Boston-based tour company, offered a tour to Virginia. The first stop was the Gettysburg Battlefield, but then the tour quickly moved on to Chesapeake Bay, Fortress Monroe, Richmond, the Natural Bridge, and the "wonderful caverns of Luray." The Natural Bridge ("among the greatest wonders of our country") and Luray's caverns swiftly became standard tourist destinations in the nineteenth century, yet it was the "rich associations connected with our country's early history and with the late war" that the company emphasized. In fact, the brochure for its fall excursions pointed out that the tour included "scores of battlefields, besides that of Gettysburg," and highlighted Virginia as a state that was "rich in association with our country's early history." The tour also included Richmond, described as one of the "most beautiful and flourishing cities of the South."[9]

Raymond's tour company employed every mode of transportation available to the nineteenth-century traveler in order to get its customers to sites in Virginia. Steamships, trains, and omnibuses took northern tourists throughout the state. In Richmond, horse-drawn carriages transported visitors to see the state capitol and its monuments, the White House of the Confederacy, St. John's Episcopal Church, and Hollywood Cemetery—all of which became standard destinations on tours of Richmond. The company also employed stagecoaches to take tourists to Virginia's interior to see the Natural Bridge.[10]

Farther south, in Georgia, nineteenth-century tourists were likely to stop in Savannah on their way to Florida. Local hotels and the region's railroad companies were eager to benefit from the northern tourist dollar. The Atlantic and Gulf Railroad's 1876–77 guide to Georgia and Florida insisted that "visitors from the North and East should make Savannah their objective point." Advertisements from the guide offer proof that hotel proprietors in Savannah understood their clientele very well. The Screven House publicized that it was the "leading first-class hotel" in the city, as evidenced by the many "first-class" travelers who chose to stay there; moreover, its meals were "supplied with the best the Northern and home markets afford." One of the features of the early southern tourist trade in Savannah and Florida was to provide a sense of "home away from home." Thus, noting that meals were prepared with foods from a "northern market" or that rooms provided "all the comforts of home and the attractions of fashionable society" proved that southern entrepreneurs understood the psychology of the northern tourist.[11]

Savannah was also advertised to northern tourists for its beauty and southern charm and as a reprieve from the hectic pace of city living. "Savannah is like no other city in the Union," J. T. Derry wrote in *Georgia: A Guide to Its Cities, Towns, Scenery, and Resources* (1878). J. B. Lippincott of Philadelphia, which marketed the book to northern tourists, published Derry's guide. "Few cities are more attractive . . . [or so] well calculated to charm the stranger and make him feel 'surely this must be a delightful retreat from the din and confusion of larger and more bustling cities.'"[12] Northern writers of the period often wrote about the desire to escape not only the winters but also the urban-industrial landscape. The fact that southern entrepreneurs sought to fulfill those desires in developing their tourist trade illustrates that they were aware of northern perceptions of the region's identity.

Historical tourism to the South got a boost during the 1907 Jamestown Exposition, which commemorated the tercentennial of the founding of the Virginia colony. The exposition provided the state of Virginia with an enormous opportunity to promote its tourist attractions. Every state in the Union was represented at the exposition with exhibits—Massachusetts built a replica of Faneuil Hall and Pennsylvania provided a replica of Independence Hall, for example. In addition, representatives from approximately 800 different newspapers from across the country were sent to cover the event.[13] Virginia was represented by a number of buildings but also by Confederate monuments, a replica of Fortress Monroe, where Jefferson Davis had been imprisoned, and an exhibit showing blacks picking cotton in a field. This image was presented as an example of southern industry but was intended to represent a "familiar southern scene." An illustration of peanuts being harvested in Virginia showed a black woman holding a bunch of peanuts, with the caption, "Nomadic bands of negroes perform this work." Such images of African Americans working were intentional, since northern tourists often expressed an interest in seeing this "familiar scene."[14]

Richmond also benefited from the crowds that came to celebrate the founding of the first permanent English colony, because it was an important stop for tourists. Guests could stay at the famed Jefferson Hotel or Ford's Hotel and could tour the city's Confederate and Revolutionary War past. The Confederate Museum, which opened in 1896, and Richmond's Confederate monuments, as well as St. John's Episcopal Church, where Patrick Henry proclaimed, "Give me liberty or give me death," were important to the city's historical tourism. Civil War battlefields in the state were also attractions, and there were several Confederate battlefields between Richmond and Jamestown. Confederate memory was such a highly visible part of the Jamestown Exposition that even the parade grounds of the exposition were named for Robert E. Lee.[15]

Confederate heritage was also well represented at the Jamestown Exposition—evidence that early on in its tourist trade Virginia recognized its importance. Not only were the parade grounds named for Lee, but the presence of Beauvoir, a replication of the last home of Jefferson Davis, helped make this point. The *Official Encyclopedic Guide to Richmond and Vicinity*, published for the occasion, focused heavily on Confederate battlefields. "These battlefields are of great interest to the tourist and the lover of history . . . and [are] where both North and South can meet on common ground and mourn their honored dead." In this instance, tourism was intended as both a boost to the local economy and a means to sectional reconciliation.[16] Thus, northern tourists who traveled to the South came to know Virginia not simply as the site of the first permanent English settlement but as a state proud of its Confederate heritage.

Northern tourists were regular visitors to Richmond and the vestiges of its Confederate past, as visitors' registers to the Confederate Memorial Institute, also known as the Battle Abbey, reveal. The Battle Abbey opened to the public in May 1921, and throughout the 1920s it averaged 10,000 visitors per year, not all of whom were from Virginia or the South. The month it opened, there were visitors from Vermont, New York, New Jersey, Pennsylvania, Illinois, Delaware, Missouri, Minnesota, and Massachusetts. Every month, hundreds of northern visitors came to see the art of the Lost Cause, and every year the Battle Abbey experienced an increase in the number of visitors traveling from northern states, evidence that the Confederate past was far from distasteful—it even was worth the price of admission.[17]

Travelers from across the United States who came south in the early twentieth century arrived by train, which was the best way to see the region's interior before the advent of the automobile. In fact, railways remained the primary mode of tourist transportation well into the 1920s, since roads and highways in southern states were in their infancy. The popular railroad line known as the Cotton Belt Route, for example, took travelers from St. Louis into Arkansas and Texas; the Norfolk & Western Railway conveyed tourists from Cincinnati to Norfolk. Rail travel was of vital importance to the tourist trade in the South. In the absence of state-sponsored tourism, railroads and later automobile clubs were vocal proponents of both regional and state tourism. The Norfolk & Western piqued midwesterners' curiosity about the South through its brochures and advertisements. For years, the railway's promotional literature employed the tagline "Virginia, the Land of Romance, Hospitality, and Beauty" to sell tickets and an image of the South that nonsoutherners had come to expect. Such tourism became part of the larger culture of reconciliation between the North and the South, and the Norfolk & Western capitalized on that image, playing up Virginia's history to market train travel. Promotional materials included maps with artistic renderings of historic places and marketed Virginia's colonial and antebellum past. The Norfolk & Western branded the two trains connecting the Midwest with Virginia the *Cavalier* and the *Pocahontas*—a nod to the romantic colonial era.[18]

Northern travelers headed south during the winter were likely to be long-term guests. New York journalist Julian Ralph wrote about his trav-

Brochure for the Norfolk & Western Railway, 1935.
(Courtesy Virginia Historical Society)

els in Dixie and revealed what he called the "secret of the peopling of Florida by Northerners," noting that "Jacksonville might easily have been mistaken for Long Branch [New Jersey] in July." Northern businessmen who had made considerable sums were the ones who could afford such luxury, and they turned Florida into a "pleasure-park" and "loafing place" for three months of the year. Moreover, Ralph observed that most of these men were likely to be accompanied by at least two women—wife, daughter, sister, or niece—prompting him to conclude that the majority of tourists in the hotels of Florida were women.[19] The popularity of the state and the thousands of visitors—and the money they brought to spend—were not lost on businessmen in other southern states along the East Coast. In the absence of state funding to develop a tourist trade, they took it upon themselves to advertise their towns and cities. Yet, as the new century dawned, the region faced more obstacles to creating tourism—specifically, building and improving roads and highways to make sure that the nation's new craze of "motor-touring" included the South.

Even before the mass production of Henry Ford's Model T led thousands of middle-class northerners and midwesterners to venture into Dixie, the state of the South's roads was on the minds of the region's leaders. O. H. Sheffield, an engineering professor at the University of Georgia, addressed this problem in a pamphlet entitled *Improvement of the Road System of Georgia*, in which he concluded that "the present system of road-working is a failure and a disgrace to civilization." Sheffield's proposal dealt with the financial concerns related to road building, which other southern states shared, by recommending the use of convict labor. This, he argued, would solve two problems. It would create a better road system for the state, and it would deter racial violence by keeping convict labor out of the free labor market. That competition with free labor, he noted, had "been the cause of serious trouble, and even of deadly conflict."[20] Most important, however, better roads would bring farmers into closer contact with markets and "increase immeasurably the bodily comfort and celerity of the traveling public."[21] His point is significant because road building in the South was important to the regional economy, whether farmers or tourists were using the roads. Southern states clearly took Sheffield's advice, since road gangs completed the majority of roads built or improved in the South during the 1920s and 1930s.[22]

Railroad travel continued to be essential to southern tourism in the early twentieth century, until state and local governments began to fund the building of roads and highways, which did not begin in earnest until the 1920s. Railroad advertising was important to selling the South and building up the region's fledgling tourist trade. The earliest railroad advertisements listed nothing more than times of service; however, this changed after the Civil War with the advent of additional rail lines and tourism travel. Northern travelers were certainly enticed to visit the "land of romance," as promoted by the Norfolk & Western Railway, but they were also invited to think of their travel in terms of Confederate memory. The Illinois Central Railroad operated a train known as the "Dixie Flyer" along what was known as the "Lookout Mountain Route," between Chicago and Jacksonville, Florida. Traveling through Dixie on a train that carried the same name helped to brand the route. Both midwesterners and southerners used the Cotton Belt Route, operated by the St. Louis Southwestern Railway. In one advertisement, the company offered to take Confederate veterans west to Texas for a reunion by offering them a "free picture of Gen. Lee" along with a copy of his farewell address "suitable for framing." In this instance, none other than Robert E. Lee—the South's most revered hero of the Civil War—was used to sell the rail service.[23]

Regional railroads with links to those coming from the North and the Midwest were equally important to the South's tourist trade. Visitors to Virginia at the turn of the twentieth century, for example, also had access to other railroads, including the Southern, the Chesapeake and Ohio, the Atlantic Coast Line, and the Baltimore and Ohio. These various lines enabled visitors to crisscross the state north to south and east to west. Similarly, in South Carolina and Georgia, visitors traveled via the Atlantic Coast Line and the Seaboard Air Line. Even as southern states worked hard to improve their roads and highways, rail travel continued to provide the quickest and safest means of getting to the region well into the 1920s.

Travel and tourism in the South expanded rapidly in the early twentieth century, but not all of it was due to the expansion of rail lines. Despite poor roads and highways, tourists were eager to take the risk and adventure that came with "motor touring," as it was then called. Wealthy travelers were the first to bring their cars to the South, especially to Florida, and during the early twentieth century they often bypassed former Confederate states in order to experience the more exotic location of Florida— often shipping their cars directly to the coastal city of St. Augustine. However, the invention and mass production of Henry Ford's Model T in 1908 made this mode of travel more affordable for the middle class, enabling the South to capitalize on northerners' fascination with the region's landscape and its history.

Three developments were important to making automobile tourism to the South possible: the improvement of roads and highways, the formation of automobile clubs and highway associations, which was encouraged nationally by the American Automobile Association (AAA), and the publication of road maps. Road and highway construction not only improved state and local economies but was even regarded as a critical step in the figurative "road" to reconciliation. Promoters of national highways saw these thoroughfares as an important step in breaking down the remaining political barriers between the sections. The Atlantic Coastal Highway, which brought travelers from Maine to Florida, and the Dixie Highway, which brought tourists from the Midwest to Florida, connected northerners to southerners in ways never before imagined. Historical geographer James Akerman argues that "the creation of the national highway system in the United States was guided by the hope that it would eliminate the last natural barriers to national integration" following the Civil War.[24]

The formation of the AAA in 1902 was also critical to both highway development and mapping. The AAA encouraged the creation of affiliate clubs throughout the United States, which were instrumental in lobbying local and state governments to build better roads as well as to pass legislation to make driving—and pedestrians—safer by posting speed limits and stop signs. These car clubs were often made up of local businessmen, who owned cars and had an economic interest in the improvement of roads to their states and locales.[25] As of 1909, there were only three state associations of the AAA in the South: the Virginia State Automobile Association based in Richmond, the Motor League of Louisiana headquartered in New Orleans, and, in Little Rock, the Arkansas Automobile Association. City clubs existed in Georgia, Tennessee, Florida, Mississippi, and Alabama, although, surprisingly, none existed in North Carolina, which became the region's leader in building good roads.[26]

The Richmond Automobile Club, a branch of the AAA formed in 1908, like the national organization, lobbied for better roads in the city and the state. The highway built between Richmond and Washington, D.C., another important tourist destination, was made possible by the insistence of the Richmond club, as well as of the Automobile Club of Virginia, which saw its potential to bring tourists from the nation's capital to Virginia's capital. The club's work to build the highway was noted in the AAA's publication *The American Motorist*, which proclaimed: "No more lively campaign in the interests of good roads is being waged anywhere in the country than that of the Richmond Automobile Club." In that same issue, the

New Orleans and Montgomery automobile clubs were applauded for their proposal to get a road built between Atlanta and New Orleans.[27]

Between 1902 and 1913, the AAA sponsored the Glidden Tours, named for financier and auto enthusiast Charles Glidden, in an effort to promote good roads throughout the country. It was not until 1911 that the AAA sponsored a Glidden Tour through the South, which took motorists from New York City to Jacksonville, Florida. The point of the tours was to promote the Good Roads movement and American-made automobiles. It was considered a race, in that the tour was led by a pace car, teams were scored, and participants competed for a prize. Southern states lobbied the AAA for years to host the tour and bring attention to the region and encourage road building. Representatives from the Atlanta Chamber of Commerce and the Jacksonville Board of Trade petitioned the AAA and convinced the organization that the tour would be used to promote the Good Roads movement in the South.[28] One of the differences of the southern tour was that it was intended for the "general tourist," and not simply for automobile makers, as in previous races.[29]

Charles Glidden was always one of the participants, and for the 1911 tour he was joined by several Atlantans, including Mayor C. S. Winn, Governor Hoke Smith, Asa Candler Jr., founder of Coca-Cola, and James Gray, editor of the *Atlanta Constitution*. Governor Smith's entry into the contest was well received—he was the first governor to participate in one of the tours, and his stature brought attention to the Good Roads movement, not just in the South but nationally. Yet Smith was clearly interested in promoting good roads in the South for the benefit of his own state and announced that he would invite the governors of each state the tour passed through to join him in his 1912 Maxwell, a car loaned to him by Benjamin Briscoe, founder of the United States Motor Company of Detroit.[30]

The contest left from AAA headquarters on Broadway in New York City with eighty cars. Atlanta had seven teams in the race, including Governor Smith's. Seventeen members of the "fairer sex" also participated in the event, including women from Georgia.[31] The race got off to a good start, and during the first section of the tour the motorcade went through New Jersey, where Governor Woodrow Wilson briefly joined the Georgia governor in his car.[32] For the first few days, the race went smoothly, and when the Glidden tourists reached Virginia, the *New York Times* proclaimed, prematurely it turned out: "Auto Tourists Find Good Roads in South."[33] At least through Staunton, tourists found the roads in better condition than expected. The participants also experienced—except for Harrisonburg,

Photograph of the Glidden Tour in Georgia, 1911. (Courtesy Georgia Archives, Vanishing Georgia Collection, cob711)

where they were harassed by the local constable—the "cheeriest welcome and proverbial Southern hospitality," which included a welcome wagon of 400 cadets from the Staunton Military Academy.[34] The only other complaint leveled by participants was the "fast driving by some of the sporty young Southerners and wild Westerners on their first Glidden Tour."[35]

But the day they left Staunton, the Glidden tourists bid farewell to good roads in Virginia. As they traveled west, the group encountered bad weather and mud ruts that were two feet deep. The road conditions between the Natural Bridge and Roanoke were some of the worst that the seasoned drivers had ever encountered. Even Charles Glidden, the tour's sponsor, claimed he had never seen such a bad stretch of road. Georgia governor Hoke Smith had to abandon his own car not far from Natural Bridge and ride in another car, which subsequently slid off the road and hit a telegraph pole. Due to bad rainstorms, women who were accompanying their husbands were "compelled to take shelter in a small farmhouse" and wait on a "relief car" to bring them back to join the rest of the touring party.[36]

Participants and newspapers followed the Glidden Tour and reported on road conditions, which were then made public. The trip from Natural Bridge on to Roanoke was so bad that the *New York Times* advised potential tourists to the South to "get an aeroplane at Natural Bridge and stay in the air until the North Carolina line is reached." Not only would the Glidden tourists "never do it again," but the article claimed that "nothing has approached in vileness the condition of the roads in Virginia."[37] This degree of bad press alarmed Virginia state officials, because reports of the tour made national news. In an effort to repair the damage, Preston Belvin, president of the Virginia State Automobile Association, wrote a letter to the *New York Times* to defend the state's roads. Belvin noted that, had the "Gliddenites" consulted with the state association, their "miseries . . . could all have been avoided." Although he admitted that Virginia had some bad roads, he also noted that they were no worse than some he had driven on in New York state.[38] This was true, as previous Glidden Tours had proved. Yet this particular tour was important to Virginia's as well as the region's reputation. The state ultimately benefited from such criticism, as it motivated legislators to invest in the improvement of its roads.

The tour through North Carolina, especially between Winston-Salem and Charlotte, was a joyride by comparison. Drivers on the tour praised the state for its good roads and hospitality. All along the way, town boosters turned out, as did welcoming crowds. In Winston-Salem, the men in the tour received boxes that included in each a pipe, tobacco, and matches. Later, in High Point, the cars passed through the main streets, where waiters, whom the *New York Times* described as "darkies," offered drivers trays loaded down with "sandwiches, coffee, cigars and ice cream." Several towns put up banners welcoming the cars; one town's banner read, "This town has a speed ordinance, and for the Glidden tour the limit is slow," which was meant to give the townspeople an opportunity to see the procession.[39] The "Gliddenites" continued their trek through South Carolina and spent two days in Atlanta, where they were feted by the locals, who held a "real Georgia barbecue" in their honor.[40] The tour continued on, with a brief stop in Savannah, and the drivers finally ended their 1,400-mile tour in Jacksonville, Florida.

The Glidden Tour of 1911 was a success on many fronts. First, southern states, except for Virginia, received very positive news coverage, which was, in effect, good advertising for tourism. Indeed, at the end of the tour, the *New York Times* reported that "the trip from New York to Florida by automobile is one of the most picturesque and interesting journeys in America."[41] Second, the tour reinforced the need for southern states, especially Virginia, to invest in their systems of roads and highways, and not simply for tourism. The tour was important to the southern economy, because it allowed towns and cities to showcase their resources for potential economic investment by northern businesses.

One of the reasons for the Glidden Tour's success in Georgia was that, exactly one year before, in October 1910, the state had held its own race to promote better roads. The event was called the "'Round the State Tour" and was sponsored by the state's newspapers to educate people about the need for good roads. Coca-Cola president Asa Candler, an automobile enthusiast, did a trial run on the 900-mile circuit of the state one month before and proclaimed that there were "no better roads to be found in the South."[42] Many towns throughout Georgia were eager for the tour to come their way. When the race began, on October 17, seventy-five cars were part of the contest, including an entry by Regina Rambo from Marietta, who drove her own automobile accompanied by two other women, including the wife of then-governor Joseph M. Brown. Rambo was well known in Atlanta society and throughout the state for her advocacy for good roads.[43]

The tour began at the *Atlanta Constitution* headquarters, and an estimated crowd of between 4,000 and 5,000 people cheered the participants. Several of the drivers were from Cincinnati, men who had participated in the Ohio Valley Exposition, at which Georgia had had an exhibit. Their involvement with the race, therefore, was regarded by both the Ohioans and the Georgians as an important step toward a mutually beneficial economic relationship. According to the *Atlanta Constitution*, "Cincinnati has long realized that she made a mistake years ago in letting the eastern cities get ahead of her in developing trade with the south."[44]

Throughout the tour, which went through Athens, Augusta, Atlanta, Macon, Albany, Valdosta, and Savannah, towns rolled out the red carpet for all the participants—not just those from Cincinnati. When it ended, the state learned from the drivers the strengths and weaknesses of their road systems, especially about the road from Valdosta to Savannah and the need to bridge the Altamaha River. Regina Rambo finished the course with a perfect score, outperforming many men in the race, and was awarded a loving cup. She was later appointed as a delegate to a regional good roads convention, and while there she cast votes—a unique honor, given that as a woman she was still denied the ballot.[45]

The 'Round the State tour and its boosters were considered important to the Good Roads movement in Georgia, yet state funding for roads was not immediately forthcoming. Agitation for better highways continued to be led by automobile clubs, local businessmen, chambers of commerce, and industrial organizations, like the American Road Builders Association. Also important to highway construction were the highway associations, which emerged in the period immediately before World War I, such as the Lincoln Highway Association and the Dixie Highway Association. The creation of the Dixie Highway, in particular, illustrates how roads were built before the Federal Highway Act of 1916 and especially before southern states appropriated funds for building roads.[46]

William Sydnor Gilbreath, president of the Detroit Automobile Club, introduced the idea of a north-south highway that would run from Michigan to Florida in 1914 at the annual meeting of the American Road Congress. Such a highway, which Gilbreath originally suggested be named the "Cotton Belt Route," was important to bringing both business and tourists to the South. As it happened, the meeting was held in Atlanta, and it probably did not hurt Gilbreath's cause that he, too, was a southerner—originally from Grenada, Mississippi. He was also an important player in mapping and developing the Lincoln Highway, the nation's first transnational highway, which ran from New York to San Francisco. He and Carl Fisher, whom Gilbreath knew from his days with the Hoosier Automobile Club of Indianapolis, conceived of the idea to build a highway that extended from the Midwest to the South, in large part because of Fisher's interest in Florida real estate, especially in Miami Beach, which he is credited with developing in the 1920s. Yet businessmen from southern states were eager to join in because of what the Dixie Highway, as it was finally named, would mean to the region's economy.[47]

Tourists from Chicago and the Midwest who wanted to travel to Florida in the days before the Dixie Highway drove 500 miles east to Washington, D.C., before heading south along Route 1. Gilbreath, who was not only an automobile enthusiast but also an expert in mapping roads, determined the route of the Dixie Highway when he "took a ruler and placed it on the map and drew a line between Chicago and Miami and realized that the line either touched or came close to major cities throughout the central part of the South."[48] He then set out by mule to map the route personally, a trip that took months to complete. His first trip by car was not much better. Automobile traffic was nonexistent, and so were gas stations. He ran into mud and "treacherous stretches of sand" and had "more than one narrow escape trying to stay on the highway." Gilbreath concluded that, if roads were not improved, "tourist travel would be cut to nothing."[49]

Southern businessmen, local governments, and automobile clubs made a firm commitment to the Dixie Highway Association, formed in

1915. Many individuals and car clubs donated money to the cause of the association, and some southern state governors provided moral support by appointing state commissioners to the association. It was strategically headquartered in Chattanooga—considered the halfway point between Chicago and Miami—the highway's final destination. Southerners were not the only ones convinced of the highway's importance to tourism. Ohio governor James Cox went before the commissioners to argue that "the Dixie Highway will live only if it proves a real factor of travel from the North to the South."[50]

When the Dixie Highway Association held its first meeting in Evansville, Illinois, in June 1915, more than 1,200 delegates arrived to lobby to have the highway cross through their cities and states—and this was just for the stretch between Chicago and Nashville. Rival factions from Kentucky and Tennessee carried large banners emblazoned with maps of proposed routes of the highway through their states.[51] Kentucky, in particular, needed a boost to its image among northern travelers, who had labeled it the "Detour State." Michigan's commissioner, moreover, asked that the highway be extended north from Chicago to Mackinaw so that it crossed through his state's resort region.[52]

If railroads were considered important routes of sectional reconciliation between the North and the South after the Civil war, highways and other roads that extended between the regions did even more to eliminate the barriers to reunion. The Dixie Highway was hailed by the *New York Times* as the "Dixie Peaceway," and the paper argued that it should be a "monument to the half century of peace within the Union." Moreover, the paper continued, as a memorial to peace, the Dixie Highway "appeals most strongly to the national imagination." One branch of the highway in Georgia, for example, followed the path along Sherman's March to the Sea, which had "laid a fair country to waste." The creation of the Dixie Highway, however, represented the accomplishments of a "new army," which used "implements of peace . . . to make a reborn country more vigorous and prosperous."[53]

Significantly, the "peaceway" was made possible by the advent of war. Indeed, one of the outcomes of World War I was that the needs of the U.S. Army spurred road building, especially in the South. Secretary of War Newton D. Baker referred to the war as being one of "motor transports," and several pieces of federal legislation made money available to southern states for highway construction.[54] In 1917, for example, Kentucky was on its way to reversing the stigma of being a detour state when it received federal aid to build a seven-mile stretch of highway through the southeastern part of the state, which was considered the last remaining barrier to travel on the Dixie Highway between Ohio and Florida. It served the purpose of assisting the army during wartime, and following the war it proved to be significant to the cause of tourism through the Bluegrass State.[55]

For all intents and purposes, the Dixie Highway was completed in 1925—ten years after it was begun. The *New York Times* enthusiastically endorsed the highway as the literal road to sectional reconciliation, playing up long-held notions of an exotic South. "The Dixie Highway links the frozen North to the tropic South . . . [and] makes this land of magic casements and tropic seas seem more accessible from the bleak North," the paper reported.[56] A motorcade celebrating the highway's tenth anniversary traveled the route from Detroit to Miami in early October of that year. As the cars passed through southern towns large and small, the motorcade was greeted by cheering crowds. In Kentucky, children stood outside their schools and greeted the motorists by waving American flags. In Tennessee, the caravan of cars passed through Chattanooga, home of the Dixie Highway Association, where the travelers were greeted with fireworks and a band that played "Dixie." On their way to Florida, the motorists actively toured the South, stopping in Dayton, Tennessee, for example, to see the courthouse where the Scopes Trial was held. Further down the road, in Georgia, they took a side trip from Atlanta to visit Stone Mountain.[57] The completion of the Dixie Highway in the 1920s and its success in bringing tourist dollars to the southern economy did encourage southern states to invest more in road construction.

Throughout the 1920s and the 1930s, the northern papers regularly reported on the condition of roads nationwide, as the sale of automobiles, as well as the number of automobile tourists, increased exponentially. This was important, as roads that were called "highways" could be in various states of construction, including concrete, macadam (crushed stone mixed with tar), oil-processed, and "improved," which essentially meant graded dirt. In 1922, a report on southern road conditions noted that improvements on the main roads to Florida and other southern resorts had been made "in anticipation of the large number of tourists from the North." The following year, it estimated that the production of American cars would be between 3 and 3.5 million, which it correctly noted would be reflected in the "increased volume of motor touring in all parts of the country."[58]

Given the long drive to Florida, travelers also needed information on accommodations, which became an increasingly important aspect of the southern tourist trade. Tourist camps, from a camping spot to a one-room edifice where travelers could rest, began to crop up along southern highways. "Many Florida cities have provided tourists camping places with piped water, firewood and other conveniences," the *New York Times* reported in 1923. There were other camps along the way, including one in Richmond, where the city "erected a tourists' rest house, with reading rooms, shower baths, laundry and other conveniences." The Richmond camp was free and was described as having "beautiful waterfalls and picturesque wooded dells."[59] Route 50 between Petersburg, Virginia, and Columbia, South Carolina, supposedly had the best hotels and was considered "the most beautiful road through eastern North Carolina."[60] By 1936, the routes south had "become a commercial enterprise . . . [and] the partners are hotels, restaurants, oil and garage companies, ferry operators, amusement concessions, roadside stand and overnight cabin owners, city societies and everyone who has any reason to welcome visitors along the wayside."[61]

New York Times columnist Frank Bohn reported in 1926 that the "movement of northern peoples toward sunnier lands" was a sign "that the new day of the American South is at hand." In his article, entitled "Southward, Man Pushes Again," Bohn asked, "What Northerner does not crave, in Winter time, the privilege of going South?"[62] Significantly, southern blacks had migrated north en masse for better wages just as northern whites were migrating by the thousands to Florida. The intermingling of northerners with southerners via tourism, Bohn concluded, marked the "close of a long period of sectional divergence."[63] Ten years later, the winter migration of northerners to Florida was estimated to be between 1 and 2.5 million persons. The paper also reported that "90 percent of northern tourists on a sunshine-seeking pilgrimage" were headed south (instead of west) and had at least seven routes to choose from. The AAA recommended that people choose their routes according to "scenery, freedom from city traffic, low total mileage, historic and interesting spots, hotels and eating places, resorts . . . and all the other items that go to make automobile touring a vacation in itself."[64]

Clearly, roads made the difference in whether southern cities and states were able to attract tourists to stay for any length of time. Most road improvements began in and around cities. In Virginia, some of the best roads were in and around Richmond. This was also true of Atlanta. Savannah could be reached by train and boat, but the city was being bypassed by automobile tourists because of the difficulty of getting to the city by car over the surrounding waterways. Harvey Granger, an attorney who moved there in 1889, dedicated his life to the improvement of roads to and from Savannah and through his efforts helped get built the section of the Atlantic Coastal Highway that eventually extended from Brunswick, Georgia, to Jacksonville, Florida. A. A. Ainsworth, a local leader in the city, lauded Harvey Granger for his work on the highway, which "spanned the marshes and rivers which have spelled isolation for Savannah." This "ribbon of concrete," he wrote, "has brought to your doors civilization which you hardly realized was in existence." Ainsworth went so far as to propose that Granger be the next governor, saying that if Granger were given the chance to do for Georgia what he had done for Savannah, its image as the "Southern Cracker" state would rapidly evolve into that of one of the "Banner States of the Union."[65]

Granger and others were deeply aware of what roads meant for tourism to the state. As he told Clark Howell, editor of the *Atlanta Constitution*, "We are not running tourist traffic bound north and west around Georgia but are bringing them through the Coastal section of Georgia." Moreover, he continued, "I am happy to say to you that a great number of these tourists are delighted to stay with us for days, weeks, and months."[66] Many of Granger's supporters agreed. Savannah businessman J. G. Hulmly told Granger, "We feel that this great Highway is not only a benefit to the State of Georgia, but to the great New England and Middle West States, in that they may [safely] pass and re-pass through the State of Georgia at all times regardless of weather conditions." The work of local boosters like Harvey Granger was extremely important to the southern tourist trade. As a result, southern cities and states became much more invested in attracting tourists to the region, and during the 1920s the South more actively developed an identity to attract tourists from the North and the Midwest.[67]

Southern cities were in the forefront of identifying tourism as a boon to their local economies and hounded state and local governments to at least build roads in the cities and their immediate environs. Members of the American traveling public were certainly interested in urban tourism as much as they were in seeing picturesque landscapes, and southern chambers of commerce and local businesses wisely developed city guides that were useful for both the tourist and the potential business investor. Indeed, the South's urban tourist literature often combined the nostalgia northerners had for the Old South with ideas of progress and innovation that suggested that the region had entered the era of the New South. Urban tourism, even in the New South, did not outpace northerners' desire to experience the rural South but still remained an important aspect of northern tourism to the South. The development of an urban tourist trade gave cities an opportunity to create their own urban persona, based on each city's setting and history, its architecture, and even the personality of its citizens.[68] Several southern cities had well developed urban personalities by the 1920s. Richmond, Atlanta, Savannah, Charleston, and New Orleans each developed distinctive identities, which were created, in part, by local leaders and chambers of commerce.

Early guidebooks to Richmond, which were sponsored by both local businesses and the chamber of commerce, reveal city leaders' attempts to showcase Richmond's progress, even while featuring its Confederate history. One such guide, *Illustrated Richmond*, sponsored by the American National Bank, noted the "marvelous metamorphosis" that had changed the city from a "crushed, devastated and demoralized rendezvous of refugees and fanatics to one of the foremost municipalities in the United States." This same guide was illustrated with photographs of Confederate monuments in full ceremony—the Davis Monument with floral arrangements, the Lee Monument fronted by a "living" Confederate flag made up of children, and a parade of the Richmond Howitzers with the battle flag in full view.[69]

Historic Richmond generally won over tourists. One travel writer described the city in the 1920s as "the tangible repository of Southern memories and of many tangible Southern souvenirs."[70] Throughout the 1920s and 1930s, several city guides to Richmond were published for tourists, and historic sites topped the list of attractions, from the Capitol to the Edgar Allan Poe "shrine" to the Confederate Museum (now the Museum of the Confederacy). Monument Avenue was also featured, as were Civil War battlefields on the outskirts of town. One travel guide correctly identified the city's personality when he wrote that "Richmond has retained in her sacred shrines the atmosphere of a by-gone day, each serving to attract thousands of visitors to the city."[71]

In the 1930s, the Richmond Chamber of Commerce advertised the city in a tourist guide entitled "Down Where the South Begins." A local radio station created the motto, and the city adopted it to let tourists know that it ("the South") began in the Capital of the Confederacy. The guide described Richmond as "the Mecca each year for hundreds of thousands of tourists who are attracted by its physical beauty, its ideal climate and the many monuments and landmarks which will ever hold a fascination for all Americans and students of history." In addition to the traditional city attractions that Richmond afforded, tourists were also encouraged to visit the historic plantations along the James River.[72] Tourists traveled to these sites in their own automobiles or via other modes of transport, which were created in response to the city's tourist trade in the late 1920s. This included renting a Drivurself Taxicab or taking the Grayline Parlor Chair Coach, which picked up visitors at Murphy's hotel and, for one dollar, took them on a "comprehensive tour" of the city, which lasted for more than an hour and a half.[73]

Charleston and Savannah, too, had their own personalities, linked to the colonial and antebellum past of the Old South. Architecturally, the cities were awash with the homes of the old southern aristocracy. Spanish moss–covered oak trees and palm trees were a reflection of their exotic locations. In these cities, tourists were more likely to encounter the "old-time negro." As historian Stephanie Yuhl explains, Charleston "failed to embrace New South innovation"; rather, the city's elite focused on fashioning a culture rooted in Charleston's colonial and antebellum past.[74] Savannah had a longer relationship with northern tourists than did Charleston and had learned early on the benefits of heritage tourism. During the expansion of northern tourism to the region in the 1920s, the Savannah Board of Trade published *Savannah: Where the Tourists Go*, for northerners traveling by automobile or by ship, as roads leading to and from Savannah were still in poor condition. The guide described the city as a "tourist paradise" and nearby Tybee Island as the "Playground of the South." Savannah had long become a stopping point for tourists headed to Florida, and the city felt that it was important to direct people to sites of historical interest linking Savannah's history to that of the nation. "Many monuments of great historical interest, buildings of colonial and antebellum fame, offer the visitor a mine of travel interest and add most materially to his appreciation of our country's noble past."[75]

Atlanta's business leaders promoted their city as a business-minded, progressive, urban center of the New South—focusing less on Civil War heritage and more on an attitude of sectional reconciliation through northern investment. In an official guide to the city published by the Atlanta Convention and Tourists Bureau in 1925, Atlanta was described as the "Metropolis of the Southeast," "The Convention Center of Dixie," and the "Gate City of the South." The guide provided a map showing the time it took to travel to the city from places as far-flung as New York, Chicago, St. Louis, Dallas, San Francisco, and Portland, Oregon. The city's "most exclusive social club" was the Piedmont Driving Club, which was made up of Atlanta's business and industrial elite. In fact, members of the city's industrial elite published their own guide in the 1920s, called *Key to Atlanta*. Promoted by a group known as Forward Atlanta, the focus of the guide was the city's resources, including its population, train service, and road and highway improvements. Stone Mountain was described as "History's Supreme Monument," and the guide was quick to dispel any notion that it was a "sectional monument." Rather it was a "national" monument, despite the fact that the intention of the monument from its inception was to honor the Confederacy. Indeed, during several incarnations of *Key to Atlanta*, the Forward Atlanta group described Stone Mountain this way: "So far from rekindling animosities now happily extinguished, it has attracted National interest, aroused National enthusiasm, and furnished the occasion for a great and impressive gesture of National good will."[76] Thus, Atlanta, despite its connections to the Civil War, chose to promote itself as business minded and forward looking.

In the 1920s, New Orleans sought to re-create its image, from the "City That Care Forgot" to "America's Most Interesting City," with an emphasis on business and industry. Yet, as historian Anthony Stanonis argues, this attempt to create a city image focused on economic investment did not work well for New Orleans—tourists who visited the city came for its leisurely atmosphere and its unique architecture. Moreover, since automobile tourists increasingly represented the bulk of visitors to the city, local leaders were forced to rethink how New Orleans was cast in order to meet the expectations of tourists. That is, if what tourists came for was "romance" writ large, then New Orleans was to be the city of history, culture, and romance and another of the South's exotic locations.[77]

Manufacturing an identity that attracted northern tourists was true for southern cities and true for the region as a whole. States, too, published tourist literature that promoted the region's romantic past. That literature often included words like "picturesque," "romance," and "hospitality," to link the region to the Old South and play into the image of the region that northerners had come to expect. States throughout the South bolstered the region's image as a place that was not only a great destination to escape northern winters but also one where northern tourists could personally engage with the Old South narrative of plantations, black servants, and rural America.

Virginia was the first southern state that northerners traveled through, and it developed its tourist image as a place where people could connect with the American past and enjoy its beaches and the beauty of the

Shenandoah Valley. In 1929, Virginia's State Commission on Conservation and Development advertised its tourist brochure, "Virginia: A Beckoning Land," in the District of Columbia's edition of *American Motorist*. The state's focus was on its history and its good roads. The ad boasted that travelers in Virginia were traveling along roads that were "open pages in the most thrilling history of the Nation." Moreover, the commission asserted, "there could be no more delightful way of teaching American history to your children" than a tour along Virginia's roads.[78]

Throughout the 1930s, the Garden Club of Virginia sponsored Historic Garden Week, a springtime "pilgrimage" to the colonial and antebellum gardens of Virginia's plantations. The purpose was to raise money for the restoration of Stratford Hall, Robert E. Lee's birthplace, but it also attracted northern tourists, including Mary Murtland Wurtz of Pittsburgh, who made the trip to see the gardens. In her journal, she wrote of her trip to Gunston Hall and other colonial gardens. She then traveled to Fredericksburg and Alexandria and eventually to the coast to see Yorktown and Carter's Grove—whose entrance was so "inconspicuous" that she drove past it several times. She and her traveling companion also visited Williamsburg, which was in the early stages of restoration. Several estates were opened to tourists during the Garden Club's annual pilgrimage, and these tours provided northerners with the opportunity to see plantations up close and helped the state establish historical tourism as a bona fide component of its economy.[79]

Historical tourism was popular in the 1920s and 1930s, and good roads and automobiles were the way to see the American landscape. State and local business leaders sought to capitalize on putting Americans in touch with their country's past, and this was true of the South. The irony was that they were using the modern tactics of advertising to sell a region that was perceived as antimodern. Virginia's State Commission on Conservation and Development led the South in this regard by establishing a highway marker program in 1927, which other southern states subsequently adopted. These markers, described as "history written on iron," were intended for automobile tourists, who could, for example, follow the route of Lee's and Grant's armies in 1864.[80]

During the 1930s, Virginians continued to spread the message of historical tourism. The creation of Colonial Williamsburg—its restoration and its marketing as an important site in the creation of American democracy—was instrumental to this development. Some tourists went out of their way to see the restoration in progress, but Colonial Williamsburg did not become a regular tourist destination until the late 1930s, at the beginning of World War II. Still, the state's official *Travel Guide to Virginia* (1937) invited tourists to spend their vacations in the "Mecca of All America." The guide featured the cities of Alexandria, Fredericksburg, Richmond, Jamestown, Yorktown, and Williamsburg, as well as the Skyline Drive through the Shenandoah Valley. In addition to the hundreds of colonial and antebellum estates and gardens, visitors were invited to "see the battlefields where freedom was won and slavery was abolished." The latter part of that invitation was interesting, since Virginia was at the heart of the former Confederacy.[81]

In the Deep South, tourists from the Midwest had also been escaping harsh winters by venturing down the Mississippi River and by train to places along the river, including Natchez and New Orleans, as well as to the beaches of the Gulf states. In the late 1920s, the Biloxi Chamber of Commerce distributed brochures promoting the Gulf Coast as the "American Riviera." Biloxi had several grand hotels and a yacht club, which sponsored a regatta and offered water excursions for northern tourists. The city was clearly reaching out to tourists from the North and Midwest by advertising that it was easily reached by rail and was just twenty-one hours from Chicago and Cincinnati and thirty-four hours from New York City. Biloxi, the pamphlet promised, offered tourists the "alluring atmosphere of the Old South with the spirit of the new in a charming four-season resort." If this was not convincing enough, the pamphlet emphasized that northern physicians recommended winter vacations to warmer locations as "necessary to the best health of their patients."[82]

State efforts to encourage investment and tourism were limited in the 1920s to an effort called the Know Mississippi Better Train, which for two weeks of the year traveled to different regions of the country promoting the state. The train consisted of a series of Pullman cars that contained exhibits on Mississippi agriculture, industry, health, and education. White citizens from all walks of life paid to take the trip. One excursion included a home demonstration agent, a teacher, a college student, a traveling salesman, and a physician, who were charged with "uphold[ing] the traditions of the South and Mississippi" and knowing quick facts about the state, such as that it had the largest cotton plantation in the world and the lowest death rate of any southern state. For several years, the train had a jazz band with singing porters to entice people during city stops to board the train and see the exhibits. This certainly played into the image of the South of contented blacks, but in 1938 the Pullman Porters Union put an

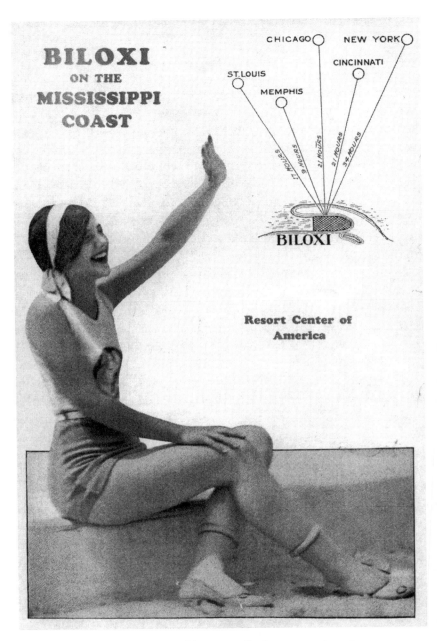

Biloxi on the Mississippi Coast, pamphlet, 1929. Biloxi encouraged tourism from the Midwest and the Northeast. (Author's collection)

end to the performances. Still, for more than a decade, the Know Mississippi Better Train served to perpetuate many of the stereotypical images nonsoutherners had of the South.[83]

Train travel to Mississippi was still the best way to see the state well into the 1930s, because the state was woefully behind other southern states in road construction and highway development. Virginia had "vile" road conditions in 1910, and the same could be said for Mississippi until the late 1930s. The state's saving grace came in the form of the annual Natchez Pilgrimage, begun in 1932, and the Mississippi Advertising Commission (MAC), formed in 1934 for the purpose of attracting tourism and investment to the state. Highway construction was vital if the state's economy was going to benefit from the millions of tourist dollars, which were currently being spent in other southern states with better roads.

In 1927, several women from Natchez's elite organized the Natchez Garden Club—for the purpose of civic improvement but specifically to preserve local architecture and landscape architecture. Five years after its founding, the club sponsored its first annual pilgrimage to draw attention to the town's antebellum homes. According to Katherine Miller, who is credited with originating the idea of the pilgrimage, "I knew we had in Natchez homes worth coming many miles to see[,] for each year numbers of tourists came and were invariably thrilled with being allowed to visit our antebellum homes." Miller and her fellow club members organized the pilgrimage so that tourists could learn about Natchez and its southern traditions and marvel at its architecture. In 1935, just three years after it was established, the pilgrimage attracted 10,000 visitors, and by the end of the decade, the club estimated that almost 50,000 tourists annually made their way to the weeklong event.[84]

The Natchez Pilgrimage offered tourists from all over the United States the opportunity to see the Old South that they had envisioned from music, radio, and other forms of popular culture. Even before the enormous success of *Gone with the Wind*, Natchez opened the doors onto the Old South by providing tourists with the chance to see large antebellum homes filled with furniture from bygone days, tours by women in hoopskirts, and "mammies in bandanas." Festivities included a Confederate ball, tableaux of historical scenes re-created in the mansions, and local black citizens singing black spirituals. This was, of course, Natchez as local whites sought to portray it, and it attracted northern and midwestern tourists by the thousands. For one week of the year, Natchez became the place "where the Old South still lives."[85]

The Chicago Motor Club, an AAA affiliate, published a special edition of its newsletter on the Natchez Pilgrimage in 1940. "It is hard to explain the charm of the spring garden pilgrimages in Mississippi," one article began. The idea of southern mistresses of antebellum homes opening their doors to the public was not "what the Yankees expected of the South." The article's author then mused about "what impels Chicagoans, Iowans, Wisconsinites, Indianans, to drive a thousand miles and more to see old homes, old gardens, decorous tableaux—and not a night club, Ferris wheel, fan dance, or futurama in sight." There was no wonder, the author concluded, when one has actually been on one of the pilgrimages. That this was called a "pilgrimage" was apropos, "because many have called the experience akin to a spiritual revival." What is more, once they arrived in Natchez, the "pilgrims" were no longer tourists but had become "old friends come to call."[86]

Traveling to see "where the Old South still lives" helped people from the North and the Midwest escape the doldrums of winter or the chaos of city living, and the success of the Natchez Pilgrimage proved to be an economic boon to both Natchez and Mississippi, attracting the attention of state leaders to the long-term impact of tourism—specifically historical tourism focusing on the Old South—on the state's economy. Many tourists to Natchez had traveled along the unpaved road and former Indian trading route known as the Natchez Trace; still others came from the Southwest along highways that led to the river town. The sheer number of tourists, who dared to venture out on Mississippi's poor roads, as well as those who avoided the state altogether for the very same reason, motivated state leaders to invest in highways that traversed the state north to south and east to west, because the state had Old South hospitality to share with its Yankee cousins.

The MAC built on the achievements of the Natchez Pilgrimage and publicized the state's newly paved highways by actively pursuing tourist dollars from the North and the Midwest. In the winter of 1937–38, the commission placed advertisements in the major newspapers of Chicago, Detroit, St. Louis, Kansas City, Toledo, Milwaukee, and Indianapolis, as well as in the *New York Times* and the *Washington Herald-Times*. The ads touted the state's four paved highways, which traversed the state north to south and east to west, and invited motorists to travel along them and enjoy the state's "wintertime splendor and warm sunshine." Moreover, the ads touted Mississippi as "America's Gateway to the Gulf" and used the illustration of a southern belle in a hoopskirt to announce that the state "opens its doors to the Nation." In addition to outdoor activities such as golfing and fishing, the MAC invited visitors to explore the state's "historic treasures," which included annual tours of Vicksburg as well as the Natchez Pilgrimage. At the bottom of the advertisement, potential tourists were directed to send their names and addresses to receive complimentary booklets highlighting the state's recreational and historic activities.[87]

Northern and midwestern tourists who saw the advertisement in their newspapers and made the request received promotional booklets that revealed a Deep South state that understood what attracted its out-of-state visitors, especially those who were not originally from the South. Moreover, the lengthy pamphlet was printed on the heels of the publishing success of *Gone with the Wind*, and the MAC capitalized on that success by promoting the state's Old South image for the next several years. The commission employed long-used narrative tactics in its brochures to entice the traveler—tourists could escape the "harsh and bleak extremes of less hospitable climates," and urban dwellers were reminded of the "crowds and congestion of nervous metropoli," which they could leave for the "relaxation of a gentle Southern sun and the pleasant welcome of a people hospitable by habit." Mississippi offered a "new vacation," although the brochures continued to use phrases familiar to northern travelers, including "valorous history," "rich pageantry," and "picturesque locale."[88]

In the mid-1930s, the illustrated booklet sent to prospective visitors represented "The Past" with images of a monument to Jefferson Davis, a photograph of Vicksburg National Military Park, southern belles in hoopskirts, and the ruins of Windsor plantation. Images that were intended to emphasize the "joy of living in the present" may have confused the northern traveler, since these included photographs of an antebellum mansion, southern belles in hoopskirts, a black carriage driver in top hat and tails, and a Confederate ball held during the Natchez Pilgrimage. In a section entitled "Mississippi at Work," the booklet appealed to northerners' fascination with southern blacks. "Those who wish to see the Southern Negro cotton economy at work—who have never heard Negroes singing in the fields—who have never watched the nation's greatest export crop in the making—need to make a pilgrimage to the cotton empire of the Yazoo-Mississippi Delta." The MAC even called attention to Parchman, the prison farm in the Delta, because the Library of Congress had called it "the best source of Negro folk music in the nation." Indeed, the Mississippi Delta, the brochure declared, "is the land of the black man, enchanted since the stars fell."[89]

MISSISSIPPI
America's Gateway to the Gulf

opens its doors
to the NATION

HISTORIC

GOLFING

FISHING

WITH four through paved highways completed—and others soon to be finished—Mississippi opens its doors to the nation and invites you to—

BE AMONG THE FIRST, THIS WINTER

★ To Motor to Mississippi—travel its new highways and thrill to its wintertime splendor and warm sunshine.

★ To Visit the Mississippi Gulf Coast and enjoy warm winter days boating, fishing, golfing, hunting or in peaceful relaxation. Hotel facilities are unexcelled and the cost of a delightful vacation will be surprisingly low.

★ To Explore Mississippi's historic treasures and join in the Vicksburg Historical Tours, March 25, 26, 27, and the Natchez Pilgrimages, March 11 to 24; March 27 to April 3.

The map on your right shows the four major U. S. Highways now completely paved. Send coupon for beautifully illustrated recreational and historic booklets.

MISSISSIPPI ✦ ✦ ✦ THE STATE
WITH A YEAR ROUND PLACE IN THE SUN

Mississippi Advertising Commission,
Jackson, Mississippi.
    I'm interested in visiting Mississippi this winter. Please send recreational and historic booklets.

NAME_____

ADDRESS_____

CITY_____STATE_____

"Mississippi, America's Gateway to the Gulf," advertisement that appeared in papers throughout the North and Midwest in 1937. (Courtesy Mississippi Department of Archives and History)

Within the image:

The Present

*

Mississippi's historic associations do not, however, overshadow the joy of living in the present. They serve rather as a backdrop to the stage of today's activity.

Each spring, in a dozen Mississippi communities, garden clubs conduct tens of thousands of visitors on tours to what are admittedly the best extant group of Southern ante-bellum homes and gardens. The pilgrimages are made to the accompaniment of elaborate tableaux, gay Confederate balls, a pageant mirroring with faith both the fantasy of an age gone by and the equally beautiful reality of spring in a Mississippi garden of today.

This image from Mississippi's tourism brochure for 1938 suggests that "The Present" still looks like the Old South. (Courtesy Mississippi Department of Archives and History)

In 1940, Mississippi hired Dixie Advertisers, an ad agency from Jackson, Mississippi, to develop a travel plan for the state. The agency developed what it called the "DownSouth" travel promotion program, intended to "sell a trip Downsouth to Mississippi" to people across the country. The slogan "DownSouth" was based on the way nonsoutherners responded to their travel to the South. "What does the average Midwesterner or northerner or easterner, who is coming below the Mason and Dixon Line[,] say when someone asks him, 'Where are you going?'" the agency asked in its proposal. The answer, it claimed, was "DownSouth," and this should become synonymous with Mississippi. Moreover, if Florida's trademark was "sunshine and fun," then Mississippi's should be linked to "Southern people extending genuine Southern hospitality."[90]

The DownSouth program continued the work of the MAC by placing advertisements in northern and midwestern newspapers and creating a

This photograph, entitled "Winter Invasion," was part of a 1940 marketing campaign by the Mississippi Advertising Commission encouraging northern tourists to escape cold winters for the warmth and hospitality of the South. (Courtesy Mississippi Department of Archives and History)

travel booklet. The media kit included press releases focused on Jackson, where "from this vantage point the glory and charm of the Old South may be relived . . . and the throbbing pulse of the New South may be felt," and on Vicksburg, "the last outpost of chivalry" and a "quaint little city . . . [with] exotic local color." Most impressive were the publicity photos that accompanied the press kit, which were taken to showcase the state. Nearly all of them were scenes of southern belles and antebellum mansions, and a few could have been still shots from the film *Gone with the Wind*, which had premiered one year before. All the photographs came complete with captions. One photograph, titled "Winter Invasion," shows three women in hoopskirts staged behind a cannon, with the caption "Seventy-five years ago three Confederate gunners would have been standing behind this cannon—not three pretty girls. Hot bloods have changed to warm friendship now; and the twin ridges of Vicksburg National Military Park are a common shrine, not a common battleground."[91]

To showcase highway development and still maintain an image of the Old South, the Mississippi Advertising Commission staged this 1940 photograph of a black driver in top hat picking up a southern belle in hoopskirt along a newly paved road into Natchez. (Courtesy Mississippi Department of Archives and History)

Between World War I and World War II, the effort by Mississippi and other southern states to attract northern travelers reflected important trends in the South's relationship to the rest of the nation. Northerners and midwesterners were definitely traveling to southern states and were doing so in search of warmer climates but also to tour sites of the region's antebellum past, including picturesque plantations and "exotic" southern blacks. Southern entrepreneurs and later southern state governments understood how the region was perceived and sought to benefit from those perceptions for purposes of both tourism and business investment.[92] Northern tourism to the South also represented an additional element in the culture of reconciliation. Tourism represented points of interaction between the former foes and an opportunity to heal old wounds. It is significant that as late as 1940 the MAC wrote of Vicksburg in the language of reconciliation, by calling it a place of "warm friendship" and a "common shrine." That reconciliation continued during World War II, when many northerners, midwesterners, and westerners were stationed at military bases throughout the South. Significantly, southern blacks were not included in those feelings of goodwill between the regions, as they remained subject to the system of Jim Crow that permeated the entire country. It took that war—and the civil rights movement that followed—to alter the nation's relationship to its black citizens, in the process changing the way the South was perceived in the national culture.

EPILOGUE

In 1946, the same year that Disney released *Song of the South*, Helen Harmon, a student at Roosevelt College, applied for a job as a typist at the Pepsodent Company in Chicago. The personnel director interviewed Harmon by telephone and asked her to report for work, but when she arrived to begin her new job Harmon was turned away and was told that Pepsodent did not hire "Negro typists." Milton Wenzler, spokesman for the company, fully admitted that this was corporate policy and also stated that if the company hired an African American, white office workers would quit. "I am afraid our employees would not like it," he answered, in response to a query by the local black press. He also revealed that "Negroes are hired only in a menial capacity." The irony of this case was not lost on the Chicago Civil Liberties Committee, which intended to pursue a lawsuit to test the city's fair employment ordinance. Pepsodent, as the committee—and most of America—knew, was the longtime sponsor of *Amos 'n' Andy*, the popular radio show based on the lives of two southern "black" characters.[1]

Although the white press did not cover Helen Harmon's story, the Associated Negro Press placed it front and center in black newspapers throughout the Midwest. Harmon's experience with Pepsodent sheds light on many aspects of the character of American society in the early years following World War II. First and foremost was that the South, as a region, did not have a monopoly on racism nor on discriminatory employment practices—this case took place in an urban-industrial center of the Midwest. Harmon's experience further reveals that northern companies like Pepsodent not only engaged in a damaging form of corporate racism by perpetuating southern black stereotypes through their sponsorship of *Amos 'n' Andy* but also followed discriminatory hiring practices, maintaining, like their southern brethren, that blacks could be hired only as menial laborers. The story also makes clear that white employees of Pepsodent shared their employer's belief in the inferiority of blacks, as evidenced by the perceived threat that they would quit rather than work with a "Negro typist." Finally, the account suggests that confronting such practices meant challenging perceptions of African Americans as contented servants of whites, a common stereotype that, although southern in origin, had become embedded in American popular culture. The quintessential southern mammy, Aunt Jemima, after all, got her start in Chicago.

Nostalgic images of the South continued to reign supreme in popular culture well into the 1950s, but the postwar civil rights movement served notice that another South existed, and it was not the romantic place of America's imagination. The work of John Popham, a journalist for the *New York Times* and its southern correspondent for several years, provides a case in point regarding the changing image of the South. On May 9, 1954, Popham wrote an article for the *New York Times*, simply entitled "The South." He painted a portrait that was in keeping with popular imagery of the region. "The past and present tilt lances in a setting as colorful as any pageantry in history," he wrote; "everywhere there is a sense of something old and stable." Popham waxed poetic about the Great Smoky Mountains and the Mississippi River, which took him from the "great pillared mansions" of Natchez, past cotton fields "dotted with sharecropper cabins," all the way down to New Orleans, "a special South within the South." He also pointed to the modern skyscrapers of Baton Rouge, as well as the "great dams of the Tennessee Valley Authority," as evidence of a more contemporary South. He concluded his paean to the region with a nod to the moonlight-and-magnolia South, writing that "for all the changes, when the mid-day sun has softened, when afternoon shadows dapple tree-shaded streets, when children return to play after their naps, there is always a Savannah or Charleston with red-brick sidewalks and colonial architecture and patio gardens to take the visitor back into the past of the South."[2]

Less than ten days after the publication of Popham's homage to Dixie, the Supreme Court handed down its decision in *Brown v. Board of Education*, which ended the legal segregation of public schools—a decision that was swiftly met by massive resistance across the South. Popham, recognized as the first northern journalist to provide extensive coverage of the region, soon discovered that his bucolic description of Dixie warranted an update. On the second anniversary of the *Brown* decision, he reported on the progress of desegregation and concluded that in the "traditional South" (that is, those states with large black populations) there was a "hardening resistance" and "militant search to circumvent the court order." Indeed, at the time of his report, the legislatures of Mississippi, Georgia, and South Carolina had passed measures that would allow them to abolish public schools altogether rather than accept racial integration.[3]

Massive resistance, and even violence, stood in stark contrast to the "pageantry" of the "old and stable" South that Popham had described for *New York Times'* readers just two years before. Yet his description was one that had a long history in journalism and popular culture. The American public shared his once-nostalgic vision of the South through the goods that they purchased or the movies that they saw, but in the 1950s this image of the region had begun to unravel. Certainly, icons of the Old South remained prominent in popular culture. Aunt Jemima was still being used to sell pancake mix, and at the beginning of the decade Hollywood produced its third iteration of *Show Boat* (1951). But now there was a new and even more powerful medium of popular culture influencing perceptions of Dixie—television.

Television alone did not alter perceptions of the South, but the response to broadcast coverage of the civil rights movement certainly contributed to this change, as did responses to television shows that perpetuated black stereotypes. Indeed, television swiftly replaced movies as the most influential medium of popular culture—Americans could now be entertained from the comfort of their own homes. Television, just as Hollywood had done years before, sought to entertain American audiences by reinventing tried-and-true radio programs. In fact, television executives immediately set their sights on the serial radio comedy *Amos 'n' Andy*—which had been on the air for twenty years—for adaptation to the small screen.

When *Amos 'n' Andy* premiered on television in 1951, the NAACP, as it had continued to do since the premiere of *The Birth of a Nation* in 1915, protested the show's depiction of African Americans, despite the fact that it had an all-black cast. This time, however, the NAACP was joined in its protest by Detroit's United Auto Workers (UAW) and by black soldiers serving in the U.S. Army. The UAW lodged its protest against the show's corporate sponsor, Blatz Brewery, and asked the company to withdraw its support. "We are deeply disturbed, not only about your program, but one or two others in which Negroes and other minority groups are portrayed as lazy, shiftless, irresponsible characters," wrote William Oliver, one of the directors of the UAW's Fair Practices and Anti-Discrimination Department.[4]

Black soldiers serving in Korea also registered their objections to the "hoary misrepresentations" portrayed on the show, one of several television programs made available to soldiers serving overseas. A group of twenty-five men from the 3rd Battalion of the 9th Infantry Regiment wrote a letter to the NAACP in New York to let the organization know how "we guys fighting in Korea feel about such derogatory trash." Not only did the letter denounce black journalists and magazines for supporting the show, but it also criticized "Negro actors and actresses [who] continue to belittle themselves and the entire race." Most important, the soldiers denounced the program as damaging to their morale and urged that there be a "more dignified outlet" for black actors and actresses on television.[5]

The protests by the UAW and African American soldiers signaled that social and political changes were on the horizon. Perhaps not coincidentally, *Amos 'n' Andy* ended its television run in 1954, the year of the *Brown* decision—a ruling that energized the southern civil rights movement. Television news coverage of the movement, moreover, revealed a crack in the veneer of popular images of the American South. Although television primarily served the corporate interests that sponsored programs, this new medium also contributed to social change by bringing attention to racial upheaval in the South—from the Emmett Till murder and the Montgomery Bus Boycott to the mobs of segregationists shouting racial epithets at black students integrating Little Rock High School in 1957.[6]

Still, this same medium, as film scholar Allison Graham argues, often stripped from shows any hint of racial discord in the region. In 1960, *The Andy Griffith Show*, based on the experiences of a small-town southern sheriff, hit the airwaves. It represented an idealized version of the region, only now the Old South was truly past. There were no black characters and therefore no reminders of the racial violence currently taking place. Between 1960 and 1965, during the peak years of the civil rights movement, Nielson ratings consistently ranked the show in the top five most watched by American viewers. The success of *The Andy Griffith Show* stood in stark opposition to reality, given that rural southern towns like Mayberry not only had black residents but were increasingly experiencing racial unrest. Yet the show's success with viewers indicates that Americans still wanted to believe in a South that was the hospitable region they had "known" from popular culture.[7]

Since World War II, the South of the American imagination has evolved to include more white stereotypes, often lower-class ones, such as that of the "cracker," the "bubba," or, more commonly, the "redneck." But more contemporary examples of the Old South continue to permeate popular culture, whether the modern-day southern belles of the 1980s show *Designing Women* or the mammy and uncle salt and pepper shakers still being sold in tourist shops around the South. Dixie may only be a state of mind, but in popular culture it remains ever present.

NOTES

Abbreviations
The following abbreviations are used throughout the notes.

AHC	Atlanta History Center, Atlanta, Georgia
AJC	*Atlanta Journal Constitution*
CUOHC	Columbia University Oral History Collection, New York, New York
GHS	Georgia Historical Society, Savannah, Georgia
Granger Papers	Mary Lois Granger Papers, Georgia Historical Society, Savannah, Georgia
JWTA	J. Walter Thompson Archives, John W. Hartman Center for Sales, Advertising & Marketing History, Duke University Rare Book, Manuscript, and Special Collections Library, Durham, North Carolina
LAB-UMD	Library of American Broadcasting, University of Maryland, College Park, Maryland
LHJ	*Ladies' Home Journal*
MAC-MDAH	Mississippi Advertising Commission, Mississippi Department of Archives and History, Jackson, Mississippi
MDAH	Mississippi Department of Archives and History, Jackson, Mississippi
MM-NYPL	Margaret Mitchell Files, Macmillan Company Records, New York Public Library, New York, New York
NYT	*New York Times*
VHS	Virginia Historical Society, Richmond, Virginia

Introduction

1 Landes, "A Northerner Views the South," 375. Landes trained with Ruth Benedict and Frank Boas at Columbia and published widely on everything from Afro-Brazilian women to Native American tribes. See Ruth Schollsberg Landes Papers, National Anthropological Archives, National Museum of American History, Washington, D.C.; Cole, "Mrs. Landes Meet Mrs. Benedict"; and Myrdal, *An American Dilemma.*

2 T. Brigham Bishop, "A Knot of Blue and Gray," Oliver Ditson, Boston, 1899; George M. Cohan, "The Wedding of the Blue and Gray," F. A. Mills, New York, 1906.

3 "Texas Tourists."

4 *On to Richmond*; Cowan, *New Invasion of the South*; *Tour of the Grand Army Club of Massachusetts*, pamphlet, September 1899, VHS.

5 Karen L. Cox, "Confederate Monument at Arlington."

6 On the reconciliation theme in films throughout the twentieth century, see Gallagher, *Causes Won, Lost, and Forgotten*; see especially the section on *Birth of a Nation*, pp. 106–7.

7 Herf, *Reactionary Modernism*, 1. Herf argues that reactionary modernists were able to reconcile an ideology about a technologically advanced nation with one that still honored a romantic German past that was not simply "backward-looking pastoralism." For a similar examination of the same trends in American society, see Wiebe, *Search for Order*; and Lears, *No Place of Grace*.

8 Ralph, *Dixie; or Southern Scenes and Sketches*, 1.

9 Wiebe, *Search for Order*, 12.

10 Ibid., 39.

11 Lears, *No Place of Grace*.

12 Ibid. Lears refers to antimodernism as a form of escapism from modernity on p. xii.

13 Kirby, *Media-Made Dixie*. James Bernhard's review in the *Journal of Southern History* describes Kirby's book as primarily "anecdotal" because, he writes, the book "lacks focus" and draws no "meaningful conclusions." Bernhard, "Book Review," 619. Lowenstein's review in *Florida Historical Quarterly* complains that Kirby "makes no serious attempt to show the effects of mass media" and is a "hodge podge" of information. See Lowenstein, "Book Review." Robert Sklar's assessment in the *American Historical Review* is that "this is a hybrid work that obscures what it accomplishes by claiming to accomplish too much." Sklar, "Book Review."

14 Helen Taylor's *Circling Dixie* surveys the impact of popular images of the South in British society.

15 Reed, *Enduring South*, 4–5, 87; see also Reed, *My Tears Spoiled My Aim*; and Reed, *Minding the South*.

16 Duck, *Nation's Region*; McPherson, *Reconstructing Dixie*; Graham, *Framing the South*.

17 Claude A. Barnett, "Role of the Press, Radio, and Motion Picture and Negro Morale."

18 Cohn, *The South*, 10, 30; "Down South Everybody's Happy," Jerome H. Remick, New York, 1917.

Chapter 1

1 Reminiscences of Jack Yellen, 1958, pp. 1–3, CUOHC; the quotation is from p. 3.

2 Lemons, "Black Stereotypes," 110.

3 "Jack Yellen, 97, Writer of Lyrics for 'Happy Days Are Here Again,'" *NYT*, April 19, 1991; Whitfield, "Is It True What They Sing about Dixie."

4 Goldberg, *Tin Pan Alley*, 46.

5 Ibid.; Spaeth, *History of Popular Music in America*, 3–6; Ewen, *Panorama of American Popular Music*.

6 "Songs for the South," *NYT*, June 16, 1861.

7 Spaeth, *History of Popular Music in America*, 94–95, 137–40; Ewen, *Panorama of American Popular Music*, 69; Daniel Decatur Emmett, "I Wish I Was in Dixie's Land," Firth, Pond, New York, 1860.

8 Ewen, *Panorama of American Popular Music*, 74; Foster's letter to Ed Christy is printed in Morneweck, *Chronicles of Stephen Foster's Family*, 398; see also Key, "Sound and Sentimentality"; and Emerson, *Doo-Dah!*, 12–13.

9 "Old Black Joe," Firth, Pond, New York, 1860.

10 Advertisement by Ticknor & Company in *The Critic: A Weekly Review of Literature and the Arts*, November 26, 1887.

11 Key, "Sound and Sentimentality," 147; Ewen, *Panorama of American Popular Music*, 94.

12 The depiction of African Americans in popular songs of the nineteenth century is examined in Dorman, "Shaping the Popular Image"; Graziano, "Use of Dialect in African-American Spirituals, Popular Songs, and Folk Songs"; Ostendorf, "Minstrelsy & Early Jazz"; and Lemons, "Black Stereotypes."

13 Dorman, "Shaping the Popular Image," 452–53.

14 Ernest Hogan, "All Coons Look Alike to Me," M. Witmark, New York, 1896.

15 Dorman, "Shaping the Popular Image," 455–56; Ewen, *Panorama of American Popular Music*, 101–2.

16 Dorman, "Shaping the Popular Image," 466. On reconciliation and Anglo-Saxonism, see Blight, *Race and Reunion*, 260; and Silber, *Romance of Reunion*, 136–37; see also Bloomfield, "Dixon's 'The Leopard's Spots.'"

17 John Martin Hammond, *Winter Journeys*, 157.

18 "Cahillogues."

19 Many of these songs can be found online at Indiana University, Lilly Library, Harmony Sheet Music collection, ⟨http://webapp1.dlib.indiana.edu/inharmony/welcome.do⟩. On the Jewish influence in popular songs about Dixie, see Whitfield, "Is It True What They Sing about Dixie."

20 Whitfield, "Is It True What They Sing about Dixie," 9.

21 Furia, *Poets of Tin Pan Alley*, 13.

22 Hamm, *Irving Berlin*, 9–10.

23 "Carolina Sunshine," words by Walter Hirsch, music by Erwin R. Schmidt, Harry Von Tilzer Music Publishing, New York, 1919.

24 "In the Evening by the Moonlight in Dear Old Tennessee," words and music by E. Clinton Keithley and Floyd Thompson, Frank K. Root & Company, New York, 1914.

25 Furia, *Poets of Tin Pan Alley*, 19–21; Reminiscences of Jack Yellen, 1958, p. 11 (first quotation), p. 25 (second quotation), CUOHC.

26 Furia, *Poets of Tin Pan Alley*, 22, 42.

27 Hamm, *Irving Berlin*, 12; "Little Puff of Smoke, Good Night—A Southern Croon," words by R. W. Lardner, music by G. Harris White, Victor Kremer Company, Chicago, 1910; "Floatin' Down the Mississippi (On Our Honeymoon)," words and music by Wendell L. Hall, Hall Music Company, New York, 1918.

28 "Are You from Dixie? ('Cause I'm from Dixie, too!)," words by Jack Yellen, music by George Cobb, M. Witmark, New York, 1913.

29 Ibid.

30 Witmark and Goldberg, *From Ragtime to Swingtime*, 132; Scheurer, *Nineteenth Century and Tin Pan Alley*, 109.

31 Hamm, *Irving Berlin*, 68–69.

32 Ibid., 5, 24–32, 50.

33 Ibid., 95; Hamm, "Genre, Performance and Ideology," 145–46.

34 "When It's Night Time Down in Dixieland," words and music by Irving Berlin, Waterson, Berlin & Snyder, New York, 1914.

35 Furia, *Poets of Tin Pan Alley*, 33; Reminiscences of Jack Yellen, 1958, p. 23, CUOHC.

36 Hamm, *Irving Berlin*, 98–99.

37 Cohan's song is mentioned in Lemons, "Black Stereotypes," 110.

38 "The Dixie Volunteers," words and music by Edgar Leslie and Harry Ruby, Waterson, Berlin & Snyder, New York, 1917.

39 Lindberg, "Popular Modernism"; quotation is from Witmark and Goldberg, *From Ragtime to Swingtime*, 68.

40 Furia, *Poets of Tin Pan Alley*, 36, 93, 245.

41 "Swanee," words by Irving Caesar, music by George Gershwin, Francis Day & Hunter, New York, 1919. On the sale of "Swanee," see Ewen, *Panorama of American Popular Music*, 183.

42 Ewen, *Panorama of American Popular Music*, 183.

43 Gershwin quoted in Wyatt and Johnson, *George Gershwin Reader*, 90, 93.

44 Ibid., 94.

45 Quotation is from Ellington, in Tucker, *Duke Ellington Reader*, 139. On "Rhapsody in Blue," see Wyatt and Johnson, *George Gershwin Reader*, 206–8.

46 Wyatt and Johnson, *George Gershwin Reader*, 222.

47 Reminiscences of Jack Yellen, 1958, p. 27, CUOHC. Anthony Harkins argues that it was during the postwar years that country musicians and promoters aggressively marketed the music to a national audience. See Harkins, *Hillbilly*, 99. Jeffrey Lange also argues that country music did not become mainstream until the postwar era. See Lange, *Smile When You Call Me a Hillbilly*, 195–97. Bill C. Malone also delineates the difference between country and popular music in the period prior to World War II in his book *Singing Cowboys and Musical Mountaineers*, 55–65. On the image of the hillbilly in popular culture, one must begin with Green, "Hillbilly Music"; see also Huber, *Linthead Stomp*, xiii. Huber argues that hillbilly music did become "an American popular music that was commercially broadcast and recorded."

48 Wilder, *American Popular Song*, 55. For a discussion of the radio program *Show Boat*, see chapter 3.

49 "Hollywood's Dernier Cri," *NYT*, June 9, 1929. In an interview with Yellen later in life, he claimed he did not like the move of the music industry from Tin Pan Alley to Hollywood, saying, "I never grew to like Hollywood." Reminiscences of Jack Yellen, 1958, p. 22, CUOHC.

50 Furia, *Poets of Tin Pan Alley*, 183.

51 Reference to "Dixie" as "the greatest war song" comes from the film trailer for *Dixie* (1943).

52 Reminiscences of Jack Yellen, 1958, p. 24, CUOHC.

Chapter 2

1 "Aunt Jemima Mills Company," Case Studies, Information Center Records, JWTA; "Account History of Aunt Jemima Pancake Flour," Account Files, Quaker Oats, JWTA. For an extended discussion of the development of the Aunt Jemima brand, see Manring, *Slave in a Box*.

2 Robinson, "Marketing Gum, Making Meanings." Robinson argues that business is not separate from culture and that advertising offers proof of that connection.

3 Schudson, *Advertising, the Uneasy Persuasion*, 209–10; McGovern, *Sold American*, 3–8. On Dixie as a brand, see Hale, *Making Whiteness*, 138–50; and Cohen, *Making a New Deal*, 101–5.

4 Kitch, *Pages from the Past*, 2–3; "Songs of Dixie," advertisement in *LHJ*, June 1891; "Game of Dixie-Land," advertisement in *LHJ*, February 1898; *A B C in Dixie* advertisement in *Town and Country*, November 26, 1904; "Folks from Dixie," advertisement of Dodd, Mead, in *Bookman; A Review of Books and Life*, August 1898.

5 Several books examine the cultural meanings of consumption, including Bronner, *Consuming Visions*; McCracken, *Culture and Consumption*; Brewer and Porter, *Consumption and the World of Goods*; Lears, *Fables of Abundance*; Strasser, *Satisfaction Guaranteed*; and Marchand, *Advertising the American Dream*. On advertising as a symbolic extension of cultural meaning, see Bronner, *Consuming Visions*, 29.

6 Wiebe, *Search for Order*, 40; Lears, *No Place of Grace*, 9–11.

7 Wiebe, *Search for Order*, 39.

8 Sivulka, *Soap, Sex, and Cigarettes*, 47.

9 Lears, *Fables of Abundance*, 124.

10 Ibid.

11 Ibid., 154; see also Strasser, *Satisfaction Guaranteed*.

12 On ad men and selling status, see McGovern, *Sold American*, 34–35; and Sivulka, *Soap, Sex, and Cigarettes*, 97.

13 "Aunt Jemima Fact Book" (1956), Account Files, Quaker Oats, JWTA.

14 Manring, *Slave in a Box*, 92–95.

15 As quoted in McGovern, *Sold American*, 31.

16 This telling is blended from two early accounts: "Account History of Aunt

Jemima Pancake Flour" (1930) and "Aunt Jemima Fact Book" (1956), both in Account Files, Quaker Oats, JWTA.

17 Bronner, *Consuming Visions*, 191–93.

18 "Account History of Aunt Jemima Pancake Flour," Account Files, Quaker Oats, JWTA.

19 Ibid.; Silvulka, *Soap, Sex, and Cigarettes*, 83, 115.

20 "Aunt Jemima Fact Book" (1956), Account Files, Quaker Oats, JWTA.

21 "Account History of Aunt Jemima Flour," Account Files, Quaker Oats, JWTA; Sivulka, *Soap, Sex, and Cigarettes*, 149.

22 Sivulka, *Soap, Sex, and Cigarettes*, 149; see also Manring, *Slave in a Box*, 76.

23 Manring, *Slave in a Box*, 76; "Consumer Recognition of the Aunt Jemima Brand," Account Files, 1885–2004, Quaker Oats, JWTA.

24 *Cleveland Call and Post* editorial, as quoted in Floyd J. Calvin, "The Digest," *Kansas City Plaindealer*, January 31, 1937.

25 "Gorham Silver" advertisement in *Life*, October 5, 1928, 92; "J. P. Lippincott Holiday Books" advertisement in *Town and Country*, November 23, 1912.

26 Marchand, *Advertising the American Dream*, 164–68. On "atmospheric advertising," see Sivulka, *Soap, Sex, and Cigarettes*, 113.

27 "Crab Orchard Whiskey" advertisement in *Life*, June 1, 1935, 8.

28 Maxwell House advertisement in *LHJ*, November 1928, Domestic Advertising Collection, JWTA.

29 "Cheek-Neale Company Account History," Colin Dawkins Papers, JWTA.

30 Ibid.

31 Maxwell House advertisement in *McCall's*, Domestic Advertising Collection, JWTA.

32 "Cheek-Neale Company Account History," Colin Dawkins Papers, JWTA.

33 General Foods advertisement, D'arcy Masius Benton & Bowles Archives, 1941–44, JWTA.

34 Maxwell House advertisement in *Saturday Evening Post*, Domestic Advertising Collection, JWTA.

35 Sammis, "How Radio Programs Are Built," 35.

36 Ibid., 35–36.

37 "On the Merry Go Round of Broadcasting," *NYT*, June 23, 1935.

38 The Selznick-Mitchell conflict over commercial tie-ins can be found in Commercial Tie-Ins, MM-NYPL.

39 "Chronological Abstract," Commercial Tie-Ins, MM-NYPL.

40 Regarding the Pepperell Manufacturing request, see G. A. Erskine to George P. Brett Jr., March 18, 1937, MM-NYPL.

41 Lois Dwight Cole to H. Y. Bingham, November 9, 1937, MM-NYPL.

42 Commercial Tie-Ins, ca. 1936–40, MM-NYPL.

43 Helen E. Sohl to Macmillan Co., April 26, 1937, MM-NYPL.

44 For *Gone with the Wind*–influenced advertisements, see Commercial Tie-Ins, ca. 1936–40, MM-NYPL.

45 Ad*Access On-line Project—Ad #BH1395 and 1397, JWTA.

46 Ad*Access On-line Project—Ad #BH1927–28, JWTA.

Chapter 3

1 Correll and Gosden, *Sam 'n' Henry*, 9, 11, 14, 51.

2 For detailed statistics on radio programs and audience share from 1926 to 1945, see Summers, *History of Broadcasting*.

3 On the development of the hillbilly stereotype, see Harkins, *Hillbilly*.

4 Jim Cox, *Sold on Radio*, 35.

5 Many scholars of early radio have discussed the phenomenon of radio minstrelsy, and still others have analyzed the role played by hillbilly acts. Yet this scholarship does not offer any in-depth analysis into how radio as a form of mass culture helped to shape Americans' perceptions of the South and southerners. The historiography on minstrelsy is rich. For a general overview of minstrelsy, see Wittke, *Tambo and Bones*; Goldberg, *Tin Pan Alley*, 31–60; Toll, *Blacking Up*; and Lott, "The Seeming Counterfeit." On minstrelsy in radio, see MacDonald, *Don't Touch That Dial*, 329–48; Hilmes, *Radio Voices*, 30–31, 76–81; and Arceneux, "Blackface Broadcasting." Discussions of hillbilly acts are found in Malone, *Country Music U.S.A.*; Lange, *Smile When You Call Me a Hillbilly*; McCusker, *A Boy Named Sue*; Hall, *Lum and Abner*; Grundy, "We Always Tried to Be Good People"; and Otto and Burns, "Black and White Cultural Interaction." Arceneaux briefly discusses hillbillies, in "Blackface Broadcasting," 68–70.

6 On the Golden Age of radio, see Barnouw, *Tower in Babel*; MacDonald, *Don't Touch That Dial*; Hilmes, *Radio Voices*; Susan J. Douglas, *Inventing American Broadcasting*; Susan J. Douglas, *Listening In*; Nachman, *Raised on Radio*; and George H. Douglas, *Early Days of Radio Broadcasting*.

7 Susman, *Culture as History*, 150–71. For a discussion of Cantril and Allport's *Psychology of Radio*, see Susan J. Douglas, *Listening In*, 130–33. On race, ethnicity, and mass culture, see Cohen, *Making a New Deal*, 143–54.

8 Susan J. Douglas, *Listening In*, 100–107.

9 On radio audience percentages, see Cantril and Allport, *Psychology of Radio*, 85–86.

10 Ibid., 96.

11 Correll and Gosden, *All about Amos 'n' Andy*, 9–29.

12 Histories of *Amos 'n' Andy* include Ely, *Adventures of Amos 'n' Andy*; and McLeod, *The Original Amos 'n' Andy*; see also Nachman, *Raised on Radio*, 272–84. The show is also discussed in numerous radio histories, including MacDonald, *Don't Touch That Dial*, 27–29; Hilmes, *Radio Voices*, 76–90; and Susan J. Douglas, *Listening In*, 100–123.

13 Ely, *Adventures of Amos 'n' Andy*, 189–90.

14 Ibid.; Vann's editorial is quoted on p. 190.

15 Gregory, *Southern Diaspora*, 56. Gregory writes that *Amos 'n' Andy* offered audiences the story of "fictional black southerners in the northern metropolis."

16 Ibid., 59.

17 Walter J. Thompson, "Among the Merry Men of Minstrelsy," *San Francisco Chronicle*, November 12, 1916.

18 Wittke, *Tambo and Bones*, 6.

19 Ibid., 8; see also Roediger, *Wages of Whiteness*, 98–116.

20 Correll and Gosden, *All about Amos 'n' Andy*.

21 "Honey and Alexander," 8–9.

22 As quoted in Arceneux, "Blackface Broadcasting," 64.

23 White, *Ar'n't I a Woman*, 27–62; see also Manring, *Slave in a Box*, 136, 193n37.

24 Hilmes, *Radio Voices*, 80.

25 Roles for black women were limited to musical performances. See "Tess 'Aunt Jemima' Gardella," in Cullen, *Vaudeville, Old and New*, 430; see also Witt, *Black Hunger*, 21–53.

26 On Widmer's acceptance by African American audiences, see "White Radio Actress in Negro Interpretations: 'Aunt Jemima' Wins Plaudits and Pleases Race," *Negro Star*, May 20, 1938. A sound clip of Widmer as Aunt Jemima can be heard at ⟨http://www.otrcat.com/aunt-jemima-p-48526.html.⟩

27 James Young lecture, "News Spreading Use of Advertising" (1934), Chicago Account Files, JWTA.

28 Avalon *Show Boat* Script, June 14, 1940, WENR Chicago, LAB-UMD.

29 Ely, *Adventures of Amos 'n' Andy*, 109–14.

30 Sinclair Minstrels Script, December 18, 1933, LAB-UMD.

31 On John Henry, see "Voodoo on the Air"; and "For Distinguished Service."

32 Photo caption, *Radioland*, March 1934.

33 Cantril and Allport, *Psychology of Radio*, 69.

34 "It's Make Believe," *NYT*, June 16, 1935.

35 "Keep Young and Beautiful"; "My Girls." On the Boswell Sisters, see "How Three Southern Belles Found Fortune on the Radio," *NYT*, February 28, 1932.

36 "Southern Charm."

37 "Ethereal Songsters," *NYT*, June 26, 1932.

38 Harkin, *Hillbilly*, 3–7.

39 Gregory, *Southern Diaspora*, 59–60.

40 Malone, *Country Music U.S.A.*, 43. Malone credits Archie Green's article "Hillbilly Music" for tracing the use of the term "hillbilly"; see also Huber and Drowne, "Hill Billy," 215–16.

41 Harkin, *Hillbilly*, 80; Lange, *Smile When You Call Me a Hillbilly*, 27–29; Malone, *Country Music U.S.A.*, 35; see also "National Barn Dance," in *Encyclopedia of Radio*, 3:1537–38.

42 "National Barn Dance," in *Encyclopedia of Radio*, 3:1537–38; see also "WLS has a Miracle Show in the Barn Dance," 86–89; and Harkin, *Hillbilly*, 80–81.

43 "Renfro Valley Folks," 16–17.

44 Ibid., 26.

45 Melick, "Hill Billy Menace," 48–49.

46 Ibid.; Harkin, *Hillbilly*, 87.

47 "Pie Plant Pete Comes East," *NYT*, July 17, 1932; "Coon Creek Girls from the Kentucky Hills," *NYT*, June 4, 1939. In the case of the Coon Creek Girls, their manager, John Lair, was responsible for creating an image of them as traditional women and sought to control them on and off stage; Oral History Interview with Barbara Greenlief.

48 "Bob Burns (1890–1956)."

49 "Judy Canova," in Kingsbury, *Encyclopedia of Country Music*, 77; Carlin, *Country Music*, 188–89; Bufwack and Oermann, *Finding Her Voice*, 103–4.

50 Hall, *Lum and Abner*, 4; "Lum and Abner," in *Encyclopedia of Radio*, 2:412–14.

51 Siegel, "Revealing Lum and Abner."

52 Hall, *Lum and Abner*, 10–14; the second quotation is from p. 34.

Chapter 4

1 "Sowing the South Forty," *NYT*, December 13, 1936; see also "The Screen in Review: Warners Start the Southern Cycle with 'Jezebel' at the Music Hall," *NYT*, March 11, 1938. On Scarlett, see Frank S. Nugent, "'Gone With,' Etc.—or the Making of a Movie," *NYT*, December 10, 1939.

2 There are a number of studies of the South in film, the most useful being Campbell, *Celluloid South*; French, *The South and Film*; Kirby, *Media-Made Dixie*; Graham, *Framing the South*; McPherson, *Reconstructing Dixie*; and Helen Taylor, *Circling Dixie*, esp. pp. 28–62. On the film image of the mountain South, see Harkins, *Hillbilly*, 141–72; and Williamson, *Hillbillyland*. On *Gone with the Wind*, see Haskell, *Frankly, My Dear*.

3 Sklar, *Movie-Made America*, 3, 4, 14. It is estimated that there were 20,000 nickelodeons in northern cities by 1910; see May, *Screening Out the Past*, 35.

4 On European influence and class, see Sklar, *Movie-Made America*, 42, 46.

5 May, *Screening Out the Past*, xii, xiv; Sklar, *Movie-Made America*, 196.

6 May, *Screening Out the Past*, xiv.

7 The American Film Institute's catalogs of films made in the United States categorize films by region, state, and themes. It is difficult to determine the actual number of films set in the South versus films set in southern states or based on a particular theme. For example, during the 1930s, the catalog has the theme "planters," meaning that a planter appears in the film. In this case, *Gone with the Wind* is not included. However, under the theme "plantations," *Gone with the Wind* is listed. Munden, *American Film Institute Catalog*.

8 *The Birth of a Nation* has been analyzed by film scholars and historians. See especially May, *Screening Out the Past*, 62–65, 80–81; Sklar, *Movie-Made America*, 58–61; Staiger, *Interpreting Films*, 140–44; Merritt, "Dixon, Griffith, and the Southern Legend"; Franklin, "Birth of a Nation"; and Michael Hammond, "A Soul Stirring Appeal to Every Briton."

9 W. E. B. Du Bois quoted in Merritt, "Dixon, Griffith, and the Southern Legend," 35; Franklin, "Birth of a Nation," 424–25.

10 Franklin, "Birth of a Nation," 425.

11 Merritt, "Dixon, Griffith, and the Southern Legend," 35; Staiger, *Interpreting Films*, 140.

12 Staiger, *Interpreting Films*, 140; May, *Screening Out the Past*, 61, 65; Merritt, "Dixon, Griffith, and the Southern Legend," 27; Claude A. Barnett, "Role of the Press, Radio, and Motion Picture and Negro Morale," 474. Dixon even tried to have the film remade as a talking version in 1933. See "Hollywood in Review: Author May Make Audible Film of 'Birth of a Nation,'" *NYT*, January 22, 1933.

13 Munden, *American Film Institute Catalog*, 146, 155.

14 Figures on film settings are drawn from ibid. On the number of films set in the antebellum South, see Gaines, *Music in the Old Bones*, 186.

15 Munden, *American Film Institute Catalog*, 657.

16 *Show Boat*, Universal Studios, 1936; Munden, *American Film Institute Catalog*, 712; Breon, "Show Boat," 99.

17 Munden, *American Film Institute Catalog*, 1205–6, 1400, 1986.

18 Johnston, *Little Colonel*.

19 *The Little Colonel*, Twentieth-Century Fox Films, 1935.

20 *The Littlest Rebel*, Twentieth-Century Fox Films, 1935.

21 "Surveying Scarlett O'Hara," *NYT*, February 19, 1939; Bosley Crowther, "Mr. Selznick and a Scarlett Future," *NYT*, October 30, 1938.

22 Letters from all the major movie studios are in the Mitchell Papers, MM-NYPL.

23 Margaret Mitchell to Harold Latham, May 25, 1936, MM-NYPL.

24 Baskette, "Gone with the Wind, Indeed!" *Photoplay*, March 1937.

25 Margaret Mitchell to Herschell Brickell, May 16, 1938, in Harwell, *Margaret Mitchell's Gone with the Wind Letters*, 202.

26 Selznick's letter is quoted in ibid., 202–3.

27 Frank S. Nugent, "The Screen in Review," *NYT*, March 11, 1938; *Jezebel*, Warner Brothers, 1938.

28 Margaret Mitchell to Virginius Dabney, July 23, 1942, in Harwell, *Margaret Mitchell's Gone with the Wind Letters*, 359.

29 Margaret Mitchell to Susan Myrick, February 10, 1939, and Margaret Mitchell to Jere Moore, February 16, 1939, in Harwell, *Margaret Mitchell's Gone with the Wind Letters*, 249, 255.

30 B. R. Crisler, "Film Gossip of the Week: General Cukor's Expeditionary Force Threatens Richmond—Director Talks," *NYT*, April 25, 1937.

31 Lucille Pratt to David Selznick, August 3, 1938, Wilbur G. Kurtz Collection, AHC; Selznick quoted in "'Scarlett' Understands Book—Except about the June Bugs," *Atlanta Journal*, January 14, 1939.

32 "Miss Leigh Gets O.K. as 'Scarlett' by UDC Head," *Atlanta Constitution*, January 22, 1939; clippings on the Atlanta Ladies' Memorial Association in Wilbur G. Kurtz Collection, AHC. Mitchell personally feared the backlash of the United Daughters of the Confederacy, because the organization was such a stickler for historical details.

33 Thomas Pryor, "Profitable Gleanings," *NYT*, January 28, 1940. Advertisements appeared in the *Atlanta Constitution*, December 15, 1939.

34 Dabney, *Below the Potomac*, 2.

35 "Gone with the Wind," *Cleveland Gazette*, December 30, 1939.

36 "Protest Film as Incitement for Lynchings," *Kansas American*, February 3, 1940.

37 Andy Razaf, "Gone with the Wind," *Kansas City Plaindealer*, January 19, 1940.

38 Dalton Trumbo quoted in McManus and Kronenberger, "Motion Pictures, the Theater, and Race Relations," 152.

39 Ibid., 154–58.

40 Ibid., 154; see also Claude A. Barnett, "Role of the Press, Radio, and Motion Picture and Negro Morale"; and Barnard, *Wendell Willkie*, 338.

41 Regester, "African American Extras."

42 Margaret Mitchell to Marcella Rabwin, February 15, 1939, in Harwell, *Margaret Mitchell's Gone with the Wind Letters*, 253; Claude A. Barnett, "Role of the Press, Radio, and Motion Picture and Negro Morale," 476.

43 On *Hearts in Dixie*, see Munden, *American Film Institute Catalog*, 335; and Claude A. Barnett, "Role of the Press, Radio, and Motion Picture and Negro Morale," 476.

44 "Scratch a Hillbilly," *NYT*, May 15, 1938.

45 "Lum and Abner [Radio Show and Movies]"; "Bob Burns (1890–1956)."

46 "Judy Canova," in Parish and Pitts, *Hollywood Songsters*, 113; "Judy Canova," in Jones, *Country Music Humorists and Comedians*, 109–10. *Pudden' Head*, *Sis Hopkins*, and *Joan of Ozark* are discussed in Munden, *American Film Institute Catalog*, 1903, 2203, 1218. *Joan of Ozark*, Republic Pictures, 1942.

47 Harkins, *Hillbilly*, 162–63; see also Williamson, *Hillbillyland*, 79–81.

48 "Disney Wants It Right: Uncle Remus Filmers Visit Turnwold," *Atlanta Constitution*, October 15, 1944; "Kurtzes to Advise on Uncle Remus Film," *Atlanta Constitution*, October 4, 1944.

49 Wright Bryan, "Changing the Name of Uncle Remus," *Atlanta Journal*, August 23, 1946.

50 Bosley Crowther, "Spanking Disney," *NYT*, December 5, 1946. Regarding more positive reviews made in newspapers beyond the South, see Campbell, *Celluloid South*, 151–52.

51 Bosley Crowther, "Spanking Disney," *NYT*, December 5, 1946; "NAACP Considers 'Uncle Remus' Dangerous," *Negro Star*, December 6, 1946.

52 "Song of the South Picketed," *NYT*, December 14, 1946.

53 "Films Chosen for Young," *NYT*, December 26, 1946.

Chapter 5

1 Margaret Mitchell to Harold Latham, January 8, 1937, MM-NYPL.

2 Ibid.

3 Archibald Henderson, "The Old South Yields to the New," *NYT*, August 15, 1926.

4 On literature and southern identity, see Duck, *Nation's Region*; Winchell, *Rein-*

venting the South; Gardner, *Blood and Irony*; Simpson, *Dispossessed Garden*; Brooks, *Language of the American South*; and Cobb, *Away Down South*, 130–31.

5 Aron, *Working at Play*, 142.

6 Sears, *Sacred Places*, 4–6.

7 Aron, *Working at Play*, 10. Aron argues that tourism and vacationing are related but that they are different types of travel. Vacationing, according to her, is defined as "pleasure trips that last at least a few days."

8 Ibid., 127.

9 There is a vast literature on tourism, which includes ibid.; Jakle, *The Tourist*; Cocks, *Doing the Town*; Schaffer, *See America First*; Selwyn, *Tourist Image* (especially pp. 1–30); and Holloway, *Business of Tourism*, 1–31. Books that treat the southern tourist trade include John D. Cox, *Traveling South*; Yuhl, *Golden Haze of Memory*; and Stanonis, *Creating the Big Easy*.

10 Selwyn, *Tourist Image*, 1, 7–8, 21.

11 Plaag, "There Is an Abundance of Those Which Are Genuine," 24–49. Several historians have defined the Lost Cause, including Wilson, *Baptized in Blood*; Foster, *Ghosts of the Confederacy*; and Karen L. Cox, *Dixie's Daughters*.

12 King, *The Great South*.

13 Ibid.; "lazy negro" appears on p. 29; "intelligent-looking" appears on p. 782.

14 Lanier, *Florida*, 218–19, 260.

15 Mooney-Melvin, "Harnessing the Romance," 36.

16 Hardy, *Down South*, 110.

17 "Richmond since the War," 303–6; Berry, *Other Side*, 93; Russell, *Letters of Matthew Arnold*, 244.

18 Hardy, *Down South*, 4–15. C. B. Berry, an Englishman, on his visit to Richmond, wrote that "things down south seemed more homelike than farther north, if less luxurious." Berry, *Other Side*, 89.

19 Russell, *Letters of Matthew Arnold*, 243–45.

20 James, *American Scene*, 370–74, 383–85.

21 Page, *In Ole Virginia*; Page, *Social Life in Old Virginia*; Dixon, *Leopard's Spots*.

22 Lanier, *Florida*, 241.

23 Derry, *Georgia*, 87–90.

24 Hardy, *Down South*, 93.

25 Harley, *Southward Ho*, 62–64.

26 Mildred Cram's husband, Allan, with whom she was traveling, made the comment about Spanish moss. Cram, *Old Seaport Towns*, 102.

27 John Martin Hammond, *Winter Journeys*, 130.

28 Brochure, *The DeSoto: Tourist Season 1896–97, Greeting* (Savannah: Watson & Powers, Proprietors, 1896), GHS.

29 Hadler, "Remus Orthography," 100–104; Kersten, "Creative Potential of Dialect Writing," 117.

30 Cram, *Old Seaport Towns*, 1, 3.

31 "Joel Chandler Harris (1845–1908)."

32 Harris, *Uncle Remus*, vii, xvii.

33 On reconciliation and Civil War memory, see Silber, *Romance of Reunion*; and Blight, *Race and Reunion*. On the cult of Anglo-Saxon supremacy, see Silber, *Romance of Reunion*, 136.

34 Mooney-Melvin, "Harnessing the Romance," 384.

35 Hardy, *Down South*, 105; Ralph, *Dixie; or Southern Scenes and Sketches*, 1.

36 Cram, *Old Seaport Towns*, 102. Mildred Cram wrote the screenplay for *Love Affair* (Warner Brothers, 1939).

37 James, *American Scene*, 386.

38 John Martin Hammond, *Winter Journeys*, 157.

39 Ibid.

40 McIntyre, "Promoting the Gothic South," 58. On historical sites and a sense of the past, see Jakle, *The Tourist*, 286.

41 McIntyre, "Promoting the Gothic South"; William Taylor, *Cavalier and Yankee*, 177–202.

42 Patrick, "Mobile Frontier."

43 Cram, *Old Seaport Towns*, 148.

44 Ibid., 151–52.

45 Ibid., 153.

46 Ibid., 30.

47 Ibid., 36–37.

48 Stanard, "Quaint Old Richmond"; quotations from pp. 444–46.

49 "Edward Stratemeyer," in *American Writers for Children before 1900*, 351–62.

50 Hope, *Bunny Brown and His Sister Sue*, 70.

51 Ibid., 76.

52 Ibid., 79.

53 Children's stories in the South were a popular genre unto themselves. See Johnston, *Little Colonel*; Darlington, *Circus Boys*; and Rathbone, *Chums in Dixie*.

54 Brown, "Negro Character as Seen by White Authors," 179, 196.

55 Conrad, "Philology of Negro Dialect," 150–54. Even authors considered sympathetic to African Americans fell short; see, for example, McDowell, "Use of Negro Dialect."

56 Yuhl, *Golden Haze of Memory*, 18.

57 Heyward, *Porgy*; Young, *So Red the Rose*.

58 On the South's literary modernists, see Duck, *Nation's Region*.

59 Harold Latham, "How the Publisher Secured the Manuscript," in Mitchell, *Gone with the Wind*, 8–9.

60 Margaret Mitchell to Harold Latham, September 9, 1938, MM-NYPL.

61 Margaret Mitchell to Thomas W. Palmer, November 25, 1938, ibid.

62 Louise Bowman to the Editor, September 1939, and H. L. Banbe to Macmillan Co., April 10, 1940, ibid.

63 John Marsh to Lois Cole, February 9, 1936, ibid.

64 Franklin Davis, "World in Review," *Kansas City Plaindealer*, May 14, 1937; Elizabeth Lawson, "Lynch Law and Pulitzer," *Cleveland Gazette*, May 29, 1937.

65 "Three Historical Novels," 48.

66 Constance Lindsay Skinner to Lois Cole, n.d., MM-NYPL.

67 All quotations are from Mitchell to Harold Latham, January 8, 1936, and September 9, 1938, ibid.

68 Margaret Mitchell Interview, typescript, September 5, 1941, ibid.

Chapter 6

1 *On to Richmond*, 5.

2 Ibid., 28–29.

3 On veterans' reunions, see Blight, *Race and Reunion*, 171–72; and Reardon, *Pickett's Charge*, 91–109.

4 This is a version of the argument James Sears has made about American culture, which can be applied to regional tourism. See Sears, *Sacred Places*, 4.

5 Ibid., 7.

6 Aron, *Working at Play*, 131.

7 See, for example, Sears, *Sacred Places*; Cocks, *Doing the Town*; and Schaffer, *See America First*.

8 Brochure, Virginia Navigation Company, 190?, VHS.

9 Brochure, *Raymond's Vacation Excursions: Five Grand Autumn Trips* (Boston, 1887), VHS.

10 Ibid.

11 *Guide to Georgia and Florida* (Atlantic and Coastal Railroad, 1876–77), pamphlet, GHS.

12 Derry, *Georgia*, 87.

13 "Sisterhood of States, Jamestown Exposition," 169–70.

14 *Glimpses of the Jamestown Exposition and Picturesque Virginia*, n.p.

15 The *National Magazine* remarked that to name the parade grounds after Lee was a great tribute to the "loved son of the great South" (p. 166).

16 *Official Encyclopedic Guide to Richmond and Vicinity Including Battlefields*, 4, 9.

17 Confederate Memorial Association, Board of Lady Managers, Visitors Register, 1921–22, 1925, vol. 1, Confederate Memorial Association Records, VHS.

18 *Virginia: The Land of Romance, Hospitality and Beauty*, pamphlet (o.s.), Norfolk & Western Railway, 1928, VHS.

19 Ralph, *Dixie; or Southern Scenes and Sketches*, 168–69.

20 Sheffield, *Improvement of the Road System of Georgia*, 26.

21 Ibid., 31.

22 Lichtenstein, "Good Roads and Chain Gangs," 86. Lichtenstein also argues that convict labor vis à vis chain gangs was preferred over traditional convict lease and was considered "a quintessential southern Progressive reform."

23 The Dixie Flyer and the Cotton Belt Route advertised regularly in the *Confederate Veteran* between 1900 and 1920.

24 Akerman, "Selling Maps, Selling Highways," 79.

25 Numerous articles address the issue of mapping roads and highway construction in the early twentieth century, including Ristow, "American Road Maps and Guides"; Hugill, "Good Roads and the Automobile"; Paxson, "The Highway Movement"; Akerman, "Selling Maps, Selling Highways"; Raitz, "American Roads, Roadside America"; LeRoy Barnett, "Why Is There a Dixie Highway in Michigan?"; McIntyre, "Promoting the Gothic South"; and "Advertising Virginia."

26 *American Motorist* 1, no. 4 (July 1909): 139.

27 *American Motorist* 1, no. 5 (August 1909): 211–12.

28 "Glidden Tour in October over Southern Highways," *NYT*, August 6, 1911.

29 "Eighty-five Cars Will Leave for the South—Conditions for the Run," *NYT*, October 8, 1911; "80 Cars Start for the South in Glidden Tour," *AJC*, October 15, 1911.

30 "Governor Smith in Glidden Tour," *NYT*, September 3, 1911.

31 "Seventy-five Cars Speed to the Southland for Famous Auto Prize," *NYT*, October 15, 1911.

32 "80 Cars Start for South in Glidden Tour," *AJC*, October 15, 1911.

33 "Auto Tourists Find Good Roads in South," *NYT*, October 17, 1911.

34 Ibid.

35 Ibid.

36 "Glidden Tour Cars Ditched in Virginia," *NYT*, October 18, 1911.

37 "Glidden Tourists Swamped in Creek," *NYT*, October 19, 1911.

38 "Virginia Roads Defended," *NYT*, October 20, 1911.

39 "South Welcomes Glidden Tourists," *NYT*, October 20, 1911.

40 "Georgia Barbecue for Glidden Party," *NYT*, October 24, 1911; "Great Reception for Gliddenites," *AJC*, October 21, 1911.

41 "Glidden Tour Ends at Jacksonville," *NYT*, October 27, 1911.

42 "No Better Roads Found in South," *AJC*, September 25, 1910.

43 "Seventy-five Cars Full of Enthusiasts Begin 900-Mile Good Roads Tour of State," *AJC*, October 18, 1911; "Miss Rambo's Feat Wins Cheers and Loving Cup," *AJC*, October 27, 1910.

44 "Warm Welcome for Cincinnati," *AJC*, September 18, 1910.

45 "Miss Rambo's Splendid Feat Wins Cheers and Loving Cup," *AJC*, October 27, 1910; "Miss Regina Rambo to Go as Delegate to Good Roads Meeting at Montezuma," *AJC*, June 5, 1911.

46 Hugill, "Good Roads and the Automobile," 332; Paxson, "The Highway Movement," 238.

47 "W. S. Gilbreath, 69, Road Expert, Dead: Automobile Club Official Had Helped to Map Route for the Dixie Highway," *NYT*, October 14, 1936; LeRoy Barnett, "Why Is There a Dixie Highway?" 16.

48 "Highway Is 25 Years Old," *NYT*, February 16, 1936.

49 Ibid.

50 "Michigan Wants Dixie Road," *NYT*, May 22, 1915.

51 "Dixie Highway Contests," *NYT*, June 25, 1915.

52 "Michigan Wants Dixie Road," *NYT*, May 22, 1915.

53 "The Dixie Peaceway," *NYT*, April 4, 1915.

54 Hugill, "Good Roads and the Automobile," 342–42; Paxson, "The Highway Movement," 244.

55 "North and South Link: Plans to Complete Seven-Mile Mountain Gap in Dixie Highway," *NYT*, October 28, 1917.

56 "The Dixie Highway," *NYT*, October 10, 1925.

57 "Kentucky Cheers Dixie 'Motorcade'" *NYT*, October 10, 1925; "Chattanooga Hails Highway Caravan," *NYT*, October 13, 1925.

58 "South Improves Motor Roads," *NYT*, August 20, 1922; "Record Automobile Year in Output and Touring," *NYT*, April 23, 1923.

59 "Improved Motor Roads for Florida Touring," *NYT*, September 16, 1923.

60 Ibid.

61 "To Florida: Many Routes South for Motorists," *NYT*, December 20, 1936.

62 "Southward, Man Pushes Again," *NYT*, February 28, 1927.

63 Ibid.

64 "To Florida: Many Routes South for Motorists," *NYT*, December 20, 1936.

65 A. A. Ainsworth to the Editor, *Savannah Morning News*, typescript, October 17, 1927, Granger Papers.

66 Harvey Granger to Clark Howell, typescript, March 9, 1929, ibid.

67 J. G. Hulmly to Harvey Granger, July 17, 1928, ibid.

68 Cocks, *Doing the Town*, 145–46.

69 *Illustrated Richmond*, n.p. Other guides similarly promoted investment in the city as well as its historic offerings. These include *City of Richmond, of Historic Fame, of Commercial Prestige* (Richmond, 1905) and *Richmond Guide Book: Sketches and Views of Richmond, Virginia*, both in VHS.

70 "Advertising Virginia."

71 "A Tourist's Guide to Richmond," *Richmond Magazine* (1932), 36, VHS.

72 *Down Where the South Begins*, Richmond Chamber of Commerce, ca. 1930s, VHS.

73 *This Year in Richmond*, Automobile Club of Virginia, pamphlet, 1929, and *Seeing Historic Richmond*, Grayline Parlor Chair Coach pamphlet, 1929, both in VHS.

74 Yuhl, *Golden Haze of Memory*, 4–5.

75 *Savannah: Where Tourists Go*, Savannah Board of Trade pamphlet, 1924, GHS.

76 *Key to Atlanta*, Industrial Bureau, Atlanta Chamber of Commerce, pamphlet, 1925–26, AHC.

77 Stanonis, *Creating the Big Easy*, 28–69.

78 *American Motorist*, District of Columbia Edition, 1929, 40.

79 *1930 Garden Club of Virginia Pilgrimage* (Garden Club of Virginia, 2000), 12, 42, VHS.

80 On the development of Colonial Williamsburg, see Greenspan, *Creating Colonial Williamsburg*; Miller, "Mapping the Boosterist Imaginary"; and *Key to Inscriptions on Virginia Highway Historical Markers* (Richmond: State Commission on Conservation and Development, n.d.), 3rd ed., pamphlet, 3, VHS.

81 *Travel Guide to Virginia* (Richmond: G. F. Gulley, 1937), pamphlet, VHS; Greenspan, *Creating Colonial Williamsburg*, 37. According to Greenspan, the total visitation to Colonial Williamsburg in 1941 was just 36,000.

82 *Biloxi* (compiled and issued by the Chamber of Commerce, Biloxi, Mississippi, 1929), pamphlet, 2–10, MDAH.

83 "Know Mississippi Better," Subject File, MDAH.

84 History of the Garden Club, Collection Description, Natchez Garden Club Records, MDAH; "Editorially Speaking" and "How the Pilgrimage Came About," *Natchez Club Affairs* (March 1935), Natchez Pilgrimages Subject File, 1931–50, MDAH; "Natchez Hopes to Attract 50,000 during Pilgrimages," ca. 1938, Natchez Pilgrimages Subject File, 1931–50, MDAH.

85 "Natchez Pilgrimage Week," typescript, Natchez Pilgrimages Subject File, MDAH; Davis, "Struggle for Public History" (for the Natchez Pilgrimage, see pp. 52–55).

86 "Pilgrims Travel to Mississippi to View Deep South of Yesterday," *Motor News*, Natchez Pilgrimages Subject File, MDAH.

87 "Mississippi: America's Gateway to the Gulf," Advertising Proof, MAC-MDAH.

88 Booklet, "Mississippi," 1937–38, MAC-MDAH.

89 Ibid.

90 "DownSouth Travel Plan for Mississippi," 1940–41, MAC-MDAH.

91 Photograph Collection, 1940, ibid.

92 The Mississippi Advertising Commission sent out a survey to other states in 1940 in order to ascertain the amount of advertising that southern states spent and how much they benefited from tourism. Those states that responded revealed that although their advertising budgets remained small (less than $20,000 per year) tourist dollars spent in southern states ranged from $36 million to over $100 million. Questionnaires & Surveys, MAC-MDAH.

Epilogue

1 "Pepsodent Won't Hire Negro Typist; FEBC Is Needed," *Kansas City Plaindealer*, April 26, 1946.

2 "The South," *NYT*, May 9, 1954; see also "John Popham, 89, Dies; Journalist Was Known for Perceptive Coverage of the South," *NYT*, December 14, 1999.

3 "The South," *NYT*, May 9, 1954; John Popham, "Desegregation: Two Years after the Ruling," *NYT*, May 13, 1956.

4 "Video Show Deplored," *NYT*, September 21, 1951.

5 "GI's in Korea Denounce 'Amos 'n' Andy' Show," *Negro Star*, September 14, 1951.

6 Kellner, *Television and the Crisis of Democracy*, 120.

7 Graham, *Framing the South*, 101, 158.

BIBLIOGRAPHY

Manuscript Sources
Atlanta, Georgia
  Atlanta History Center
    Gone with the Wind Papers, 1936–89
    Wilbur G. Kurtz Collection
College Park, Maryland
  Library of American Broadcasting, University of Maryland
    General Collection, Radio Scripts
    Jerry Lee On-Line Photo Archives
    Pamphlet Collection
    Schaden Collection
Durham, North Carolina
  Duke University, John W. Hartman Center for Sales, Advertising & Marketing
      History, Rare Book, Manuscript, and Special Collections Library
    D'arcy Masius Benton & Bowles Archives
    J. Walter Thompson Archives
Hattiesburg, Mississippi
  University of Southern Mississippi
    De Grummond Children's Literature Collection
Jackson, Mississippi
  Mississippi Department of Archives and History
    Know Mississippi Better Subject File
    Natchez Pilgrimages Subject File
    Mississippi Advertising Commission
New York, New York
  Columbia University
    Oral History Collection
  New York Public Library
    Margaret Mitchell Files, Macmillan Company Records, 1889–1960
Richmond, Virginia
  Virginia Historical Society
    Battle Abbey Photographs Collection
    Cole Sheet Music Collection
    Confederate Memorial Association Records
    Confederate Memorial Institute Records
    Douglas Southall Freeman Scrapbook
    Lewis Ginter Papers

Savannah, Georgia
  Georgia Historical Society
    Mary Lois Granger Papers
    Rare Pamphlet Collection
    Savannah Automobile Club Guidebook and Photograph Collection

Published Works

"Advertising Virginia: Tourism in the Old Dominion in the Twenties and the Great Depression." *Virginia Cavalcade* 44, no. 1 (1994): 28–39.

Akerman, James R. "Selling Maps, Selling Highways: Rand McNally's 'Blazed Trails' Program." *Imago Mundi* 45 (1993): 77–89.

Albert, Dora. "That Old Showboater Captain Henry." *Radioland*, June 1934, 15.

The American Film Institute Catalog of Motion Pictures Produced in the United States. Vol. 3. Berkeley: University of California Press, 1993.

The American Film Institute Catalog of Motion Pictures Produced in the United States. Vol. 4. Berkeley: University of California Press, 1999.

American Motorist. Washington: American Automobile Association, 1902–20.

Arceneux, Noah. "Blackface Broadcasting in the Early Days of Radio." *Journal of Radio Studies* 12, no. 1 (2005): 61–73.

Aron, Cindy S. *Working at Play: A History of Vacations in the United States.* New York: Oxford University Press, 1999.

Baldwin, Brooke. "The Cakewalk: A Study in Stereotype and Reality." *Journal of Social History* 15, no. 2 (Winter 1981): 205–18.

Barnard, Ellsworth. *Wendell Willkie: Fighter for Freedom.* Boston: University of Massachusetts Press, 1971.

Barnett, Claude A. "The Role of the Press, Radio, and Motion Picture and Negro Morale." *Journal of Negro Education* 12, no. 3 (1943): 474–89.

Barnett, LeRoy. "Why Is There a Dixie Highway in Michigan?" *Michigan History* (July/August 2002): 16–19.

Barnouw, Erik. *A Tower in Babel: A History of Broadcasting in the United States to 1933.* New York: Oxford University Press, 1966.

Baskette, Kirtley. "Gone with the Wind, Indeed!" *Photoplay Magazine*, March 1937, 21–23, 102.

Becker, Jane S. *Selling Tradition: Appalachia and the Construction of an American Folk, 1930–1940.* Chapel Hill: University of North Carolina Press, 1998.

Bernhard, James. "Book Review." *Journal of Southern History* 44, no. 4 (November 1978): 619.

Berry, C. B. *The Other Side: How It Struck Us.* New York: E. P. Dutton, 1880.

Blight, David. *Race and Reunion: The Civil War in American Memory.* Cambridge: Belknap, 2001.

Bloomfield, Maxwell. "Dixon's 'The Leopard's Spots': A Study in Popular Racism." *American Quarterly* 16, no. 3 (August 1964): 387–401.

"Bob Burns (1890–1956)." *Encyclopedia of Arkansas History & Culture.* ⟨http://www
.encyclopediaofarkansas.net/encyclopedia/entry-detail.aspx?search=1&entryID=
2185⟩ (accessed October 6, 2009).

Breon, Robin. "Show Boat: The Revival, the Racism." *TDR* 39, no. 92 (1995): 86–105.

Brewer, John, and Roy Porter, eds. *Consumption and the World of Goods.* New York:
Routledge, 1993.

Bronner, Simon J., ed. *Consuming Visions: Accumulation and Display of Goods in
America, 1880–1920.* New York: W. W. Norton, 1989.

Brooks, Cleanth. *The Language of the American South.* Athens: University of Georgia
Press, 1985.

Brown, Sterling A. "Negro Character as Seen by White Authors." *Journal of Negro
Education* 2, no. 2 (April 1933): 179–203.

Bufwack, Mary A., and Robert K. Oermann. *Finding Her Voice: Women in Country
Music, 1800–2000.* Nashville: Country Music Foundation Press, 2003.

"Cahillogues." *What's on the Air* 1, no. 11 (1930): 24.

Campbell, Edward D. C., Jr. *The Celluloid South: Hollywood and the Southern Myth.*
Knoxville: University of Tennessee Press, 1981.

Cantril, Hadley, and Gordon W. Allport. *The Psychology of Radio.* New York: Harper,
1935.

Carlin, Richard, ed. *Country Music: A Biographical Dictionary.* New York: Taylor &
Francis, 2003.

Carver, Martha, and Claudette Stager, eds. *Looking Beyond the Highway: Dixie Roads
and Culture.* Knoxville: University of Tennessee Press, 2006.

Cobb, James C. *Away Down South: A History of Southern Identity.* New York: Oxford
University Press, 2005.

Cocks, Catherine. *Doing the Town: The Rise of Urban Tourism in the United States:
1850–1915.* Berkeley: University of California Press, 2001.

Cohen, Lizabeth. *Making a New Deal: Industrial Workers in Chicago.* Cambridge:
Cambridge University Press, 1990.

Cohn, David L. *The South.* Look at America Series. Boston: Houghton Mifflin,
1947.

Cole, Sally. "Mrs. Landes Meet Mrs. Benedict: Culture Patterns and Individual
Agency in the 1930s." *American Anthropologist* 104, no. 2 (2002): 533–43.

Conrad, Earl. "The Philology of Negro Dialect." *Journal of Negro Education* 13, no. 2
(1944): 150–54.

Correll, Charles, and Freeman Gosden. *All about Amos 'n' Andy and Their Creators.*
New York: Rand McNally, 1929.

———. *Sam 'n' Henry.* Chicago: Shrewesbury Publishing Company, 1926.

Cowan, John F. *A New Invasion of the South.* New York: Board of Officers Seventy-
first Infantry, 1881.

Cox, Jim. *Sold on Radio: Advertisers in the Golden Age of Broadcasting.* Jefferson, N.C.:
McFarland, 2007.

Cox, John D. *Traveling South: Travel Narratives and the Construction of American Identity*. Athens: University of Georgia Press, 2005.

Cox, Karen L. "The Confederate Monument at Arlington: A Token of Reconciliation." In *Monuments to the Lost Cause: Women, Art, and the Landscape of Memory*, edited by Cynthia Mills and Pamela H. Simpson, 149–62. Knoxville: University of Tennessee Press, 2004.

———. *Dixie's Daughters: The United Daughters of the Confederacy and the Preservation of Confederate Culture*. Gainesville: University Press of Florida, 2003.

Cram, Mildred. *Old Seaport Towns of the South*. New York: Dodd, Mead, 1917.

Cripps, Thomas. *Slow Fade to Black: The Negro in American Film, 1900–1942*. New York: Oxford University Press, 1977.

Cullen, Frank, ed. *Vaudeville, Old and New*. New York: Routledge, 2007.

Dabney, Virginius. *Below the Potomac*. New York: D. Appleton-Century, 1942.

Darlington, Edgar B. P. *The Circus Boys in Dixie Land; or, Winning the Plaudits of the Sunny South*. New York: Saalfield, 1911.

Davidson, Archie. "Meet the Sinclair Minstrels." *Radio Stars*, May 1934, 52–53, 81.

Davis, Jack E. "A Struggle for Public History: Black and White Claims to Natchez's Past." *Public Historian* 22, no. 1 (Winter 2000): 45–63.

Derry, J. T. *Georgia: A Guide to Its Cities, Towns, Scenery, and Resources*. Philadelphia: J. B. Lippincott, 1878.

Dixon, Thomas. *The Leopard's Spots*. New York: Doubleday, 1902.

Dorman, James H. "Shaping the Popular Image of Post-Reconstruction American Blacks: The 'Coon Song' Phenomenon of the Gilded Age." *American Quarterly* 40, no. 4 (December 1988): 450–71.

Douglas, George H. *The Early Days of Radio Broadcasting*. Jefferson, N.C.: McFarland, 1987.

Douglas, Susan J. *Inventing American Broadcasting, 1899–1922*. Baltimore: Johns Hopkins University Press, 1987.

———. *Listening In: Radio and the American Imagination*. New York: Random House, 1999.

Duck, Leigh Anne. *The Nation's Region: Southern Modernism, Segregation, and U.S. Nationalism*. Athens: University of Georgia Press, 2006.

Dunning, John. *On the Air: The Encyclopedia of Old-Time Radio*. New York: Oxford University Press, 1998.

Ely, Melvin Patrick. *The Adventures of Amos 'n' Andy: A Social History of an American Phenomenon*. New York: Free Press, 1991.

Emerson, Ken. *Doo-Dah!: Stephen Foster and the Rise of American Popular Culture*. Cambridge: Da Capo Press, 1998.

Encyclopedia of Radio. 3 vols. New York: Routledge, 2003.

Estes, Glenn E., ed. *American Writers for Children before 1900*. Vol. 2 of *Dictionary of Literary Biography*. Detroit: Gale Group, 1985.

Ewen, David. *The Life and Death of Tin Pan Alley: The Golden Age of Popular Music*. New York: Funk and Wagnalls, 1964.

————. *Panorama of American Popular Music: The Story of Our National Ballads and Folk Songs, the Songs of Tin Pan Alley, Broadway and Hollywood, New Orleans Jazz, Swing, and Symphonic Jazz.* Englewood Cliffs, N.J.: Prentice-Hall, 1957.

Faris, John T. *Seeing the Sunny South.* Philadelphia: J. B. Lippincott, 1921.

Field, Harvey, and Paul F. Lazarsfeld. *The People Look at Radio.* Chapel Hill: University of North Carolina Press, 1946.

"For Distinguished Service." *Radio Stars,* November 1933, 34.

Foster, Gaines M. *Ghosts of the Confederacy: Defeat, the Lost Cause, and the Emergence of the New South, 1865–1913.* New York: Oxford University Press, 1987.

Franklin, John Hope. "'Birth of a Nation': Propaganda as History." *Massachusetts Review* 20, no. 3 (1979): 417–34.

French, Warren, ed. *The South and Film.* Jackson: University Press of Mississippi, 1981.

Furia, Philip. *The Poets of Tin Pan Alley: A History of America's Great Lyricists.* New York: Oxford University Press, 1990.

Gaines, Janet Howe. *Music in the Old Bones: Jezebel through the Ages.* Carbondale: Southern Illinois University Press, 1999.

Gallagher, Gary W. *Causes Won, Lost, and Forgotten: How Hollywood and Popular Art Shape What We Know about the Civil War.* Chapel Hill: University of North Carolina Press, 2008.

Gardner, Sarah E. *Blood and Irony: Southern White Women's Narratives of the Civil War, 1861–1937.* Chapel Hill: University of North Carolina Press, 2004.

Georgia: A Guide to Its Towns and Countryside. Athens: University of Georgia Press, 1940.

Glimpses of the Jamestown Exposition and Picturesque Virginia. Chicago: Laird & Lee, 1907.

Graham, Allison. *Framing the South: Hollywood, Television, and Race during the Civil Rights Struggle.* Baltimore: Johns Hopkins University Press, 2003.

Graziano, John. "The Use of Dialect in African-American Spirituals, Popular Songs, and Folk Songs." *Black Music Research Journal* 24, no. 2 (Autumn 2004): 261–86.

Green, Archie. "Hillbilly Music: Source and Symbol." *Journal of American Folklore* 78, no. 309 (July–September 1965): 204–28.

Greenspan, Anders. *Creating Colonial Williamsburg.* Washington: Smithsonian Institution Press, 2002.

Gregory, James N. *The Southern Diaspora: How the Great Migrations of Black and White Southerners Transformed America.* Chapel Hill: University of North Carolina Press, 2005.

Grundy, Pamela S. "We Always Tried to Be Good People": Respectability, Crazy Water Crystals, and Hillbilly Music on the Air, 1933–1935." *Journal of American History* 81, no. 4 (March 1995): 1591–1620.

Hadler, Jeffrey. "Remus Orthography: The History of Representation of the African-American Voice." *Journal of Folklore Research* 35, no. 2 (1998): 100–104.

Hale, Grace Elizabeth. *Making Whiteness: The Culture of Segregation in the South, 1890–1940.* New York: Vintage, 1999.

Hall, Randal L. *Lum and Abner: Rural America and the Golden Age of Radio*. Lexington: University Press of Kentucky, 2007.

Hamm, Charles. "Genre, Performance and Ideology in the Early Songs of Irving Berlin." *Popular Music* 13, no. 2 (May 1994): 143–50.

———. *Irving Berlin: Songs from the Melting Pot: The Formative Years, 1907–1914*. New York: Oxford University Press, 1997.

Hammond, John Martin. *Winter Journeys in the South*. Philadelphia: J. B. Lippincott, 1916.

Hammond, Michael. "'A Soul Stirring Appeal to Every Briton': The Reception of *The Birth of a Nation* in Britain, 1915–1916." *Film History* 11, no. 3 (1999): 353–70.

Hardy, Lady Duffus. *Down South*. London: Chapman and Hall, 1883.

Harkins, Anthony. *Hillbilly: A Cultural History of an American Icon*. New York: Oxford University Press, 2003.

Harley, Reverend Timoth. *Southward Ho! A Tour through Georgia*. London: Sampson Low, Marston, Searle & Rivington, 1886.

Harris, Joel Chandler. *Uncle Remus: His Songs and His Sayings*. New York: D. Appleton, 1880.

Harwell, Richard, ed. *Margaret Mitchell's Gone with the Wind Letters*. New York: Macmillan, 1976.

Haskell, Molly. *Frankly, My Dear: "Gone with the Wind" Revisited*. New Haven: Yale University Press, 2009.

Herf, Jeffrey. *Reactionary Modernism: Technology, Culture, and Politics in Weimar and the Third Reich*. Cambridge: Cambridge University Press, 1984.

Hilmes, Michele. *Radio Voices: American Broadcasting, 1922–1952*. Minneapolis: University of Minnesota Press, 1997.

Holloway, J. Christopher. *The Business of Tourism*. 5th ed. Edinburgh: Longman, 1988.

"Honey and Alexander: First Citizens of Shanty Town." *Radio Varieties*, January 1940, 8–9.

Hope, Laura Lee. *Bunny Brown and His Sister Sue in the Sunny South*. New York: Grosset & Dunlap, 1921.

Huber, Patrick. *Linthead Stomp: The Creation of Country Music in the Piedmont South*. Chapel Hill: University of North Carolina Press, 2009.

———, and Kathleen Drowne. "Hill Billy: The Earliest Known African American Usages." *American Speech* 83, no. 2 (Summer 2008): 214–21.

Hugill, Peter J. "Good Roads and the Automobile in the United States, 1880–1929." *Geographical Review* 72, no. 3 (1982): 327–49.

Illustrated Richmond: Souvenir and Guide. Richmond: Clyde W. Saunders and C. W. Bowers, 1908.

Jakle, John A. *The Tourist: Travel in Twentieth-Century North America*. Lincoln: University of Nebraska Press, 1985.

James, Henry. *The American Scene*. London: Chapman and Hall, 1907.

"Joel Chandler Harris (1845–1908)." *New Georgia Encyclopedia*. ⟨http://www.georgia encyclopedia.org/nge/Article.jsp?id=h-525⟩ (accessed March 18, 2010).

Johnson, Clifton. *Highways and Byways from the St. Lawrence to Virginia*. New York: Macmillan, 1913.

———. *What to See in America*. New York: Macmillan, 1919.

Johnston, Annie Fellows. *The Little Colonel*. Shirley Temple Edition. New York: A. L. Burt, 1935.

Jones, Loyal. *Country Music Humorists and Comedians*. Urbana: University of Illinois Press, 2008.

"Keep Young and Beautiful." *Radio Stars*, July 1935, 6, 70.

Kellner, Douglas. *Television and the Crisis of Democracy*. Boulder, Colo.: Westview Press, 1990.

Kersten, Holger. "The Creative Potential of Dialect Writing in Later-Nineteenth-Century America." *Nineteenth-Century Literature* 55, no. 1 (2000): 92–117.

Key, Susan. "Sound and Sentimentality: Nostalgia in the Songs of Stephen Foster." *American Music* 13, no. 2 (Summer 1995): 145–66.

King, Edward. *The Great South: A Record of Journeys in Louisiana, Texas, the Indian Territory, Missouri, Arkansas, Mississippi, Alabama, Florida, Georgia, South Carolina, North Carolina, Kentucky, Tennessee, Virginia, West Virginia, and Maryland*. Hartford: American Publishing Company, 1874.

Kingsbury, Paul, ed. *The Encyclopedia of Country Music*. New York: Oxford University Press, 1988.

Kirby, Jack Temple. *Media-Made Dixie: The South in the American Imagination*. Baton Rouge: Louisiana State University Press, 1978.

Kitch, Carolyn. *Pages from the Past: History and Memory in American Magazines*. Chapel Hill: University of North Carolina Press, 2005.

Landes, Ruth. "A Northerner Views the South." *Social Forces* 23, no. 3 (March 1945): 375–79.

Lange, Jeffrey. *Smile When You Call Me a Hillbilly: Country Music's Struggle for Respectability, 1939–1954*. Athens: University of Georgia Press, 2004.

Lanier, Sidney. *Florida: Its Scenery, Climate, and History*. Philadelphia: J. B. Lippincott, 1875.

Lears, T. J. Jackson. *Fables of Abundance: A Cultural History of Advertising in America*. New York: Basic Books, 1994.

———. *No Place of Grace: Antimodernism and the Transformation of American Culture, 1880–1920*. New York: Pantheon, 1981.

Lemons, J. Stanley. "Black Stereotypes as Reflected in Popular Culture, 1880–1920." *American Quarterly* 29, no. 1 (Spring 1977): 102–16.

Levette, Jay Davidson. "Auto-Tourist Talk." *American Speech* 9, no. 2 (April 1934): 110–14.

Lichtenstein, Alex. "Good Roads and Chain Gangs in the Progressive South: 'The Negro Convict Is Slave.'" *Journal of Southern History* 59, no. 1 (February 1993): 85–110.

Lindberg, Ulf. "Popular Modernism? The 'Urban' Style of Interwar Tin Pan Alley." *Popular Music* 22, no. 3 (October 2003): 283–98.

Lott, Eric. "'The Seeming Counterfeit': Racial Politics and Early Blackface Minstrelsy." *American Quarterly* 43, no. 2 (1991): 223–54.

Lowenstein, Ralph L. "Book Review." *Florida Historical Quarterly* 57, no. 3 (January 1979): 382–83.

"Lum and Abner [Radio Show and Movies]." *Encylopedia of Arkansas History & Culture.* ⟨http://www.encyclopediaofarkansas.net/encyclopedia/entry-detail. aspx?entryID=77⟩ (accessed October 6, 2009).

MacDonald, J. Fred. *Don't Touch That Dial: Radio Programming in American Life, 1920–1960.* Chicago: Nelson-Hall, 1979.

Malone, Bill C. *Country Music U.S.A.* 2nd rev. ed. Austin: University of Texas Press, 2002.

———. *Singing Cowboys and Musical Mountaineers: Southern Culture and the Roots of Country Music.* Athens: University of Georgia Press, 2003.

Manring, M. M. *Slave in a Box: The Strange Career of Aunt Jemima.* Charlottesville: University Press of Virginia, 1998.

Marchand, Roland. *Advertising the American Dream: Making Way for Modernity, 1920–1940.* Berkeley: University of California Press, 1986.

May, Lary. *Screening Out the Past: The Birth of Mass Culture and the Motion Picture Industry.* New York: Oxford University Press, 1980.

McCracken, Grant. *Culture and Consumption: New Approaches to the Symbolic Character of Consumer Goods and Activities.* Indianapolis: Indiana University Press, 1988.

McCusker, Kristine. *A Boy Named Sue: Gender and Country Music.* Jackson: University of Mississippi Press, 2004.

McDowell, Tremaine. "The Use of Negro Dialect by Harriet Beecher Stowe." *American Speech* 6, no. 5 (1931): 322–26.

McElya, Micki. *Clinging to Mammy: The Faithful Slave in Twentieth-Century America.* Cambridge: Harvard University Press, 2007.

McGovern, Charles F. *Sold American: Consumption and Citizenship, 1890–1945.* Chapel Hill: University of North Carolina Press, 2006.

McIntyre, Rebecca C. "Promoting the Gothic South." *Southern Cultures* 11, no. 2 (2005): 33–61.

McLeod, Elizabeth. *The Original Amos 'n' Andy: Freeman Gosden, Charles Correll, and the 1928–1943 Radio Serial.* Jefferson, N.C.: McFarland, 2005.

McManus, John T., and Louis Kronenberger. "Motion Pictures, the Theater, and Race Relations." *Annals of the American Academy of Political and Social Science* 244, Controlling Group Prejudice (March 1946): 152–58.

McPherson, Tara. *Reconstructing Dixie: Race, Gender, and Nostalgia in the Imagined South.* Durham: Duke University Press, 2003.

Melick, Weldon. "The Hill Billy Menace." *Radioland,* June 1935, 48–49.

Merriman, Alan P. "Music in American Culture." *American Anthropologist* 57, no. 6 (December 1955): 1173–81.

Merritt, Russell. "Dixon, Griffith, and the Southern Legend." *Cinema Journal* 12, no. 1 (1972): 26–45.

Miller, James S. "Mapping the Boosterist Imaginary: Colonial Williamsburg, Historical Memory, and the Construction of Managerial Memory." *Public Historian* 28, no. 4 (Fall 2006): 51–74.

Mitchell, Margaret. *Gone with the Wind.* Special 25th Anniversary Edition. New York: Macmillan, 1961.

Mooney, H. F. "Popular Music since the 1920s: The Significance of Shifting Taste." *American Quarterly* 20, no. 1 (Spring 1968): 67–85.

Mooney-Melvin, Patricia. "Harnessing the Romance of the Past: Preservation, Tourism, and History." *Public Historian* 14, no. 2 (Spring 1991): 35–48.

Morford, Henry. *Morford's Short-Trip Guide to America.* New York: Baker, Pratt, 1881.

Morneweck, Evelyn Foster. *Chronicles of Stephen Foster's Family.* Pittsburgh: University of Pittsburgh Press, 1944.

Munden, Kenneth W. *The American Film Institute Catalog.* Vol. 2. New York: R. R. Bowker, 1971.

"My Girls." *Radioland,* October 1933, 73.

Myrdal, Gunnar. *An American Dilemma: The Negro and Modern Democracy.* New York: Harper, 1944.

Nachman, Gerald. *Raised on Radio.* New York: Pantheon, 1998.

Newell, Georgie Willson. *Natchez and the Pilgrimage.* Kingsport, Tenn.: Kingsport Press, 1935.

Niles, John J. "Shout, Coon, Shout!" *Music Quarterly* 16, no. 4 (October 1930): 516–30.

The Official Blue Book of the Jamestown Ter-Centennial. Norfolk, Va.: Colonial Publishing, 1907.

The Official Encyclopedic Guide to Richmond and Vicinity Including Battlefields. Jamestown Exposition Edition. Richmond, Va.: Richmond Press, 1907.

Official Guide to the City of Atlanta. Atlanta Convention and Visitors Bureau, 1936.

On to Richmond by Post 23 G.A.R. Trenton: John L. Murphy Printer, 1881.

Oral History Interview with Barbara Greenlief, April 27, 1996. Interview R-0020. Southern Oral History Program Collection (#4007), Southern Historical Collection, Wilson Library, University of North Carolina at Chapel Hill.

Ostendorf, Berndt. "Minstrelsy and Early Jazz." *Massachusetts Review* 20, no. 3 (Autumn 1979): 574–602.

Otto, John S., and August M. Burns. "Black and White Cultural Interaction in the Early Twentieth Century South: Race and Hillbilly Music." *Phylon* 35, no. 4 (1974): 407–17.

Page, Thomas Nelson. *In Ole Virginia: Marse Chan and Other Stories.* New York: Charles Scribner's, 1887.

———. *Social Life in Old Virginia before the War.* New York: Charles Scribner's, 1895.

Parish, James Michael, and Michael R. Pitts. *Hollywood Songsters: Singers Who Act and Actors Who Sing.* Vol. 1. 2nd ed. New York: Routledge, 2003.

Patrick, Rembert W. "The Mobile Frontier." *Journal of Southern History* 29, no. 1 (February 1963): 3–18.

Paxson, Frederic L. "The Highway Movement, 1916–1935." *American Historical Review* 51, no. 2 (1946): 236–53.

Plaag, Eric W. "'There Is an Abundance of Those Which Are Genuine': Northern Travelers and Souvenirs of the Antebellum South." In *Dixie Emporium: Tourism, Foodways, and Consumer Culture in the American South*, edited by Anthony J. Stanonis, 24–49. Athens: University of Georgia Press, 1988.

Preston, Howard L. *Dirt Roads to Dixie: Accessibility and Modernization in the South, 1885–1935*. Knoxville: University of Tennessee Press, 1991.

"Radioland's Popularity Poll Winner." *Radioland*, May 1935, 52.

"Radioland Survey." *Radioland*, February 1934, 28.

"The Radio Parade." *Radioland*, September 1933, 68.

Raitz, Karl. "American Roads, Roadside America." *Geographical Review* 88, no. 3 (July 1998): 363–87.

Ralph, Julian. *Dixie; or Southern Scenes and Sketches*. New York: Harper, 1896.

Rathbone, St. George. *Chums in Dixie; or the Strange Cruise of a Motorboat*. Chicago: M. A. Donohue, 1912.

Reardon, Carol. *Pickett's Charge in History and Memory*. Chapel Hill: University of North Carolina Press, 2003.

Reed, John Shelton. *The Enduring South: Subcultural Persistence in Mass Society*. Chapel Hill: University of North Carolina Press, 1972.

———. *Minding the South*. Columbia: University of Missouri Press, 2003.

———. *My Tears Spoiled My Aim and Other Reflections on Southern Culture*. Fort Washington, Pa.: Harvest Books, 1994.

Regester, Charlene. "African American Extras in Hollywood during the 1920s and 1930s." *Film History* 9, no. 1 (1997): 95–115.

"Renfro Valley Folks: Hill Billy Life and Music of Long Ago Lives Again in Kentucky's Renfro Valley." *Radio Varieties*, October 1940, 16–17.

Rhodes, Marylou. *Landmarks of Richmond: Places to Know and See in the Nation's Most Historic City*. Richmond: Garrett and Massie, 1938.

Richmond Guide Book: Sketches and Views of Richmond, Virginia. Richmond: M. A. Burgess, 1913.

"Richmond since the War." *Scribner's Monthly* 14 (1877): 303–12.

Ristow, Walter W. "American Road Maps and Guides." *Scientific Monthly* 62, no. 5 (1946): 397–406.

Robinson, Daniel. "Marketing Gum, Making Meanings: Wrigley in North America, 1890–1930." *Enterprise & Society* 5, no. 1 (2004): 4–44.

Roediger, David R. *The Wages of Whiteness: Race and the Making of the American Working Class*. New York: Verso, 1991.

Rosenburg, Bernard, and David Manning White, eds. *Mass Culture: The Popular Arts in America*. New York: Free Press, 1957.

Russell, George W. E., ed. *The Letters of Matthew Arnold, 1848–1888*. New York: Macmillan, 1895.

Sammis, Edward R. "How Radio Programs Are Built: The Story of How the Showboat Hour Came to Be Created and How the Imaginary Cruise of Cap'n Henry Up and Down the Mississippi River Has Grown into a National Institution." *Radioland*, September 1933, 34–37.

Schaffer, Marguerite S. *See America First: Tourism and National Identity, 1880–1940*. Washington: Smithsonian Books, 2001.

Scheurer, Timothy E., ed. *The Nineteenth Century and Tin Pan Alley*. Vol. 1 of *American Popular Music: Readings from the Popular Press*. Bowling Green, Ohio: Bowling Green State University Popular Press, 1989.

Schudson, Michael. *Advertising, the Uneasy Persuasion: Its Dubious Impact on American Society*. New York: Basic Books, 1984.

Sears, John F. *Sacred Places: American Tourist Attractions in the Nineteenth Century*. New York: Oxford University Press, 1989.

Selwyn, Tom, ed. *The Tourist Image: Myths and Myth Making in Tourism*. New York: John Wiley, 1996.

Sheffield, O. H. *Improvement of the Road System of Georgia*. Washington: Government Printing Office, 1893.

Siegel, Norman. "Revealing Lum and Abner." *Radio Stars*, December 1933, 32–33.

Silber, Nina. *Romance of Reunion: Northerners and the South, 1865–1900*. Chapel Hill: University of North Carolina Press, 1995.

Simpson, Lewis P. *The Dispossessed Garden: Pastoral and History in Southern Literature*. Athens: University of Georgia Press, 1975.

"The Sinclair Minstrels." *Radioland*, October 1933, 41.

"Sisterhood of States, Jamestown Exposition." *National Magazine*, May 1907, 169–70.

Sivulka, Juliann. *Soap, Sex, and Cigarettes: A Cultural History of American Advertising*. Belmont, Calif.: Wadsworth, 1998.

Sklar, Robert. "Book Review." *American Historical Review* 84, no. 1 (February 1979): 279–80.

———. *Movie-Made America: A Cultural History of American Movies*. New York: Vintage, 1994.

Smith, Jessica Carney, ed. *Images of Blacks in American Culture: A Reference Guide to Information Sources*. Santa Barbara, Calif.: Greenwood, 1988.

"Southern Charm." *Radio Stars*, August 1938, 50, 73.

Spaeth, Sigmund Gottfried. *A History of Popular Music in America*. New York: Random House, 1948.

Staiger, Janet. *Interpreting Films: Studies in the Historical Reception of American Cinema*. Princeton: Princeton University Press, 1991.

Stanard, Mary Newton. "Quaint Old Richmond." *Century*, February 1921, 443–50.

Stanonis, Anthony J. *Creating the Big Easy: New Orleans and the Emergence of Modern Tourism, 1918–1945*. Athens: University of Georgia Press, 2006.

Strasser, Susan. *Satisfaction Guaranteed: The Making of the American Mass Market.* New York: Pantheon, 1989.

Summers, Harrison B. *History of Broadcasting: Radio to Television, a Thirty-Year History of Programs Carried on National Radio Networks in the United States, 1926–1956.* New York: Arno Press/New York Times, 1971.

Susman, Warren I. *Culture as History: The Transformation of American Society in the Twentieth Century.* New York: Pantheon, 1985.

Taylor, Helen. *Circling Dixie: Contemporary Southern Culture through a Transatlantic Lens.* New Brunswick, N.J.: Rutgers University Press, 2001.

Taylor, William. *Cavalier and Yankee: The Old South and American National Character.* New York: Oxford University Press, 1961.

"Texas Tourists." *Prairie Farmer*, December 29, 1877, n.p.

"Three Historical Novels." *New Yorker*, August 15, 1936, 48.

Toll, Robert. *Blacking Up: The Minstrel Show in Nineteenth-Century America.* New York: Oxford University Press, 1977.

Tucker, Mark, ed. *The Duke Ellington Reader.* New York: Oxford University Press, 1993.

Twelve Southerners. *I'll Take My Stand: The South and the Agrarian Tradition.* New York: Harper, 1930.

"Voodoo on the Air." *Radio Stars*, June 1933, 33–49.

Wallace, Michele. "Uncle Tom's Cabin: Before and After the Jim Crow Era." *TDR* 44, no. 1 (2000): 137–56.

Waller, Gregory. *Main Street Amusements: Movies and Commercial Entertainment in a Southern City, 1896–1930.* Washington: Smithsonian Institution Press, 1995.

Weinberger, Julius. "Economic Aspects of Recreation." *Harvard Business Review* 15 (Summer 1937): 455–61.

"What Radio Fans Want to Know." *Radio Stars*, December 1933, 65.

White, Deborah Gray. *Ar'n't I a Woman? Female Slaves in the Plantation South.* New York: W. W. Norton, 1999.

Whitfield, Stephen J. "Is It True What They Sing about Dixie?" *Southern Cultures* 8, no. 2 (2002): 8–37.

Wiebe, Robert H. *The Search for Order, 1877–1920.* New York: Hill and Wang, 1967.

Wilder, Alec. *American Popular Song: The Great Innovators, 1900–1950.* New York: Oxford, 1992.

Williamson, J. W. *Hillbillyland: What the Movies Did to the Mountains & What the Mountains Did to the Movies.* Chapel Hill: University of North Carolina Press, 1995.

Wilson, Charles Reagan. *Baptized in Blood: The Religion of the Lost Cause, 1865–1915.* Athens: University of Georgia Press, 1982.

Winchell, Mark Royden. *Reinventing the South: Versions of a Literary Region.* Columbia: University of Missouri Press, 2006.

Witmark, Isidore, and Isaac Goldberg. *From Ragtime to Swingtime: The Story of the House of Witmark.* 1939. Reprint, New York: Da Capo Press, 1976.

Witt, Doris. *Black Hunger: Soul Food and America*. Minneapolis: University of Minnesota Press, 2004.

Wittke, Carl. *Tambo and Bones: A History of the American Minstrel Stage*. Ca. 1930. New York: Greenwood Press, 1968.

"WLS Has a Miracle Show in the Barn Dance." *Radio Stars*, July 1934, 86–89.

Wyatt, Robert, and John Andrew Johnson, eds. *The George Gershwin Reader*. New York: Oxford University Press, 2004.

Yuhl, Stephanie A. *A Golden Haze of Memory: The Making of Historic Charleston*. Chapel Hill: University of North Carolina Press, 2005.

INDEX

Cohan, George M.: "Wedding of the Blue and Gray," 2, 25; "Yankee Doodle Dandy," 25
Cohn, David, 8
Cole, Lois, 51, 126–27, 128
Colonial Williamsburg, Virginia, 152–53
Columbian Exposition (Chicago, 1893), 40–41, 65
Confederacy: "Dixie's Land" associated with, 11; and tourism, 112, 113, 114, 132, 134–35, 149, 151, 153, 157
Confederate colonel, 7, 36, 89
Confederate Memorial and Literary Society, 113
Confederate Museum (White House of the Confederacy), 2, 113, 133, 134, 149
Conrad, Earl, 125–26
Consumerism: and pastoral images of Old South, 3–4, 8, 37; and modernization, 5, 27, 37; and advertising, 36, 37, 38–42; and world's fairs, 40; and women, 41, 42, 46–47, 54; and tourism, 132
Convict labor, 137, 180 (n. 22)
Coon Creek Girls, 75, 76–77, 175 (n. 47)
Coon songs, 13, 15–16, 18, 19, 24, 31, 65
Coquette (film, 1929), 85
Correll, Charles, 58, 62, 68
Cosmopolitan, 46
Cotton Belt Route, 138, 143, 181 (n. 23)
Country music: and hillbilly music, 30, 73, 74–77, 170 (n. 47); and World War II, 31, 170 (n. 47)
Crab Orchard whiskey, 44
Cram, Mildred, 119–22, 129, 178 (n. 26)
Crinoline and Romance (film, 1923), 86
Crosby, Bing, 32, 69, 71
Crowther, Bosley, 90, 103
Cukor, George, 93–94
Cumberland Ridge Runners, 74–75

Dabney, Virginius, 93, 95
D. Appleton & Company, 116, 119
Darwin, Charles, 118
Daughters of the American Revolution, 3

Davis, Bette, 32, 90, 92
Davis, Jefferson, 134, 157
Davis, Owen: Jezebel, 92
Designing Women (television show), 166
Detroit Automobile Club, 144
Dialect: and Foster's "Old Folks at Home," 12; and Tin Pan Alley, 24; of blackface performers, 24, 49, 63, 64–65, 66; in songs about South, 28, 31; and radio, 49, 61, 62; and Song of the South, 103, 104; and literature, 116, 118, 123, 125–26; and inferiority of blacks, 126
Disney, Walt, 83, 100, 103, 104, 163
Dixiana (film, 1930), 87
"Dixie" (song, 1859), 11–12, 16, 32, 66, 89, 146
Dixie (film, 1943), 32
Dixie Advertisers, 159
Dixie Belle Gin, 43
Dixie Flyer, 138, 181 (n. 23)
Dixie Highway, 75, 139, 143, 144, 145, 146
Dixie Highway Association, 143, 144–45, 146
"Dixie Volunteers, The" (song, 1917), 25, 27
Dixon, Thomas, Jr.: literature of, 2, 6, 85, 108, 114; The Leopard's Spots, 3, 16, 114, 128; The Clansman, 83; and Birth of a Nation, 83, 84–85, 176 (n. 12)
Dorsey, Tommy, 13
Doubleday Press, 114
DownSouth program, 159–60
Du Bois, W. E. B., 84
Dunbar, Paul Laurence: and coon songs, 15; Folks from Dixie, 36
Dunham, Katherine, 97
Dunne, Irene, 87

Edison, Thomas, 82
Ellington, Duke: "Swanee River Rhapsody," 12; on jazz, 30; and film, 97
Ely, Melvin, 63, 68
Emmett, Daniel Decatur: popularity of, 10, 11, 12, 32; "Dixie," 11–12, 16, 32, 66, 89, 146

Kirby, Jack Temple, 5, 168 (n. 13)
Know Mississippi Better Train, 153, 155
Kronenberger, Louis, 97
Ku Klux Klan, 25, 93, 108
Kurtz, Annie, 103
Kurtz, Wilbur, 93, 100, 103

Ladies' Home Journal, 41, 44, 46, 49
Ladies' Memorial Association, 94
Laemmle, Carl, 86
Lair, John, 75, 175 (n. 47)
Landes, Ruth, 1, 167 (n. 1)
Landscape: and tourism, 109, 112, 115, 131,
    133, 138, 148, 150, 152, 155; and literature,
    111, 118, 120, 123, 128, 129, 131
Lanier, Sidney: *Florida*, 111, 114
Latham, Harold, 90, 106, 127, 128
Lauck, Chester, 77, 99
Lears, T. J. Jackson, 4, 38
Lee, Robert E., 44, 134, 138, 152, 180
    (n. 15)
Leigh, Vivien, 94
Leisure: perpetuated by slavery, 10, 73;
    and advertising, 37, 39, 43, 46, 47, 66;
    and southern belles, 72, 73; and images
    of South, 94; and tourism, 112, 119,
    131, 151
Leslie, Edgar, 25
Lewis, Jerry Lee, 13
Life magazine, 43, 65
Lincoln Highway Association, 144
Lippincott, J. P., 43
Literature: and culture of reconciliation,
    2, 43; and idealization of past, 4; and
    perceptions of South, 5, 6, 80, 81, 106,
    108, 120, 131; and regional icons, 7;
    plantation images in, 10, 114, 116, 118,
    120, 123, 126, 128, 131; and sentimental-
    ized images of South, 16, 50, 90; and
    black stereotypes, 16, 83, 111, 112–13,
    115–16, 118–23, 125, 128; advertising of,
    36; children's literature, 36, 123, 125,
    179 (n. 53); and film, 83–85, 86, 88, 90;
    and Lost Cause, 93, 110, 113, 126; and
    northern publishing industry, 106, 108;

and landscape, 111, 118, 120, 123, 128, 129,
    131; and dialect, 116, 118, 123, 125–26;
    and tourism, 116, 126–29. *See also* Travel
    literature
Little Colonel, The (film, 1935), 32, 88–89,
    90, 98
"Little Puff of Smoke, Good Night—
    A Southern Croon" (song, 1910), 19
Littlest Rebel, The (film, 1935), 32, 88,
    89–90
Lost Cause: regional myths associated
    with, 1; and literature, 93, 110, 113, 126;
    and *Gone with the Wind*, 94, 106; and
    tourism, 135
Louisiana: films set in, 86. *See also* New
    Orleans
Lucas, Sam, 15
Lum and Abner (radio show), 61, 77, 80, 99
Lynching: racist stereotypes justifying,
    16; images of South contrasted with,
    24; and *Gone with the Wind*, 95; and
    race riots, 118

Mack and Moran (vaudeville minstrel
    act), 64
Macmillan Company, 50–52, 90, 106,
    126–27
Macy's department store, 51–52
Malone, Pick, 64, 65
Mammies: as regional icon, 7, 33; in songs,
    17, 19, 24, 28; and artwork of sheet
    music, 19; and advertising, 34, 36, 37,
    38, 39–43, 65–66, 164; and *Gone with
    the Wind*, 43, 49–50; and black stereo-
    types, 65; and radio, 65–66; in film, 86,
    89, 90, 97–98; and tourism, 155, 166
Mapping: and tourism, 139, 144, 150
Marketing: southern imagery used in, 5;
    and Tin Pan Alley, 17; and advertising,
    41–42, 46
Marsh, John, 51, 127–28
Mass media: radio as, 60; film as, 82;
    television as, 105, 165
Maxwell House coffee: sponsorship of
    Maxwell House Show Boat radio show,

"Negro wench": and minstrelsy, 65
Neumann, Kurt, 81
New Orleans, 131, 149, 151
New South, 95, 148, 150, 160
New York City: music publishing industry
    in, 13, 15, 17, 18–19; as setting for film, 83
New Yorker magazine, 128
New York Journal, 46
New York Southern Society, 127
New York Times: and radio, 72–73; and
    hillbilly music, 76; and film, 81, 90, 92,
    98–99, 103; and tourism, 140, 141–42,
    147, 156; and culture of reconciliation,
    146; and changing image of South,
    164–65
Nickelodeons, 82, 175 (n. 3)
North: southern blacks' migration to,
    2, 25, 32, 58, 63, 69, 85, 147, 173 (n. 15);
    narrative of southern identity originat-
    ing in, 5, 60, 110; advertising industry
    based in, 39, 54; and radio, 61–62; and
    hillbilly music, 75; publishing industry
    in, 106, 108, 109, 110, 114, 118–19, 126;
    South compared to, 112–13, 115, 119;
    tour companies of, 132–33; economic
    investment in South, 143
North Carolina, 142
Northerners: perceptions of South, 1, 6,
    7, 11, 22, 80, 111; and tourism to South,
    7, 109–10, 112–16, 119, 123, 125, 126, 128,
    129, 130–35, 137–38, 146, 147, 148–49,
    150, 151, 152, 153, 155, 156, 157, 159, 162;
    and music publishing industry, 11; and
    racial stereotypes, 54
Northern whites: attitudes toward
    African Americans, 2, 12, 163; attitudes
    toward immigrants, 2, 25, 119; migra-
    tion to Florida, 147
Nostalgia: and imagined South, 6, 11, 164,
    165; and songs, 33; and advertising, 36,
    37–38; and film, 81, 83, 93, 94, 98; and
    Gone with the Wind, 81, 93, 94; and tour-
    ism, 148
Nugent, Frank, 81, 92
N. W. Ayer & Sons, 60

Okeh Records, 74
Old South Perfumers, 54
"Ol' Man River" (song, 1927), 31
Ossiebrink, Luther, 75

Padgett, Pat, 64, 65
Page, Thomas Nelson: and images of
    South, 5, 108, 118; *In Ole Virginia*, 114;
    Social Life in Old Virginia, 114; *The
    Negro*, 119; and dialect, 125
Paramount Pictures, 88
Parker Pen Company, 51
Pastoralism: modernity contrasted with,
    3, 168 (n. 7); and consumerism, 3–4, 8,
    37; and regional icons, 7, 38; and Tin
    Pan Alley, 9; and advertising, 38; and
    tourism, 109, 132
Pepperell Manufacturing, 51
Pepsodent Company, 163
Philadelphia Courier, 63
Photoplay magazine, 92
Pick and Pat (radio show), 64
"Pickaninnies": and songs, 18, 19; and
    advertising, 36, 38; and film, 89, 90;
    and literature, 125
Pickens Sisters, 59, 71–73
Pickford, Mary, 76, 85
Piedmont Driving Club, 150–51
Pie Plant Pete, 76–77
Plantation images: as regional icon, 7;
    in songs, 9–10, 22; in advertising,
    10, 36, 44; in literature, 10, 114, 116,
    118, 120, 123, 126, 128, 131; in film, 83,
    86, 87, 88, 93–94, 175 (n. 7); in travel
    literature, 110, 111, 115, 120–22, 123;
    and tourism, 150, 151, 152, 155, 156,
    157, 160, 162
Popham, John, 164–65
Popular culture: and historical studies
    of southern identity, 5; and percep-
    tions of southern identity, 5, 6, 7, 8,
    155, 166. *See also* Advertising; Film;
    Literature; Radio; Tourism
Puddin' Head (film, 1941), 100
Pullman Porters Union, 153, 155

Quaker Oats, 42, 66

Race records, 27
Race relations: sentimentalization of, 11, 39, 71; and songs, 24, 33; and *Birth of a Nation*, 85; and *Gone with the Wind*, 94, 96, 97; and film, 94, 96–97, 98, 104–5; and radio, 98; and *Song of the South*, 103; and literature, 115, 116, 118, 121–22, 125
Racial stereotypes. *See* Black stereotypes
Racial violence: and popularity of coon songs, 15, 16; images of South contrasted with, 24; and *Gone with the Wind*, 95–96; and race riots, 118; and convict labor, 137; and school segregation, 165. *See also* Lynching
Racism: and coon songs, 15; rise in, 25; and minstrelsy, 63; and *Birth of a Nation*, 83, 84, 85, 98; and literature, 108, 112, 113, 118; and hiring practices, 163
Radio: and perceptions of South, 5, 7, 59, 61, 80, 131, 155, 173 (n. 5); and regional icons, 7, 58, 59, 80; and minstrel songs, 10, 13, 16; and coon songs, 16; and music publishing industry, 19, 27; and Dixie songs, 24; and songs about South, 27, 30; national networks, 30, 58, 59, 62, 80; and hillbilly music, 30–31, 74–76; Maxwell House coffee sponsoring *Maxwell House Show Boat*, 31, 47, 49–50, 65, 69, 70–71; and advertising, 37, 38, 42, 47, 49, 60, 63, 69; and minstrelsy, 49, 58, 59, 60, 61, 62–69, 71, 173 (n. 5); and black dialect, 49, 61, 62; and hillbilly acts, 59, 60, 61, 62, 73, 74–77, 80, 98, 99, 173 (n. 5); as mass media, 60; and southern identity, 60, 62, 63, 64, 69, 80, 173 (n. 5); studies of, 60–61, 62; and tourism, 149
Radio Guide, 50
Radioland, 49, 69, 70, 71, 76
Radio Stars, 69, 71, 80
Radio Varieties, 64
Ragtime, 15, 16, 24, 28

Railroads: and tourism, 131, 132, 133, 135, 137–38, 145, 151, 153, 155; and culture of reconciliation, 145
Rainbow on the River (film, 1936), 81
Raleigh, Henry, 46–47
Ralph, Julian, 4, 119, 135, 137
Ransom, John Crowe, 8
Rastus: and Cream of Wheat, 38
Reconciliation, culture of: and veterans' reunions, 1, 2, 25, 118, 130; in American culture, 1–3; and songs, 2, 16, 25; and literature, 2, 43; and tourism, 2, 130, 131, 132, 134, 135, 145, 147, 150, 160, 162; and advertising, 54; and roads, 139, 145, 146
Reconstruction, 2
Reed, John Shelton, 6
Regional icons: and radio, 7, 58, 59, 80; and film, 7, 83; and advertising, 36–43, 46–47, 165. *See also specific icons*
Remick, Jerome, 18
Renfro Valley Folks (radio show), 75
Republic Pictures, 98, 99–100
Resor, Helen, 40
Resor, Stanley, 40
Rice, Glen, 76
Richmond: and travel literature, 112–13, 114, 119, 123; and tourism, 130–33, 134, 135, 139, 147, 149–50
Richmond Automobile Club, 139
Richmond Times-Dispatch, 93
River of Romance (film, 1929), 86
RKO Radio Pictures, 90
Robeson, Paul, 87, 97
Robinson, Bill "Bojangles," 89
Roosevelt, Eleanor, 75
Ross, Lanny, 50, 69
'Round the State Tour (Georgia), 143
R. T. Davis Milling Company, 39, 40, 41
Ruby, Harry, 25
Rudy Vallee Show (radio show), 77
Rural life: agrarian tradition in South, 4, 8, 9, 32; value of, 4, 72; and radio, 61, 74, 80; and modernity, 76; and film, 100; and tourism, 109, 119, 120, 149, 151. *See also* Pastoralism

Southern identity: in popular culture, 5, 6, 7, 8, 155, 166; and advertising, 36, 47; and radio, 60, 62, 63, 64, 69, 80, 173 (n. 5); and literature, 108, 119, 127; and tourism, 131, 133, 148, 151

Southern Literary Renaissance, 126–27

Southern whites: migration of, 73, 100; stereotypes of, 73–74, 76, 77, 80, 100, 111, 166; and *Gone with the Wind*, 94, 95, 96

Southern writers: and images of South, 114, 118, 126–27; and northern publishers, 127

Status: and advertising, 39, 46, 47

Steamships: and tourism, 131, 132, 133

Stern, Joseph, 18

Stowe, Harriet Beecher: *Uncle Tom's Cabin*, 118

Stratemeyer, Edward, 123, 125

Stratemeyer Syndicate, 123

Susman, Warren, 60

Tarkington, Booth: *Magnolia*, 88

Television: and perceptions of South, 6, 82, 165; as influential form of mass media, 105, 165

Temple, Shirley, 32, 88, 89, 90

Three Georgia Crackers, 77, 99

Till, Emmett, 166

Tin Pan Alley: and sentimental images of South, 9, 10, 17, 22, 24, 27; and Jewish immigrant songwriters, 9, 16; and legacy of minstrel songs, 10; and black stereotypes, 15; and ragtime, 16; and mass marketing, 17; and sheet music, 18; and manufacture and distribution of popular songs, 18–19, 30; and race records, 27; and jazz, 27, 28; and radio, 30, 71; and film, 31, 32

Tourism: historical tourism, 2, 120, 133–34, 138, 149, 150, 151, 152–53, 156, 157; and culture of reconciliation, 2, 130, 131, 132, 134, 135, 145, 147, 150, 160, 162; and perceptions of South, 7, 108–9, 127, 131, 166; and *Gone with*

the Wind, 95, 96, 106, 127–29, 160; and travel literature, 108, 109–16, 119–23, 125, 129, 133, 135, 137, 149, 153; and landscape, 109, 112, 115, 131, 133, 138, 148, 150, 152, 155; and automobiles, 112, 126, 129, 135, 137, 138–46, 150, 151, 152; and literature, 116, 126–29; and roads, 129, 131, 135, 137–48, 151, 152, 155, 156; and steamships, 131, 132, 133; and railroads, 131, 132, 133, 135, 137–38, 145, 151, 153, 155; and advertising, 131, 133, 135, 137, 138, 149, 150–51, 152, 153, 155, 156–57, 159–60, 181 (n. 23), 183 (n. 92); and accommodations, 146–47, 150; urban tourism, 148–49; vacationing contrasted with, 178 (n. 7)

Tourist camps, 147

Travel Guide to Virginia, 153

Travel literature: and perceptions of South, 4, 7, 15, 108, 109, 111, 118–19; and tourism, 108, 109–16, 119–23, 125, 129, 133, 135, 137, 149, 153; in magazines, 109–10, 123, 126; plantation images in, 110, 111, 115, 120–22, 123; and North compared to South, 112–13; and dialect, 118, 123, 125, 126; and black stereotypes, 121–23

Truman, Harry, 104

Trumbo, Dalton, 96–97

Turner, Joseph Addison, 100

Twain, Mark, 116

Twentieth-Century Fox, 88, 97

Two Black Crows, The, 64

Uncle Ben: and advertising, 38

"Uncle" figure: and advertising, 36, 38, 39; and film, 89–90; and tourism, 166

Under Southern Stars (film, 1937), 32

United Auto Workers (UAW), 165, 166

United Daughters of the Confederacy (UDC), 2, 3, 94, 128, 176 (n. 32)

Urbanization: and perceptions of South, 3, 33; and value of agricultural life, 4; and songs about South, 10, 22; and mass consumption, 37; and pastoral

38100939R00126

Made in the USA
San Bernardino, CA
30 August 2016